"Worse Than Slavery"

THE FREE PRESS

New York   London   Toronto   Sydney   Tokyo   Singapore

"Worse Than Slavery"

PARCHMAN FARM AND THE
ORDEAL OF JIM CROW JUSTICE

✠

DAVID M. OSHINSKY

THE FREE PRESS
A Division of Simon & Schuster Inc.
1230 Avenue of the Americas
New York, NY 10020

THE FREE PRESS and colophon are trademarks
of Simon & Schuster Inc.

Designed by Carla Bolte

Manufactured in the United States of America

10 9 8 7 6 5 4 3 2 1

Library of Congress Cataloging-in-Publication Data

Oshinsky, David M., 1944–
    Worse than slavery: Parchman farm and the ordeal of Jim Crow
justice/ David M. Oshinsky.
      p. cm.
    Includes bibliographical references and index.
    ISBN 0-684-82298-9
    1. Mississippi State Penitentiary—History. 2. Criminal justice,
Administration of—Mississippi—History. 3. Prisoners—Mississippi—
History. I. Title.
HV9476.M72M576   1996
365´.9762—dc20   95-52880
                                               CIP

Grateful acknowledgment is made of permission to reproduce illustrations from the following
sources: Mississippi Department of Archives and History, pages 2, 7–9, 10 (top), 11–13, and 15;
Library of Congress (*Documentary Portrait of Mississippi: The Thirties*, edited by Patti Carr Black,
1982), pages, 3, 4, 5, and 6 (top); archives of Parchman Penitentiary, pages 1, 10 (bottom), and 16;
Samuel Charters, *The Blues Makers*, 1991, page 14.

FOR MY SON MATTHEW,
a father's jewel

The abuses of [our criminal justice] system have often been dwelt upon. It had the worst aspects of slavery without any of its redeeming features. The innocent, the guilty, and the depraved were herded together, children and adults, men and women, given into complete control of practically irresponsible men, whose sole object was to make the most money possible.

—Frank Sanborn, keynote address, in *Ninth Atlanta Conference on Negro Crime*
(edited by W. E. B. Du Bois), 1904

The convict's condition [following the Civil War] was much worse than slavery. The life of the slave was valuable to his master, but there was no financial loss . . . if a convict died.

—L. G. Shivers, "A History of the Mississippi Penitentiary," 1930

The most profitable prison farming on record thus far is in the State of Mississippi . . . which received in 1918 a net revenue of $825,000. . . . Given its total of 1,200 prisoners—and subtracting invalids, cripples, or incompetents—it made a profit over $800 for each working prisoner.

Proceedings of the Annual Congress of the American Prison Association, 1919

I have visited Parchman repeatedly and I have found that their cotton was very profitable but that profit was secured by reducing the men to a condition of abject slavery.

—Hastings Hart, reporting to the Russell Sage Foundation, 1929

On the whole, the conditions under which prisoners live in [Parchman], their occupation and routine of living, are closer by far to the methods of the large antebellum plantation worked by numbers of slaves than to those of the typical prison.

—David Cohn, Where I Was Born and Raised, 1935

One . . . he's a gitten' de leather,
Two . . . he don't know no better,
Three . . . cry niggah, stick yo' finger in yo' eye,
Four . . . niggah thought he had a knife,
Five . . . got hit off'n his visitin' wife,
Six . . . now he'll git time for life,
Seven . . . lay it on trusty man!
Eight . . . wham! wham! he gotta wu'k tomorra,
Nine . . . he gotta chop cotton in de sun,
Ten . . . dat's all, trusty men, you's done.

—The cadence of "Black Annie," the strap used at Parchman Farm

Self-supporting prison systems must, in the end, become slave camps. Slavery is the partner of the lash. The wielder of the lash is brutalized along with the victim, and brutes will sometimes kill.

—Southern Regional Council, *The Delta Prisons: Punishment for Profit,* 1968

Contents

Acknowledgments

This project began in the reading room of the Mississippi Department of Archives and History in Jackson—a wonderfully supportive environment. I would like to thank Hank Holmes, Nancy Bounds, and the reference staff for making a northerner feel very much at home. I am especially grateful to Anne Lipscomb Webster for her skill, her interest, and her boundless energy. I am indebted as well to archivists at the University of Mississippi Library; the Southern History Collection at the University of North Carolina, Chapel Hill; the Library of Congress; and the Barker History Center at the University of Texas, Austin.

A number of Mississippians provided support along the way. Jan Hillegas generously shared her research on lynchings and executions. Attorney Ron Welch took me to Parchman, tutored me about prison issues, and showed me the finer side of Southern life and banjo-picking. Vera Richardson helped me gather research material. Jim Young and Ed King filled in crucial gaps about Parchman and civil rights. Parchman officials Dwight Presley and Gene Meally supplied valuable information about the prison; Lieutenant Tony Champion was a superb guide; and longtime inmates James Louis, Robert Phillips, Horace Carter, Delbert Driskill, and Matthew Winter offered remarkable first-hand testimony about convict life.

I would also like to acknowledge Rutgers University for supplying research and travel funds during the life of this project, and the National Endowment for the Humanities for its generous senior fellowship. At Rutgers, my close friends and generous colleagues, Willam O'Neill and Maurice Lee, were a source of strength for me in difficult times, and Chris Stacey did superb work as a research assistant.

At The Free Press, I have had the rare pleasure of working with a fine copy supervisor, Loretta Denner, as well as with two superb editors and good friends. Joyce Seltzer played the major role in getting this book off the ground. Her enthusiasm was contagious; her patience more than I deserved. When Joyce left for Harvard University Press, Bruce Nichols stepped in and brought the book to conclusion. I owe Bruce, in particular, a debt of gratitude that he alone understands.

My agent, Gerry McCauley, provided encouragement, support, and friendship in expert doses. He has the overwhelming respect of the authors he represents because of the personal and professional interest he takes in their lives.

Finally, I would like to acknowledge my parents for their love and endless generosity; my children, Matthew, Efrem, and Ari, for the joy they provide and the patience they have shown; and Jane Rudes, for making my daily life brighter in more ways than I can possibly list—or repay.

Prologue

Northerners, provincials that they are, regard the South as one
large Mississippi. Southerners, with their eye for distinction, place
Mississippi in a class by itself.

—V. O. Key, Jr.

I

Throughout the American South, Parchman Farm is synonymous
with punishment and brutality, as well it should be. Parchman is the
state penitentiary of Mississippi, a sprawling 20,000-acre plantation
in the rich cotton land of the Yazoo Delta. Its legend has come down
from many sources: the work chants and field hollers of the black
prisoners who toiled there; the Delta blues of ex-convicts like Eddie
"Son" House and Huddie "Leadbelly" Ledbetter; the novels of
William Faulkner, Eudora Welty, Shelby Foote, and, most recently,
John Grisham, who seem almost mesmerized by the mystique of the
huge Delta farm. One of Faulkner's characters in *The Mansion*, a
young attorney, tells his luckless client: "It's Parchman . . . destination doom. . . . You can't escape. You can't make it." And Washington "Bukka" White, who served hard time there, sings these words
in his "Parchman Farm Blues":

1

Prologue

Oh listen men: I didn't mean no harm
If you want to do good . . . stay off
the Parchman Farm."[1]

Parchman is the quintessential penal farm, the closest thing to slavery that survived the Civil War. Its story covers the bleak panorama of race and punishment in the darkest corner of the South. It begins in antebellum times, on the Mississippi frontier, though Parchman itself would not be constructed until 1904. And it continues to this day, a story filled with warnings and consequences, and perhaps lessons, for a nation deeply divided, black and white.

II

In the fall of 1833, a local judge wrote to Mississippi governor Charles Lynch about an "unfortunate circumstance" in his jurisdiction. During a routine street brawl, he explained, a quick-tempered fellow named Clark had beaten his opponent senseless, "and then, drawing his knife, had cut out the eyes of the unfortunate man," leaving him "dependent on the public for his support." The community wanted to punish Clark, who had escaped "to parts unknown," the judge added. "We are therefore anxious that you take this subject into consideration [by offering] a sufficient reward so that he will be apprehended."[2]

The governor did not reply. There is no evidence that a reward was offered or that Clark was ever tried for his offense. The incident was similar to hundreds of others on the isolated Mississippi frontier, where formal authority was weak, if not invisible, and lethal violence permeated everyday life. "No state in the Union," complained a local newspaper, "[has] a worse penal code, or a more lax execution of criminal law."[3]

This probably was true. Admitted to statehood in 1817, Mississippi had experienced an explosive population growth in succeeding decades, as white farmers from Georgia and the Carolinas left their worn-out plots for the fertile lands and deep river highways of the "Old Southwest." By 1840, Mississippi had become the nation's leading cotton producer, with black slaves comprising more than half of its 375,000 people. The great bulk of whites were rough back-country folk, well armed, fiercely democratic, deeply sensitive to insults and signs of disrespect. Whiskey flowed freely in their world, and personal disputes were often settled in the dirt-floor taverns or dueling fields outside town. Most men "wore pistols and bowie-knife," a contemporary recalled, "and a row once a day was the rule, not the exception."[4]

With its cheap, fertile land and scattered rural population, Mississippi had no large or medium-sized cities. Only the river ports of Natchez and Vicksburg could boast of sidewalks, brick buildings, or paved streets before the Civil War, and neither town had more than 6,500 people. What distinguished both places, however, was the fabulous wealth of their elite new planter class (Natchez was said to have the greatest concentration of millionaires in the South) and the lawlessness of their citizens. In his remarkable diary of street life in antebellum Natchez, William Johnson chronicled endless shootings and brawls. Men squared off at the slightest provocation, gouging and biting; using their heads as battering rams; cutting out tongues; hurling bricks; swinging swords, canes, and iron bars; stabbing with their dirks; and firing pistols. The diary ended abruptly in 1851, when Johnson himself was shot and killed.[5]

Even by frontier standards, the violence seemed extreme. Some blamed it on hot weather, heavy drinking, and deadly weapons; others pointed to physical isolation, obsessions with honor and vengeance, and a system of slave labor that strengthened the belief that all whites belonged to the master class, making one white man as good as the next. For these reasons, and perhaps more, fatal duels took a frightful toll among the "gentlemen" of antebellum Mississippi, and ordinary killings appeared too numerous to count. In a typical month, a Jackson newspaper reported a "bloody affair" in Port Gibson, a "grisly murder" in Jefferson County, "another murder" in Vicksburg, a "homicide in Newton," a "fatal difficulty" in Jackson, an "outrageous murder" in Sunflower County, a "Negro shot dead," two assassination attempts, the ambush of a sheriff, and a "domestic squabble" in which "Mr. Lockhair, a man generally respected by his neighbors while sober, was killed by his own son."[6]

At times, the local courtrooms became extensions of the streets. In numerous cases, people acquitted of crimes were beaten by waiting crowds until they "confessed." One man had turpentine poured on his body "to restore his feeling senses." Another was "maimed most inhumanely [with the mob] cutting off his nose and ears and scarifying his body to the very ribs!" In Natchez, a defendant *convicted* of manslaughter was set upon by the victim's family, "stabbed in three or four places," crudely dismembered, and left for dead "in the hall of the court." "What is Mississippi coming to?" the local newspaper wailed. "It would seem that no man's life or property is respected. We blush for the name posterity will be forced to ascribe to her."[7]

It did not take nearly that long. By the 1830s, Mississippi was viewed as a place of violent moods and minimal restraint, where passion took precedence over the law. And that reputation grew ever larger as vigilante groups sprang up to battle street crime in the brawling river towns. In 1835, a "tumultuous mob" dragged six "captured and crestfallen gamblers" to a makeshift gallows in Vicksburg. "It was the next morning," a witness reported, "before their bodies were cut down and buried together in a ditch."[8]

The national press soon dubbed Mississippi the "lynching state," a distinction it would hold for a century as its victims changed from white to black. In 1837, an obscure lawyer named Abraham Lincoln charged that "dead men [are] literally hanging from the boughs of trees by every roadside" in Mississippi. And Davy Crockett, the legendary frontiersman, described the mobs that gathered in Natchez and Vicksburg as "lynchers." "When an individual escapes punishment by some technicality of the law, or perpetrates an offense not recognized in courts of justice," he wrote, "they seize him, and inflict such chastisement as they conceive adequate to the offense."[9]

III

Crockett's words rang true. Though Mississippi had a harsh criminal code in place, there were not nearly enough sheriffs or judges to enforce it. In 1838 Governor Alexander McNutt complained that crime *and* vigilantism had reached epidemic proportions because criminals had almost no fear of the law. "Very few are brought to trial," he noted, "and still fewer are punished." There were but a handful of jails in Mississippi, and the largest one in Natchez was described as a "crumbling dungeon" where prisoners "lie gasping in a . . . state of nudity," their unwashed bodies "freighted with disease." In some counties, the sheriff either leased his inmates to a planter or chained them to a tree.[10]

The state's early criminal codes emphasized the swift, painful justice of common law and biblical teachings. "We have but four kinds of punishment," a Mississippi official admitted: "the whipping post, the pillory, the hot iron, and the halter." For dozens of offenses, including murder, arson, burglary, forgery, and Negro stealing, the law decreed death at the gallows. For petty theft, the offender was to be whipped on his bare back or branded on the face with the letter *T.* For the crime of mayhem, such as biting off an ear or gouging out an eye, the culprit paid a fine and stood in the stocks for several hours on successive days.[11]

These codes lost their impact over time. The penalties were too inflexible and severe. Juries became squeamish about sentencing common criminals to death, and governors seemed to pardon all but the most heinous offenders. In 1832, for example, a convicted forger was granted executive clemency on the grounds that capital punishment did not properly fit his crime. A year later, Governor H. G.

Prologue

Runnels set aside the sentence of a Vicksburg woman after being flooded with petitions from her neighbors. The community could not accept "so horrid an exhibition," said one, "as the naked back of a decrepit old woman lacerated by the whip of a public executioner."[12]

This sentiment gained strength in the 1830s as the turmoil of daily life served to ignite cries for serious reform. The more educated classes worried about Mississippi's social stability as well as its image to the rest of the world. "Truly," warned the *Holly Springs Banner,* "we are gaining an unenviable character abroad!"[13]

After bitter debate, the Mississippi legislature revised the state's criminal code in 1835, abandoning corporal punishment and restricting the death penalty to a handful of major crimes. In their place came "time sentences" in a penitentiary, a humanitarian and pragmatic change. Punishment would be less brutal, more precise, and far more certain than before. Juries could now convict the guilty without seeing them tortured or killed.

This new code, however, was meant for white folk alone. Slaves "had no rights to respect," wrote one authority, "no civic virtue or character to restore, no freedom to abridge." Slaves were the property of their master, and the state did not normally intervene. In the words of one Natchez slaveholder, "Each plantation was a law unto itself."[14]

In 1836, the legislature authorized $75,000 to build a state penitentiary in Jackson, the new capital. Known as the Walls, it was modeled after the New York State prison at Auburn, an institution praised throughout the United States and Europe for its advanced methods of penal reform. The Auburn system combined two popular theories of that time: congregate working quarters and complete solitary confinement. By day, the prisoners labored together in silence; by night, they slept alone in tiny cells. Conditions were spartan; food and clothing were purposely inferior to what the lower classes enjoyed. Prisoners were to be trained in religious instruction and taught the value of hard work. At Auburn, as in Jackson, the inmates were "constantly employed."[15]

For the next twenty-five years, the Walls would stand as Mississippi's most impressive civic reform. Its population was overwhelmingly white and male, reflecting a society in which slaves were punished by the master and white women were seen as "virtuous" and "pure." At its peak in 1860, the prison operated as a textile mill, making low-grade cotton cloth, turning small yearly profits, and working its 150 inmates in monastic silence, their eyes downcast, their thoughts, it was hoped, on repentance and the Lord. When Union troops reached the Walls in 1863, they discovered a "great manufactory"—and promptly burned it down. The Civil War would paralyze and liberate Mississippi in countless ways.

PART ONE

After Slavery, Before Parchman

CHAPTER ONE

Emancipation

I think God intended the niggers to be slaves. Now since man has deranged God's plan, I think the best we can do is keep 'em as near to a state of bondage as possible. . . . My theory is, feed 'em well, clothe 'em well, and then, if they don't work . . . whip 'em well."

—A Yazoo Delta planter, 1866

I

In the tumultuous summer of 1861, a Mississippi planter named William Nugent rode off to war with a regiment from Vicksburg. He did not expect a very long fight, viewing a Southern victory as all but inevitable. Nugent worried instead about his own mortality—about dying on a faraway battlefield without "leaving an heir behind to . . . represent me hereafter in the affairs of men." His early letters home were filled with bluster and pride. "I feel that I would like to shoot a Yankee," he told his young wife. "The North will yet suffer for this fratricidal war she has forced upon us—Her fields will be desolated, her cities laid to waste, and the treasuries of her citizens dissipated in the vain attempt to subjugate a free people."[1]

Nugent was mistaken, of course. By war's end, only the South matched his grim portrait of destruction, and no other state had suf-

fered more than his own. The fields of Mississippi had been "desolated" by fire and flood and simple neglect. The cities had been flat-
tened by Grant's artillery and pillaged by Sherman's roaming troops.
Following the seven-week siege of Vicksburg in 1863, Union soldiers had marched through the heart of Mississippi, burning houses,
killing livestock, and trampling crops. Writing to his wife in 1864,
Nugent described the damage near Jackson, which had just been
put to the torch: "The largest plantations are . . . grown up in
weeds . . . ; fences are pulled down & destroyed; houses burned; negroes run off. . . . The prospects are gloomy enough and may be
worse. I think the present year will wind it up and . . . see me at
home again."[2]

Nugent was among the lucky ones: he came back alive. More
than a third of Mississippi's 78,000 soldiers were killed in battle or
died from disease. And more than half of the survivors brought home
a lasting disability of war. Visitors to the state were astonished by the
broken bodies they saw at every gathering, in every town square.
Mississippi resembled a giant hospital ward, a land of missing arms
and legs. In 1866, one-fifth of the state budget went for the purchase
of artificial limbs.[3]

Few could escape the consequences of this war. Mississippi was
bankrupt. Its commerce and transportation had collapsed. The railroads and levees lay in ruins. Local governments barely functioned.
In Desoto County, just below Memphis, Judge James F. Trotter portrayed a landscape "enveloped in shadows, clouds and darkness."
"Wherever we turn our eyes," he said, "we witness the sad memori-
als of our misfortunes, melancholy evidence of our sufferings, and of
the cruelty and savage ferocity of our late enemies. . . . Our one con-
solation is the hope that we have reached the bottom."[4]

Desperate planters and farmers struggled simply to survive. Their
slaves had been freed; their currency was worthless; their livestock
and equipment had been stolen by soldiers from both sides. In the
fertile Yazoo Delta, "plows and wagons were as scarce as mules, with

no means to buy new ones. The cavalryman fortunate enough to have been paroled with his horse . . . was the envy of his neighbor."[5]

Many of these farms were now tended by women and elderly men, the war having wiped out more than one-quarter of the white males in Mississippi over the age of fifteen. In his popular travel account, *The Desolate South,* author John T. Trowbridge described a visit to Corinth, Mississippi, near the Shiloh battlefield, in the winter of 1866. The "bruised and battered" town was filled with "lonely white women," he wrote, "crouched shivering over the hearth." In Natchez, reformer Carl Schurz found an old gentleman—"delicate hands; clothes shabby"—cutting down "a splendid shade tree" on the grounds of his once magnificent home. When Schurz asked him why, the man replied, "I must live. My sons fell in the war. All my servants have left me. I sell firewood to the steamboats passing by."[6]

Even Schurz, who despised the slaveholding class, was moved by the suffering of its members. Their cause had been morally indefensible, he believed, but their "heroic self-sacrifice" had been very real indeed. Schurz returned to the North "troubled with great anxiety." He worried most about the rising tide of white anger he saw in places like Natchez and Vicksburg—an anger directed mainly against blacks, the traditional victims of violence and exploitation in the South.

There were reasons for concern. With slavery abolished, Mississippi was moving toward a formal—and violent—separation of the races. Deeply rooted customs were now being written into law. The state legislature had just passed the South's first Jim Crow ordinance, prohibiting Negroes from riding in railroad coaches set aside for whites. Following suit, the city of Natchez had segregated its river walkways in order to keep black men and white women apart—the right bluff for use "of the whites, for ladies and children and nurses; the central bluff for bachelors and the colored population; and the lower promenade for whites."[7]

Blacks who challenged these rules faced arrest, humiliation, and sometimes worse. On a steamboat ride down the Mississippi River, Trowbridge noticed "a fashionably dressed couple" come on board near Vicksburg.

> Terrible was the captain's wrath. "God damn your soul," he said, "get off this boat." The gentleman and lady were colored, and they had been guilty of unpardonable impudence in asking for a stateroom.
>
> "Kick the nigger!" "He ought to have his neck broke!" "He ought to be hung!" said the indignant passengers, by whom the captain's prompt action was strongly commended.
>
> The unwelcome couple went quietly ashore and one of the hands pitched their trunk after them. They were in a dilemma: their clothes were too fine for deck passage and their skins were too dark for cabin passage. So they sat down on the shore to wait for the next steamer.
>
> "They won't find a boat that'll take 'em," said the grim captain. "Anyhow, they can't force their damned nigger equality on to me!"
>
> Afterwards I heard the virtuous passengers talking over the affair. "How would you feel," said one with solemn emphasis, "to know that *your wife was sleeping in the next room to a nigger and his wife?*"[8]

This hatred had many sources. The ex-slave had become a scapegoat for the South's humiliating defeat. John F. H. Claiborne, Mississippi's most prominent historian, blamed him for causing the war and for helping the North to prevail. Others saw the freedman as a living symbol, a daily reminder, of all that had changed. For the planter, emancipation meant the loss of human property and the disruption of his labor supply. For the poor white farmer, it meant even more. Emancipation had not only crushed his passionate dreams of slaveholding; it had also erased one of the two "great distinctions" between himself and the Negro. The farmer was white and free; the Negro was black—but also free. How best to preserve the remaining distinction—white supremacy—would become an obsession in the post–Civil War South.[9]

Throughout Mississippi, these tensions seemed particularly severe. That, at least, was the opinion of northerners who visited the South, or were stationed there, after the war. Whitelaw Reid of the *New York Tribune* was struck by the enormous hostility he found in the Magnolia State, where blacks greatly outnumbered whites and where a free Negro majority created unique possibilities for political and economic change. "More or less, the same feeling had been apparent in Tennessee, Georgia, Alabama, and Louisiana," he wrote in 1866, "but it was in Mississippi that I found its fullest expression. However these man may have regarded the negro slave, they hated the negro freeman. However kind they may have been to negro property, they were virulently vindictive against a property that had escaped from their control."[10]

II

By the time of the Confederate surrender in April 1865, more than half of Mississippi's 400,000 blacks were already free. Some of them had fled to Union lines from their poorly guarded plantations; others had been abandoned by their owners as the enemy approached. "The arrival among us of these hordes was like the oncoming of cities . . . ," wrote a chaplain in Grant's army. "There were men, women, and children in every stage of disease or decrepitude, often nearly naked, with flesh torn by the terrible experiences of their escapes." Those who survived were put to work as paid laborers, loading supplies, clearing land, and chopping wood. They lived in awful squalor, the chaplain reported, their "ignorance" causing "a veritable moral chaos" in the camps.[11]

Emancipation came late, often grudgingly, to other parts of the state. Former slaves sketched a memorable scene—a kind of ritual—in which the master lined them up, told them they were no longer his property, and asked (or demanded) that they stay on to help with the crop. "My white folks talked plain to me," recalled a freedman from Adams County, south of Natchez. "Dey said real sad like: 'Charlie, you is bin a dependence but now you kin go effen you is so desirous. But effen you wants to stay wid us . . . dare is a house fur you, en wood to keep you warm. . . . Do jist ez you please.' "[12]

But others described a different reality, filled with false promises from the master. An ex-slave from Amite County, on the Louisiana border, remembered the day that "Marse Bill blowed dat big horn an' all de slaves cum right ter de big house an' he tole dem dat dey was free now, but dat he wanted dem ter stay wid him till de crop wus made an' he wud pay dem fur it." At year's end, however, the field hands received no wages because Marse Bill had charged them dearly for rent and supplies. "All dey made de boss tuk it, and 'iffen you moved to er nudder plantashunm yo' had to go wid nuffin."[13]

Some slaves were not even told they were free. Their masters, believing emancipation to be illegal or immoral, refused to spread the word. This caused particular problems in the deep interior counties of Mississippi, where towns were scattered, plantations were isolated, and news could be tightly controlled. "I heered it talked about . . . but I wuz kinda skeered to ask . . . ," said an ex-slave from the Yazoo Delta. "I did one day tho when I asked Ole Miss, 'Miss dey tells me de niggers is free, is dey?' She say, 'No! and you'd better come on and go to work 'fore you gits tored up.' Dey did free us tho about three or fo months after dis."[14]

These planters sought a way to control black labor now that slavery had expired. This would not be easy because the freedmen had interests of their own. They were determined to explore the countryside, to experience the novelties of town life, and to feel freedom under their feet. Mobility was both a precious right and a liberating force for ex-slaves. It permitted them to leave a hated master, to bargain for better conditions, to search for loved ones who had been cruelly sold away. "We have not one of our old hands on the plantation this year," a Mississippian reported in 1867. "They are scattered to the four winds."[15]

Emancipation

Emancipation provided legal relief from the pace and discipline of slavery, and it allowed blacks to protest old grievances by simply moving on. A freedwoman from Simpson County, south of Jackson, could not forget the flogging of her grandmother, "wid her clothes stripped down to her waist, her hands tied 'hind her to a tree . . . it just made a 'pression on my childest mind." An ex-slave from South Mississippi could still hear the crack of the whip and the futile pleadings of her mother: "O, marse, I is neber gwine to run 'way er gin. O, please, I is gwine to stay here." And a freedman from the Yazoo Delta could not forgive the brutal beatings suffered by his father: "My pa an' ma wasn't owned by de same masters. . . . At night pa would slip over to see us an' ole Marse wuz mos' always on de look out fer everything. When he would ketch him he would beat him so hard 'till we could tell which way he went by de blood. But pa, he would keep a comin' to see us an' takin' de beatins."[16]

The extent of this mobility is difficult to gauge. Among the hundreds of ex-slaves interviewed in the 1930s, about 40 pecent claimed to have moved during the war itself or in the months immediately following emancipation. But most remained where they were, living as tenants or field hands on the same land they had worked all along. And those who did leave often went a very short distance—to a neighboring plantation, perhaps, or the nearest crossroads town. The exhilaration of moving was tempered by feelings of insecurity and fear. "We wanted to be free at times, den we would get scart an' want to stay slaves," a freedman recalled. "We was tol all kinds of things but didn't know jes what to believe." Some returned to their home plantations. "[We] was jes' lak cows an' hogs," said an ex-slave from central Mississippi. "We would stray off an' didn't know whar to go an' fus thing would go right back to Ole Marse."[17]

Southern whites took a different point of view. Emancipation had ended slavery but had not destroyed the assumptions upon which slavery was based. The fact that many blacks abandoned their plantations in 1865 simply reinforced the image of the lazy, indolent field hand, shuffling aimlessly through life. In white eyes, the Negro viewed his freedom in typically primitive terms—as a license to roam the countryside in search of pleasure and trouble.

By most accounts, the Negro found both. Newspapers reported that "idle darkies" were clogging the roads, stealing crops and live-stock, jostling whites from sidewalks, and fouling the air with "cigar smoke and profanity." The white response left no doubt that rough times lay ahead. "The infernal sassy niggers had better look out, or they'll get their throat cut," warned one Mississippian. "Let a nigger come into *my* office without tipping his hat, and he'll get a club over it," said another. In Natchez, a local editor predicted an all-out race war unless the Negro acknowledged his permanent inferiority to whites. "One *must* be superior—one *must* be dominant," he wrote. "If the negro should be the master, the whites must either abandon the territory, or there will be another civil war in the South . . . and [it will] be a war of extermination."[18]

Others simply wanted the stealing to stop. A woman from the Delta complained that the "poor deluded negro," equating freedom with license, had stripped the region bare. "Not even a cabbage head in the garden or a chicken on its roost is safe, and I guess (I am not a Yankee) it is the same throughout the South."[19]

In fact, some Yankees thought much the same thing. Northern officials in Mississippi were often appalled by the freedman's "law-less" behavior. But unlike Southerners, these officials were more likely to view him as a victim of circumstance, not as a congenital thief. To be free and black in Mississippi "is first to beg, then to steal, and then to starve," a Union officer observed. "That is their reality." A colonel from Illinois took the longer view: "Slavery has made them what they are; if they are ignorant and stupid, don't expect much of them; and give them at least time to [improve] before judg-ing them by the highest standards."[20]

Such views were anathema in the white South, where slavery had long been viewed as a civilizing influence upon an inferior race.

Bondage had been good for the Negro, it was argued, because the system kept his primitive instincts in check. And freedom would be bad for the Negro because those checks had been removed. Southerners "understood" such things. They knew that slavery had been a response to the African's inferiority, and not its cause. They knew that the freedman needed constant attention—and a whip at his back. "The negro is [their] sacred animal," said a Mississippi planter. "The Yankees are about negroes like the Egyptians were about cats."[21]

III

Some whites talked about leaving Mississippi—moving west to Texas and California, where they would not have to mingle with Negroes or compete with them for work. "We ain't made to live together under this new style of things," said a migrating farmer. "Free niggers and me couldn't agree." There also was talk about "colonizing" the blacks in Mexico or some other distant place. But this notion had little support in a state so utterly dependent upon Negro sweat and toil. As one editor put it: "Every white man would be glad to have the entire race deported—except his own laborers."[22]

Many believed that blacks would perish in freedom, like fish on the land. The Negro's "incompetence," after all, had been essential to the understanding—and defense—of slavery itself. "Where shall Othello go?" a planter asked in 1865. "Poor elk—poor buffaloe—poor Indian—poor Nigger—this is indeed a white man's country." One newspaper predicted that the freedman would be extinct within a hundred years. Another gave him less time than that. "The child is already born who will behold the last negro in the State of Mississippi," mused the *Natchez Democrat*. "With no one to provide for the aged and the young . . . and brought unprepared into competition with the superior intelligence, tact, and muscle of free white labor, they must surely and speedily perish."[23]

After Slavery, Before Parchman

In the fall of 1865, Governor Benjamin G. Humphreys addressed the "negro problem" before a special session of the Mississippi legislature. A planter by profession and a general during the war, Humphreys had campaigned for office in a "thrice-perforated" army coat shot through with Yankee lead. Like other leading Confederates, he had at first been excluded from participating in the South's postwar political affairs. But President Andrew Johnson had pardoned the general, and hundreds like him, in remarkably short order. Humphreys received his pardon on October 5, 1865, just three days after winning the governor's race in a landslide.[24]

His speech about the Negro was a major event, the first of its kind by a Southern governor since the Confederate defeat. "Under the pressure of federal bayonets," Humphreys began, ". . . the people of Mississippi have abolished the institution of slavery." That decision was final; there could be no turning back. "The Negro is free, whether we like it or not; we must realize that fact now and forever."[25]

But freedom had its limits, Humphreys continued. It protected the Negro's person and property but did not guarantee him political or social equality with whites. Indeed the "purity and progress" of both races required a strict caste system, with blacks accepting their place in the lower order of things. And that place—literally—was the cotton field of the South. Since economic recovery depended on a ready supply of Negro labor, the new system, like the old one, must reward the faithful field hand and punish the loafer. Such was the rule of the plantation, said Humphreys, and the "law of God."

In the following days, the legislature passed a series of acts known collectively as the Black Codes. Their aim was to control the labor supply, to protect the freedman from his own "vices," and to ensure the superior position of whites in southern life. "While some of [these acts] may seem rigid and stringent to sickly modern humanitarians," the legislators declared, "the wicked and improvident, the vagabond and meddler, must be smarted [and] reformed." Others agreed. The Mississippi Black Codes were copied, sometimes word for word, by legislators in South Carolina, Georgia, Florida, Alabama, Louisiana, and Texas.[26]

The Black Codes listed specific crimes for the "free negro" alone: "mischief," "insulting gestures," "cruel treatment to animals," and the "vending of spiritous or intoxicating liquors." Free blacks were also prohibited from keeping firearms and from cohabiting with whites. The penalty for intermarriage, the ultimate taboo, was "confinement in the State penitentiary for life."

At the heart of these codes were the vagrancy and enticement laws, designed to drive ex-slaves back to their home plantations. The Vagrancy Act provided that "all free negroes and mulattoes over the age of eighteen" must have written proof of a job at the beginning of every year. Those found "with no lawful employment . . . *shall be deemed vagrants,* and on conviction . . . fined a sum not exceeding . . . fifty dollars." The Enticement Act made it illegal to lure a worker away from his employer by offering him inducements of any kind. Its purpose, of course, was to restrict the flow (and price) of labor by forcing plantation owners to stop "stealing" each other's Negroes.

Given the huge number of cases, the vagrant could not expect a normal trial. Town officials were put in charge of these proceedings, with the sheriff usually meting out justice by himself. If the vagrant did not have fifty dollars to pay his fine—a safe bet—he could be hired out to any white man willing to pay it for him. Naturally, a preference would be given to the vagrant's old master, who was allowed "to deduct and retain the amount so paid from the wages of such freedman."

These codes were vigorously enforced. Hundreds of blacks were arrested and auctioned off to local planters. Others were made to scrub horses, sweep sidewalks, and haul away trash. When news of this crackdown reached the North, a storm of protest arose that there had been little change in the South, despite the sacrifice of 300,000 Yankee lives. "We tell the white men in Mississippi," warned the

Chicago Tribune, "that the men of the North will convert [their] state into a frog pond before they will allow such laws to disgrace one foot of soil in which the bones of our soldiers sleep and over which the flag of freedom waves."[27]

IV

These were not just empty words. In the winter of 1867, the U.S. Congress passed a sweeping Reconstruction Act over President Johnson's angry veto. The act divided the South into five military districts; required the individual states to write new constitutions providing for black manhood suffrage; and compelled their legislatures to ratify the Fourteenth Amendment before applying for readmission to the Union.*

In Mississippi, this act created a new political majority almost overnight. More than 80,000 black voters were registered by federal officials, as opposed to fewer than 60,000 whites. Not surprisingly, these freedmen joined the party of Abraham Lincoln and the Emancipation Proclamation. By 1870, black Republicans in Mississippi were serving as sheriffs, mayors, and state legislators. (Local newspapers routinely described them as "ranting niggers" and "stinking scoundrels.") Their ranks included John R. Lynch, the first black Speaker of the Mississippi House of Representatives, and Hiram B. Revels, the first Negro to serve in the U.S. Senate. Revels would

---

* This act mixed idealism, self-interest, and hypocrisy in fairly equal doses. Northern whites had long treated Northern blacks, who numbered about 250,000, as second-class citizens. Few blacks had the right to vote in the North; indeed, at the very moment this bill was being debated, whites in Ohio, Kansas, and Minnesota were busy defeating referenda that would have guaranteed male Negro suffrage in their own states. In truth, the Reconstruction Act was partly designed to encourage the South's four million ex-slaves to remain where they were. As Senator Roscoe Conkling of New York put it, the best way to keep blacks from "bursting in hordes upon the North" was to "give them liberty and rights in the South, and they will stay there and never come into a cold climate to die."

Emancipation

make history—some called it "historic revenge"—by completing the unexpired term of Jefferson Davis, the state's most famous son.

Reconstruction in Mississippi has sometimes been portrayed as an orgy of waste and corruption, led by Northern profiteers ("carpet-baggers"), Southern opportunists ("scalawags"), and ignorant blacks. In reality, the Reconstruction governments were more compassionate and democratic than any the state had known before. Money was raised to build hospitals, expand state asylums, and repair public works devastated by war. The remaining Black Codes were repealed, and racial distinctions were wiped from the statute books. In 1870, the legislature passed Mississippi's first public education law, guaranteeing four months of free schooling each year to all children, regardless of race. It appeared as if real change were coming to a culture frozen in time.[28]

The appearance was deceiving. As Reconstruction unfolded in Mississippi, black hopes and white fears collided with murderous force. Violence was central to the South's code of personal behavior, its compulsion to settle private matters outside the law. It had always been so in Mississippi—from the gentleman's *code duello* to the common man's head-splitting brawls, from the festive public hangings to the dutiful whipping of slaves. After completing an extensive tour of the South during Reconstruction, a prominent journalist noted that the "respectable people of Mississippi are astonishingly tolerant of acts which would arouse a Northern community to the utmost." There was, he added, a "willingness to see men take the law into their own hands; and what is still worse, to let them openly defy the laws, without losing . . . the respect of the community."[29]

Much of this violence owed nothing to race. Mississippi had a well-deserved reputation as America's most dangerous state. When travelers described its primitive river ports and inland hamlets as the "worst spots" in the nation, local residents did not normally disagree. In 1866, the mayor of Jackson resigned after failing to mobilize public opinion against brawling and lawlessness in his town. Among Jackson's worst offenders were the white lawmakers who battled each other with pistols, knives, and fists. On a May afternoon in 1870, three separate fights erupted in the capital chamber and spilled out into the streets. In one of them, Representative M. J. Manning landed "a good right-hand" on "the fly-trap" of Senator J. C. Shoup, "splitting his lip considerably." In another, Senator J. H. Pierce, the "Panola Giant," defeated Representative J. S. B. Cogge-shall, the "Street Car Conductor," by "planting his right 'digit' in the conductor's left 'peeper,'" and gouging out the eye. Pierce was de-clared the winner and "champion of the Mississippi Legislature."[30]

In 1871, Governor James Lusk Alcorn claimed that the "suppres-sion of the pistol and the knife will do as much in Mississippi as the suppression of the sword did in England for asserting the sanctity of human life." Some Englishmen thought so, too. A visitor from Lon-don, one of Europe's more raucous cities, was amazed at the speed with which chance encounters and trivial slights escalated into grisly homicides. Even dinner conversations in Mississippi, he wrote, had a "smack of manslaughter about them."[31]

Outsiders could never quite fathom the casual nature of these as-saults. Killing seemed easy in Mississippi, and natural to all classes of men. "The heart is sickened . . . with the frequency of life taken sud-denly and by violence," a Northerner lamented. "Two neighbors, life-long friends, perhaps members of the same church, have a slight difference; high words pass; instead of giving reason sway, or refer-ring the subject to the courts, or to friends, one rushes for his pistol or shot gun." A presidential emissary offered this observation to An-drew Johnson after traveling through the South on an inspection tour in 1865: "Mississippians have been shooting and cutting each other . . . to a greater extent than in all the other states of the Union put together."[32]

With emancipation, the focus clearly changed. Violence—and

vigilante action—took on a distinctly racial air. The ex-slaves could no longer count on the "protection" that went along with being the master's valuable property. And their new rights and freedoms made them natural targets for angry, fearful whites. A federal official noted that blacks of Mississippi were now more vulnerable than mules, because the "breaking of the neck of the free negro is nobody's loss." A Southern editor put it crudely but well: "When detected in his frequent delinquencies, Sambo will have no 'maussa' to step in between him and danger."[33]

Now danger was everywhere. Northern senators charged that "two or three black men" were being lynched in Mississippi every day. The true numbers will never be known, because local authorities did not bother to investigate "nigger killings," and the newspapers carefully played them down. The only evidence came from federal authorities in Mississippi and from the intended victims themselves. One Union officer wrote to his superiors that freedmen in his area were being whipped and murdered for offenses more imagined than real. A suspected horse thief, he said, "was beheaded, skinned, and nailed to the barn." In Vicksburg, a group of "colored citizens" begged the governor for help. "The rebels are turbulent," they wrote, "and are arming themselves . . . to murder poor negroes. Gov., ain't there no pertiction?"[34]

The answer, increasingly, was no. There were never enough soldiers to prevent race violence in Mississippi, and the mobs grew bolder as federal troops were cut back over time. Besides, Northern officers did not always oppose vigilante action, particularly when "sexual" crimes were said to be involved. In one instance a general told mob leaders that they "had done right" to lynch a Negro charged with insulting a white woman. In another, a captain allowed a freedman accused of rape to be run to death by hounds.[35]

Much of this violence was the work of local rifle clubs like White Rose, Seventy-Six, and Sons of the South. But the biggest group by far was the "invisible empire" known as the Ku Klux Klan, comprising white men from all classes and regions of Mississippi. Its local anthem went like this:

> Niggers and [Republicans], get out of the way.
> We're born of the night and we vanish by day.
> No rations have we, but the flesh of man—
> And love niggers best—the Ku Klux Klan.
> We catch 'em alive and roast 'em whole.
> And hand 'em around with a sharpened pole.[36]

Klan violence was often random, spontaneous, and poorly planned, but it spread quickly and took every imaginable form. There were attacks on freedmen who voted, ran for office, sat on juries, and testified against whites. In hard-scrabble Monroe County, a Klan mob made "fried nigger meat" of a Republican leader by disemboweling him in front of his wife. In the fertile cotton lands, Klansmen enforced plantation discipline by whipping "lazy" workers and detaining ex-slaves who tried to move on. A freedman from Marion County recalled his "old massa" telling him, "Now you show up t'morrer an' get your-self behind a mule or I'll land you in de chain gang for stealin,' or set the Klu Klux on you." The freedman added: "That's how come I ain't stole f'om dat day to this un."[37]

Among the Klan's favorite targets were Northern white teachers who had traveled south to instruct black children about the rights and responsibilities of freedom. Local white opinion of these teachers was very harsh. The historian of Oktibbeha County described them as "obnoxious agitators" who "incited the darkeys against their old friends, the Southern whites." How? By teaching blacks that freedom meant thinking for themselves.[38]

For the most part, native whites viewed the very idea of black education as a contradiction in terms. Why confuse the Negro by raising false hopes about his naturally humble station in life? "These country niggers are like monkeys," a white woman explained to a local teacher. "You can't *learn* them to come in when it rains."[39]

Most Klan attacks took place in the poor hill country, where white farmers were struggling with crop failures, fears of black competition, and the numbing losses of war. It was here that teachers were threatened, beaten, and sometimes killed. "The violence centered on the schools of the Negroes . . . ," wrote one historian. "By the summer of 1871, in a number of counties, not a school remained in operation."[40]

The worst Klan violence occurred in Meridian, near the Alabama line. Badly damaged by Sherman's troops in 1863, Meridian, a railroad center, had become a magnet for ex-slaves fleeing the cotton fields in search of better jobs and simple adventure. This influx had led white residents to form vigilante groups for "self-protection," with mixed results. One mob action in 1865 was triggered by the disappearance of a planter named William Wilkinson. Local whites, assuming that Wilkinson had been robbed and murdered by his own field hands, formed a posse to round up the suspects. The mob surrounded Wilkinson's plantation, roughed up several freedmen, and was preparing to lynch them when federal troops intervened. The next morning, a lonely soldier came upon Wilkinson in a Meridian brothel, "quite alive, though somewhat disheveled by the two days he had spent celebrating his cotton sale."[41]

As Meridian's black population expanded in the late 1860s, tensions increased between local Republicans, who ran the town government, and local vigilantes, who vowed to bring it down. Both groups formed their own militias; both held emotional rallies and parades. In 1870, two black county supervisors were assassinated. An explosion seemed inevitable.

It came in the spring of 1871, at the trial of three blacks charged with inciting arson in the town. Almost everyone came to the courtroom well armed, as Mississippians had been doing for years. This time shots rang out, killing the white Republican judge and several black spectators. The crowd surged forward, chasing down one defendant, whose body they riddled with bullets, and hurling another from the roof. ("When this failed to kill him," a witness reported, "his throat was cut.") For the next three days, local Klansmen rampaged through Meridian, murdering "all the leading colored men of the town with one or two exceptions." Despite frantic pleas for help, federal troops in Mississippi did not arrive in time. When the slaughter finally ended, more than twenty-five blacks were dead. So, too, was Republican rule in this hill country town.[42]

The Meridian riot demonstrated that the black community—poorly armed, economically dependent, and new to freedom—could not effectively resist white violence without federal help. And it showed that such help might be lacking at the very moment it was needed most. By 1871, Northern sympathy for the freedman's troubles had begun to wane. Military occupation was simply not working in the South; even General Sherman, the U.S. Army commander, despaired of propping up weak and provocative state governments with more federal troops. As black Meridian buried its dead that spring, the failure of Reconstruction was clear. The freedman stood dangerously alone.[43]

Meridian set the stage for a full-blown epidemic of racial violence in the South. And Mississippi, with its vigilante tradition and vulnerable black majority, would lead the region in every imaginable kind of mob atrocity: most lynchings, most multiple lynchings, most lynchings of women, most lynchings without an arrest, most lynchings of a victim in police custody, and most public support for the process itself. Widely defended as the only effective deterrent against the murder and rape of white women by Negro men, mob violence would be directed at burglars, arsonists, horse thieves, grave robbers, peeping toms, and "trouble-makers"—virtually all of them black.[44]

For the victims of mob violence, there was no hope of redress.

Emancipation

The traditional protections of slavery were gone. In a perverse way, emancipation had made the black population more vulnerable than before. It now faced threats from two directions: white mobs and white courts. Like the Ku Klux Klan, the criminal justice system would become a dragnet for the Negro. The local jails and state prisons would grow darker by the year. And a new American gulag, known as convict leasing, would soon disgrace Mississippi, and the larger South, for decades to come.

✠

CHAPTER TWO

The Mississippi Plan

It is not the shame or the hard labor to which we object; it is the
slow torturous death inflicted by the demonic-like contractor who
takes us to the Yazoo Delta to "wear our lives away." It is fearful, it
is dreadful, it is damnable.

—W. G. Orr, Okolona, Mississippi, writing to Governor Robert Lowry
about the evils of convict leasing, 1884

I

On a Mississippi Delta plantation in 1866, a black field hand named
Viney was caught stealing a pig. Her employer and former master,
Wilmer Shields, well understood the motive for her crime: Viney's
children had nothing to eat. Yet Shields did not hesitate to summon
the sheriff in Natchez, a considerable distance away. "If I can induce
the [law] to come so far she shall be arrested and prosecuted," Shields
told a friend. "If not I will drive her from the place, first making her
pay for the 40 lb. hog."[1]

This incident reflected the new rules of punishment in the
post–Civil War South. Not every black would be as luckless as Viney,
nor every white as unbending as Wilmer Shields. Much would de-

pend on circumstance: the mood of the employer, the importance of the worker, the nature of the crime. But something fundamental had changed. Throughout the South, thousands of ex-slaves were being arrested, tried, and convicted for acts that in the past had been dealt with by the master alone. The theft of a pig could now mean a few years at hard labor instead of a beating behind the barn. An offense against Mr. Shields had become an offense against the state.

Southern whites had long viewed criminal behavior as natural to the Negro. They took his stealing for granted, as a biological flaw. An "honest darkey," most believed, was as rare as a Negro virgin of fifteen. "You can't find a white streak in 'em, if you turn 'em wrong side outwards and back again . . . ," one planter observed. "All the men are thieves, and all the women are prostitutes. It's their natur' to be that way, and they'll never be no other way."[2]

With freedom, "black crime" moved well beyond the plantation. Stealing was the most common offense. From Florida to Virginia, from the Carolinas to Texas, came reports of ex-slaves' looting "pigs, turkeys, chickens, melons, and roasting ears" from white families who seemed perilously close to poverty themselves. "The negroes are so destitute they will keep stealing," wrote a Mississippi woman in 1866. "They think, the last one of them, that they have a right to what belongs to their former owners." General Edmund Ord, the military commander of her district, did not disagree. The Negroes are "plundering for food," he cabled from Vicksburg. "Owners are leaving the country for safety—and there is reason to fear a war of races if the blacks are not fed."[3]

But hunger did not explain it all. Stealing had always been common among slaves, though its intensity, and punishment, varied by place. Some masters had cracked down hard on theft; others had excused it "on grounds of congenital black character"—that is, the Negro was a "born thief." Some had even encouraged their slaves to steal from neighboring plantations; others had looked the other way. And those slaves who stole regularly from their masters had often viewed it as a "payback"—a response to being underfed or exploited, an act of defiance from below. In some cases, slaves had described their stealing as a mere recycling of the master's property: "If chicken eat corn, only turn massa corn into massa chicken; he no tief. If hog root through potato row, he no tief; only turn massa potato into massa hog. If nigger eat corn, and chicken, and hog, he no tief; all massa's yet." The problem, however, was that stealing would become a way of life for many ex-slaves, whose victims, increasingly, were those for whom the law offered the least possible protection: fellow blacks.[4]

Across the South, white reaction was intense. There were calls to bring back the gallows for serious property crimes, and the whipping post for misdemeanors such as vagrancy and petty theft. In Alabama, vigilantes punished hundreds of "thieving niggers" on their own. Some were flogged; others were lynched. In Mississippi, farmers were urged to gun down loitering freedmen and "let the buzzards hold an inquest over [their] remains." In Georgia, an editor suggested military force: "If the white people of the South find that the negro continues to steal all they raise, they may possibly conclude to raise troops and see whether the negroes will steal them."[5]

It did not take long for the new outlines of crime and punishment to emerge. The fear of white men assaulting one another—a matter of some concern in previous years—had been replaced by the problem of blacks stealing animals, household items, and crops. Whites "look upon the negroes with a kind of horror," as "a body of men [who] are going to rob them . . . ," explained a federal official in Mississippi. "I believe the white people down there are generally inclined to think that stealing is a baser crime than killing, and that breaking a man's head is not half so mean and contemptible as cutting his purse."[6]

Law enforcement now meant keeping the ex-slaves in line. "Whenever larceny, burglary, arson, and similiar crimes are committed in the South," said a Charleston attorney, "no one is suspected [anymore] save negroes." And almost no one save Negroes went to trial. When a local newspaper described a typical day at the Richmond police court in the late 1860s, it could have been writing about the one in Vicksburg or Atlanta, in Galveston or New Orleans. "Africa was on the rampage," it reported in the distinctive prose of that time and place. "The dock was thronged with forlorn, degraded, and sulky eboshins," including "a negro city buck," "a kinky-headed culprit," "a flat-nosed, bullet-headed, asp-eyed little darkey," "a decriped old negress," and "a lady of color" charged with "stealing three pounds of butter from John (not Jim) Crow."[7]

As convictions mounted, Southern prisons turned black. "In slavery times," a freedman recalled, "jails was all built for the white folks. There warn't never nobody of my color put in none of them. No time . . . to stay in jail; they had to work; when they done wrong they was whipped and let go." After emancipation, this pattern was reversed. By 1866, the Natchez city jail held sixty-seven black prisoners and just eleven whites. In Grenada, to the north, there were seventeen blacks and one white. In Columbus, to the east, there were fifty-three blacks and no whites. Almost overnight, the jailhouse had become a "negro preserve."[8]

For the ex-slave, the ways of the state seemed no gentler than the ways of the master. Indeed, the punishments could be more severe. "You kno' you niver heard tell uf a slave bein' sent ter de pen," said a freedman from Pike County, Mississippi. "En now de niggers goes ter de pen ebber time de courts meet. Dey had better wish dey wus slaves."[9]

II

Throughout the South, emancipation placed enormous strains on a modest prison system gutted by war. Many of the jails and penitentiaries had been destroyed. There was no money to repair them or to house the flood of criminals now pouring through the courts. In Mississippi—a state with more blacks and less revenue per capita than any other—these problems were particularly severe. The penitentiary at Jackson had been torched in 1863; the local jails were crumbling from neglect. "Emancipation . . . will require a system of prisons," a state official observed at war's end. "The one in Jackson was nearly full *when the courts had little to do with the negroes.* How will it be now?"[10]

The answer was provided by a businessman named Edmund Richardson. Born in North Carolina in 1818, Richardson had parlayed an inheritance of $2,800 and a few slaves into an empire of cotton plantations and general stores throughout Mississippi. When the Civil War began, his assets totaled $1 million; when it ended, almost everything was gone. "Somehow he had saved five hundred bales of cotton," wrote a sympathetic biographer. "In a year he was out of debt and soon had capital in his business. It was quite a comeback."[11]

Richardson moved quickly. In 1868, he struck a bargain with the federal authorities in Mississippi. Richardson needed cheap labor to work some land he had bought in the sparsely settled Yazoo Delta; the state had a gutted penitentiary overflowing with ex-slaves. The result was a contract that allowed Richardson to work these felons outside the prison walls. He promised to feed them, clothe them, guard them, and treat them well. The state agreed to pay him $18,000 a year for their maintenance and an additional sum for their transportation to and from his primitive Delta camps. Richardson got to keep all of the profits he derived from the labor of these convicts.

Richardson's contract began the era of convict leasing in Mississippi. At the time, it seemed a stop-gap measure to deal with rising crime rates until a new prison could be built. It did not turn out that way. Before convict leasing officially ended, a generation of black prisoners would suffer and die under conditions far worse than anything they had ever experienced as slaves. Few of them would spend much time inside a state prison or a county jail. They would serve their sentences in the coal mines, sawmills, railroad camps, and cotton fields of the emerging New South.

Richardson set down the guidelines that others would follow. He separated his convicts by race, keeping the whites in Jackson and sending the blacks to his primitive Delta farms. According to the *Penitentiary Report of 1871,* "146 colored males" and "6 colored females" were shipped to the Delta, while "61 white males" and "25 colored males" (the old and disabled) remained at the state penitentiary, or Walls. There were no white female convicts at this time, because Southern custom frowned upon their incarceration. When Alabama sent its first white woman, a murderess, to the penitentiary in 1850, state officials expressed amazement at finding a "lady so destitute of virtue and honor."[12]

Richardson's black convicts did the "nigger work": building levees, clearing swampland, and ploughing the fields. The *Penitentiary Report* lied shamelessly about conditions on his farms. "Few punishments had to be administered," it said, "and labor in most cases has been cheerfully performed." The report added, almost in passing, that 119 convicts had escaped since 1868 and that dozens more had died of gunshot wounds and disease.

No one seemed to care. The stories about Richardson focused on his incredible success and wealth. Convict leasing had helped him earn a fortune, a fact noted by businessmen throughout the South. By 1880, he had built a mansion in New Orleans, another in Jackson, and a sprawling plantation house known as Refuge in the Yazoo Delta. His holdings included banks, steamboats, and railroads. He owned three dozen cotton plantations and a controlling interest in Mississippi Mills, the largest textile plant in the Lower South. His New Orleans–based brokerage house, Richardson and May, handled more than 250,000 bales of cotton each year.

The press called him the "greatest of Southern financiers" and the "largest cotton planter in the world, not excepting the Khedive of

Egypt." Publicly, Richardson described himself as a model employer, the "darkey's" best friend. Time and again, he reminded visitors at Refuge that his "favorite slaves," given to him as wedding gifts in 1840, were still working for him as house servants in 1880, "never desiring to change their happy condition."[13]

III

Convict leasing was a system that pitted rich people against poor people, whites against blacks, and ex-masters against former slaves. Its profits would be widely resented and narrowly shared. Yet the system arose during the "radical Reconstruction" of Mississippi, an era of promising racial change. It was tolerated by state Republican leaders, black and white, who owed their offices to the power of Negro votes. In 1870, Governor James Lusk Alcorn condemned the "shocking spectacle of a group of [convicts] followed by keepers with loaded rifles, ready to shoot them as though they were dogs." A few months later, unable to find a better alternative, Alcorn extended Richardson's contract for another two years.[14]

But convict leasing did not fully take hold in Mississippi until after 1875, when the Republican party was routed and the federal troops went home. In the fall of that year, local Democrats launched their infamous Mississippi Plan, designed to win back the state government—and ensure white supremacy—through terror, coercion, and fraud. A white Democrat described the political campaign of 1875 as a "revolutionary crusade." A black Republican called it the "most violent time that ever we have seen."[15]

In "redeeming" Mississippi from the clutches of "black power" and "Yankee control," the Democrats provided a model for other Southern states to follow. They proved that whites from different classes and regions could be united by simple appeals to race. And they showed that a determined minority could win any election if their tactics were intimidating enough.

In Mississippi, angry planters threatened to drive "nigger Republicans" from their fields. Merchants denied them credit, and newspapers published blacklists of their names. But violence was the key to this campaign, and it erupted first in Vicksburg, the rough-and-tumble Mississippi River port, when a white mob forced the "resignation" of Sheriff Peter Crosby, a black Republican accused of widespread corruption. Crosby responded by forming a posse of local freedmen to help him take his office back. On December 7, 1874, five hundred blacks, armed with knives and pistols, were met by a well-drilled white militia near the outskirts of town. The battle quickly became a rout, and then a massacre. The militia, using cavalry and long-range rifles, tore through Crosby's poorly trained men. When the fighting ended, white units went on a rampage. Three hundred blacks were murdered in a matter of days; white deaths were listed at two.[16]

In desperation, the Republican legislature authorized Governor Adelbert Ames, a former Union general, to organize and equip two regiments of state militia, composed largely of black recruits. Ames raised hundreds of men but hesitated to use them, fearing that their deployment would spark a full-scale war between the races. Instead, he pleaded for assistance from Washington, which had lost the will to intervene. "The freedom of a race is at stake," Ames wrote. "We do hope the North will stand true to the rights of the colored man."[17]

In the following months, as federal authorities did nothing, white vigilantes roamed the Mississippi countryside terrorizing Republican rallies and their largely Negro crowds. When blacks resisted, retaliation was extreme. At a political barbecue in Clinton, a number of armed and drunk white men were killed in a gun battle with local freedmen who had come well prepared to defend themselves. "The news spread rapidly," wrote a local historian, "and the county was wild with excitement. Soon special trains with companies of armed men came . . . to aid the whites." Led by the Vicksburg militia, they launched an "indiscrimate assault on blacks," killing "between twenty and thirty" before returning to their homes.

White opinion viewed the slaughter as part of a "glorious struggle" against the "mongrelism, ignorance, and depravity" of radical Republican rule. In the words of one defender, "this lesson of Anglo-Saxon supremacy, written in blood, will ever remain the most important of many lessons taught in the modest college town of Clinton to the rising young manhood of a proud and untrammeled Commonwealth."[18]

Dozens more died in places like Rose Hill, Satartia, Columbus, and Drew. "If they don't like a negro here," said a white man from violent Pike County, "he is pretty apt to be killed." These murders occurred at public meetings, in broad daylight, without the slightest hesitation or disguise. There was little fear of punishment because white opinion strongly supported these crimes. *"Mississippi is a white man's country,"* declared the *Yazoo City Banner, "and by the Eternal God we'll rule it."*[19]

On election day 1875, thousands of black voters stayed home or were turned away at the polls. Fraud was so rampant that Republican candidates received a scant seven votes in Yazoo County, where blacks outnumbered whites by three to one. The official results showed Democrats winning two-thirds of the congressional seats and both houses of the state legislature. There were no apologies or second thoughts. In the words of one Democratic leader: "We were *forced* to a choice between the evils of negro rule and the evils of the questionable practices to overthrow it. We chose what we thought was the lesser evil, and it is now not to be regretted."[20]

Time would prove him wrong. The events of 1875 would linger for generations in a closed society of racial caste and stifling one-party rule. From this point forward, every issue, every candidate, every public decision would be held hostage to the bugaboo of race. And every possible corruption, from lynching to ballot stuffing, would be excused or defended as a "necessary evil." Before departing Mississippi for his Northern home, Governor Ames summed up the devastating consequences of this election for the blacks he had left behind: "Yes, a *revolution* has taken place—by force of arms—and a race are disenfranchised. They are to be returned to a condition of serfdom—an era of second slavery."[21]

IV

When the Mississippi legislature convened in 1876, crime and punishment were among its primary concerns. The new Democratic majority was extremely sensitive to the issue of black "lawlessness" and to growing white demands for tougher penalties and controls. The Democrats were fascinated by the potential of convict leasing. They knew that white taxpayers would never fund an expensive penitentiary, whatever their worries about crime. They believed that convicts could provide at least a partial solution to the needs of Mississippi's labor-starved employers. And they assumed that the profits generated by leasing would quiet any moral rumblings about the treatment of black criminals, who were, after all, the dregs of an "inferior" race.

Early in 1876, the legislature passed a major crime bill aimed directly at the Negro. Known as the Pig Law, it redefined "grand larceny"—offenses punishable by up to five years in state prison—to include the theft of a farm animal or any property valued at ten dollars or more. Arrests shot up dramatically; the number of state convicts quadrupled, from 272 in 1874 to 1,072 by 1877. According to one official, the Pig Law did nothing to stop crime but quite a lot to spur convict leasing. "The affinity of 'our Brother in Black' for fresh pork," he observed, "was in no wise impaired by it."[22]

As the legislature increased the penalties for minor property crimes, the local courts moved to weaken the protections only recently afforded black defendants. By 1875, wrote one historian,

"Negroes appeared in smaller and smaller numbers on the jury panels, [although] their complete elimination did not occur until after 1890." Blacks were rarely represented by counsel, and their testimony was often restricted to cases in which whites were not directly involved. "You can't believe a thing a negro says," one judge remarked. "They will tell you just what they think you want to hear."[23]

The Pig Law did not stand alone. It was followed a few weeks later by "AN ACT to provide for leasing the . . . convict labor of the State." All prisoners, it declared, may "work outside the penitentiary in building railroads, levees or in any private labor or employment." With the gates now officially open, Mississippi leased more than a thousand of its convicts in one fell swoop. They included the likes of Rause Echols, "colored of Lauderdale County," who was handed a three-year sentence for stealing an "old suit of clothes." And Lewis Luckett of Canton, Mississippi, "a pure and simple negro, black as the ace of spades," who received a two-year sentence for the theft of a hog. Robert Hamber, "colored of Chickasaw County," got five years for stealing a horse. His case bore out the suspicion that no freedman was too feeble or unfit to work on a convict labor gang. Described by neighbors as an "imbecile and a cleptomaniac," Hamber had recently been discharged from the state lunatic asylum on the remarkable grounds that he was an "idiot."[24]

The Leasing Act was designed for black, not white, convicts. It cleverly ensured this distinction by setting aside the old penitentiary in Jackson to house prisoners serving ten years or more. The intent, said lawmakers, was to keep the most dangerous criminals behind well-guarded prison walls. In truth, however, the real issue was race. Though far fewer in number, white convicts received longer sentences than blacks because the courts of Mississippi did not normally punish whites for anything except the most heinous of crimes.

The Leasing Act also permitted the towns and counties to work their convicts outside the local jails—in theory, anyone who had breached a local ordinance and was sentenced to one year or less.

In practice, it applied to those who could not pay the fines and court costs that accompanied almost every trial. The end result was a stream of black bodies to the county chain gangs and local plantations.

The chain gang took people like Walter Blake, a "crap-shooting little colored boy" who received a $50 fine for illegal gambling and a $132 bill for court costs, a sum he could not possibly raise. Blake spent a full year working off his debt. A "negro thief" named Julius Hoy found himself reduced to virtual peonage during his stay on the Covington County chain gang. "He is being charged 60 cents per day for board," a local attorney noted, "and at present the fine and accumulated board amounts to approximately $89.20, and it will never be possible for him to serve out his time."[25]

Other county convicts went straight to the fields. Their paths can be traced in the meticulous record books left by David Hearn, a private contractor in the Yazoo Delta. One of his entries is for Henry Gale, a freedman sentenced to ninety days, a $5.00 fine, and $9.95 in "costs" for being "a tramp."

Fine:	$5.00
Mayor's Fee	3.90
Officer's Fee	3.25
Jail Fee	2.80
Total	14.95

Hearn paid the various charges, took control of Henry Gayle, and leased him to a local planter for $8.00 a month. The judge, mayor, sheriff, and jailer split the $14.95. Hearn received $24.00 from the planter, who got himself a field hand for ninety days at a fraction of the normal cost. Only Henry Gayle would suffer the consequences of this deplorable system, but he was hardly in a position to complain.[26]

V

The exclusive right to lease state convicts quickly became Mississippi's most prized political contract, coveted by planters, businessmen, and speculators across the board. It passed from Colonel Edmund Richardson, who had spent a small fortune bribing legislators, to General Nathan Bedford Forest, first Grand Wizard of the Ku Klux Klan, to Colonel Jones S. Hamilton, a gambler-turned-financier from Wilkinson County, south of Natchez. Hamilton had commanded a batallion of Confederate cavalry during the Civil War. He was already a legend of sorts in Mississippi—portrayed by contemporaries as a reckless, quick-tempered adventurer who could "spend a fortune with the same speed and facility with which he could make it."

Hamilton owned the Jackson gas works, a racetrack, and a number of hotels. He would later use the profits he made from convict leasing to buy a piece of the Gulf and Ship Island Railroad, an operation maintained, in large part, by the prisoners under his control. The railroad would help spur the great timber boom in Mississippi by opening its vast pine forests for exploitation. It would also make Hamilton a millionaire.[27]

The new lease, a four-year contract signed in 1876, was a bit less generous than the Richardson deal. Hamilton got no money from the state. He agreed to provide for the maintenance of his convicts and to pay a monthly fee of $1.10 for each one he leased. With contract in hand, he placed advertisements in the local press:

J. S. HAMILTON & CO.,
LESSEES MISSISSIPPI PENITENTIARY
Jackson, Mississippi

Contractors for the Building or Repairing of all kinds of Public Buildings, Court Houses, Jails, Churches. Etc., Etc. Also for Bridges, Trestles, Rail Road and Levee Work. All work fully guaranteed.

After Slavery, Before Parchman

His profits were enormous. Unlike Colonel Richardson, who had used most of the convicts on his own land, Hamilton subleased the great bulk of them to other interests, especially the railroads, at a monthly rate of nine dollars per head. He became a middleman, a latter-day version of the slave broker who supplied fettered Africans to the great plantations of the antebellum South.[28]

From a business standpoint, the subleasing was ideal. It plugged the major weakness of the old system: the high fixed cost of labor. Under the sublease, an employer was not stuck with a set number of prisoners over a long period of time. He did not have to feed, clothe, and guard them when there was little work to be done. He could now lease convicts according to his specific, or seasonal, needs.

In terms of human misery, however, this system could hardly have been worse. The convict now found himself laboring for the profits of three separate parties: the sublessee, the lessee, and the state. There was no one to protect him from savage beatings, endless workdays, and murderous neglect. "It is to be supposed that sub-lessees [take] convicts for the purpose of making money out of them," wrote a prison doctor, "so naturally, the less food and clothing used and the more labor derived from their bodies, the more money in the pockets of the sub-lessee." If a convict died or escaped, his employer lost nothing. Colonel Hamilton would profitably supply a replacement—at nine dollars per month.[29]

Hamilton's convicts worked at jobs that free labor did not like to do, in places were free labor sometimes feared to go. Employers preferred them over Asians ("too fragile"), Irish ("too belligerent"), and local blacks ("too slow"). "They do 30 percent work more than free laborers," said one report, which praised their "hard, steady" pace. When the Greenville Railroad needed workers to lay track in the scorching heat of the Yazoo Delta, it subleased convicts. When the Mississippi Central needed men to dynamite a tunnel near Kosciusko, it subleased convicts. When the New Orleans and Northeastern needed labor to clear a malarial swamp south of Hattiesburg, it subleased convicts at a premium daily rate of $1.75 a head. According to witnesses, the men were chained for days in knee-deep pools of muck, "their thirst driving them to drink the water in which they were compelled to deposit their excrement."[30]

As the railroad boom tailed off in the late 1880s, most convicts were transferred to the emerging Yazoo Delta plantations, where workers were still scarce and the competition for them was fierce. "The crop [here] is being considerably damaged by want of sufficient labor," a landowner complained. "I hope you will send additional convicts without a moment's delay." At times, these planters requested "darkies" and "niggers" as if emancipation had never really occurred. "When you get a moment," wrote one, "won't you send a slave out to fix my cemetery fence?"[31]

The plantation records of this era tell a story of endless brutality and neglect. The prisoners ate and slept on bare ground, without blankets or mattresses, and often without clothes. They were punished for "slow hoeing" (ten lashes), "sorry planting" (five lashes), and "being light with cotton" (five lashes). Some who tried to escape were whipped "till the blood ran down their legs"; others had a metal spur riveted to their feet. Convicts dropped from exhaustion, pneumonia, malaria, frostbite, consumption, sunstroke, dysentery, gunshot wounds, and "shackle poisoning" (the constant rubbing of chains and leg irons against bare flesh). "This farm is too hot for me and i am sick and i cant see veary far and i look to be punish at any time for not doing my task when i know i am not abel," wrote a weary convict from the Delta. "Please dont think i am mean for writing this for i am not i has dun all i can . . . but i wish for the governor to know i has not ben treated rite. i would like to go back to the Walls but i afraid of bing punish for [asking] to leave."[32]

Occasionally a local doctor or health official would be sent out to inspect these plantations. His main job, aside from signing the death certificates, was to separate the prisoners who were well enough to work from the ones who were hopelessly ill. Those in the latter group were either pardoned by the governor or shipped back to the prison hospital in Jackson. Among their ranks were Albert Robinson, a burglar, "in the last stage of consumption"; Sam Milsap, a petty thief, "having from two to three fits a day"; Alex Graves, a moonshiner, "suffering with a fractured skull"; Moses Mullins, an arsonist, who "lost all of his toes from frostbite"; and "Convict #723" from Bolivar County, whose "open bullet wound" was discharging "very offensive" pus. "He keeps the Cage in bad odor," the doctor noted, and "can do no work in his present condition."[33]

Some of these officials were paid to write favorable reports by the lessees, but others wrote honestly about what they observed. After treating "an emaciated consumptive, 17 years old," on a Delta plantation, the attending physician noted that the word *unsanitary* did not begin "to express the filthy conditions of the convict cage": bloodstained dirt floor, overflowing waste buckets, and vermin-covered walls. And a doctor sent to study the "unusual mortality among convicts on W. F. Randolph's place at Bogue Philia" could barely contain his rage. The convicts spent their days in blazing, shadeless fields, he charged, and their nights chained up outdoors. "As long as the state expects to get this work done for less money than it is worth, they will find that at the end of the year they have paid the balance in men."[34]

In the 1880s, the annual mortality rate for Mississippi's convict population ranged from 9 to 16 percent. Blacks suffered far more than whites, who rarely left the penitentiary walls. In 1882, for example, 126 of 735 black state convicts perished, as opposed to 2 of 83 whites. Not a single leased convict ever lived long enough to serve a sentence of ten years or more. It is little wonder that George Washington Cable, the noted social reformer, described leasing in Mississippi as the "system at its worst."[35]

And that was not all. Hundreds of black children were leased because the state penal code did not distinguish between adult and juvenile offenders. By 1880, at least one convict in four was an adolescent or a child—a percentage that did not diminish over time. "The boys are put in degrading stripes and herded with the adult criminals," wrote a leading reformer. "I do not know what the prison officials are doing toward their reformation, but I do know that the law takes no account of them."[36]

White taxpayers refused to "waste" money on the needs of "incorrigible" young blacks. When a state legislator pressed for a juvenile reform school in the late nineteenth century, he acknowledged that the "opposition to my bill is principally that negroes form a large majority of the prisoners." As a compromise, he proposed that "schooling and moral instruction" be limited to the evenings, after "10 or twelve hours of work" had been performed in the fields. His bill was defeated on the ground that "it was no use trying to reform a negro."[37]

Black children remained a vital part of Mississippi's powerful convict labor machine. In the 1870s, the machine included Robert Day (age twelve; height four feet, nine inches; complexion black) serving a life sentence for murder, and James Harrington (age thirteen; height five feet, one inch; complexion black), serving ten years for "burglary with intent to rape." In the 1880s, it added Mary Gay of Vicksburg, "a negro child, but little over six years old," sentenced to thirty days "plus court costs" for stealing a hat. And in 1901, it snared young Will Evans, a "flat-nosed negro" from Washington County, whose "vital facts" were these:

Height: 4 feet, 5 inches.
Occupation: Errand Boy.
Term: 2 years.
Weight: 70 pounds.
Crime: Grand Larceny.
Habits of Life: Good.
Use of Tobacco: Yes.
Education: Very Little.

Build: Child
Style of Whiskers Worn When Received: None

Young Will was sent to prison for stealing some change from the counter of a dry goods store. He was eight years old.[38]

VI

In the winter of 1884, a squad of battered convicts arrived in Vicksburg by steamer from a nearby Delta farm. The men were chained together, frostbitten, and barely alive. Their filthy, half-naked bodies were covered with blisters and scars. "They presented such a shocking spectacle," wrote one official, "that the city authorities of Vicksburg refused to permit them to march through the streets, and had them conveyed in covered wagons to the railway stop." Their final destination was the prison hospital in Jackson, forty miles to the east, where worn-out convicts were routinely sent to die.[39]

The Vicksburg incident was a milestone of sorts. It marked the first serious challenge to convict leasing in Mississippi after a decade of profits and praise. All at once a window had opened, exposing abuses too shameful to ignore. Angry editorials appeared, aimed at negligent officials and brutal lessees. Lawmakers promised to investigate, and the courts took a peek of their own. What they found, in the words of one observer, was a system of "fiendish cruelty," which "could only [flourish] in an ex-slave state where ex-slaves made up the majority of its convicts."[40]

One revelation followed another. Late in 1884, a committee of the legislature acknowledged that prisoners had been savagely abused by sublessees throughout the state. Some had been murdered by sadistic guards; others, "unable to work, had been driven to death while fettered in chains." When the Hinds County grand jury paid a surprise visit to the prison hospital in Jackson, it found twenty-six recent arrivals from the convict railroad camps. "All [bear] marks of the most brutal and inhuman treatment," the jurors reported:

> Most of them have their backs cut in great wales, scars, and blisters, some with the skin peeling off in places as the result of severe beatings. . . . All of them [have] the stamp of manhood blotted out of their faces. . . . They are lying there dying, some of them on bare boards . . . with live vermin crawling over their [bodies].[41]

The battle against leasing initially was fought on humanitarian grounds, with opponents focusing on the cruel treatment of convicts, not on the profits made by the elite. Among the leaders of this early struggle were editors John Martin of *The New Mississippian* and Roderick Gambrell of *The Sword and Shield*. Both men were moral reformers who railed against liquor and gambling as well as the convict lease. And both men criticized Colonel Hamilton, the high-living, racetrack-owning wheeler-dealer who seemed to embody all shades of evil.

To Hamilton, this meant a duel. Though banned by statute in 1820, dueling was still regarded in some quarters as the honorable way of settling a dispute. It appeared to be a leading cause of death among Mississippi's embattled newspaper editors, four of whom had been gunned down in Vicksburg alone. The most recent incident had occurred in 1875 in the town of West Point, after the Republican editor accused his Democratic competitor of climbing the courthouse flag pole to "view the ladies of the visiting D'Este theater troupe" as they dressed for the show. Meeting on the dusty main street, the two had fired pistols at each other from point-blank range. "Both gentlemen displayed extraordinary coolness," a witness noted. The Republican editor was killed in his tracks; the Democrat was unhurt. A few days later, an editor from nearby Aberdeen was shot dead by the D'Este Troupe's leading actor in a dispute over a "harshly-worded" theater review.[42]

Colonel Hamilton confronted Roderick Gambrell on the Capitol Street Bridge in Jackson. Both men hit their mark, the "young editor being carried off dead, while Hamilton was borne home seriously wounded." At his murder trial in 1887, the colonel was acquitted by a jury after fifteen minutes of deliberation. For the rest of his long life, he would proudly display the bullet that doctors pulled from his chest.

Within months of Gambrell's death, editor John Martin followed him to the grave. He was killed in a duel with General Wirt Adams, a "gallant Confederate soldier," a friend of Colonel Hamilton, and a partner in Gulf and Ship Island Railroad. "Adams fired three shots; Martin six. Both men were shot through the heart and died within six feet of each other."[43]

Nobody was surprised; crusading editors in Mississippi did not often die in their sleep. "It has been a matter of wonderment," wrote one newspaper, "that [Martin's] brilliant but . . . aggressive pen did not sooner bring him to a violent end—for such must . . . come to all editors who pursue the peculiar line of journalism he saw fit to adopt."[44]

The killings of Gambrell and Martin did not ease the pressure for reform. Others stepped forward to take their place. The patrician *Natchez Democrat* now condemned leasing as "dark and shameful," while the rural *Chickasaw Messenger* called it *"a stain upon our manhood,"* the ultimate Southern disgrace. In the following months, opposition grew amid reports that 15 percent of Mississippi's convicts had died in 1887 (as opposed to less than 1 percent in states like Ohio and Illinois, which kept their prisoners in penitentiaries, under careful state control). According to former attorney general Frank Johnston, convict leasing in Mississippi had produced an "epidemic death rate without the epidemic."[45]

Opponents also played up the large number of convict breakouts from poorly guarded plantations and railroad camps; the annual rate was at least 10 percent. Thus, one state prisoner in four either perished or escaped in an average year. Among whites in Mississippi, the image of black criminals roaming the countryside was a nightmare come true, and the publicity surrounding these escapes served to focus attention on the system's brutality in an unintended way. Time and again, these fugitives were described in newspaper reports as emaciated, frostbitten, and badly scarred by the lash. From shade trees and store windows hung the wanted posters of battered convicts on the loose. The one for Joe Martin, "colored of Pike County," offered a fifty-dollar reward:

> Age 21 years; Ht. 5 ft 8 inches; complexion ginger cake; hair and eyes black; scar on neck under right jaw; scar on right side of chin; scar on tip of penis; scar on front of right upper arm from bullet wound; 2 scars on point of right elbow; 4 dim scars on right kneecap; scar just below left buttock; scar on left groin from syphilis. Thoroughly spotted from jail itch. Laborer. Sentenced . . . for life, for the crime of murder.[46]

VII

In the summer of 1890, 134 delegates—including Isaiah T. Montgomery of Mound Bayou, the lone black and Republican among them—assembled at the state capitol to write a new constitution for Mississippi. Their mission seemed clear. The delegates had come to disenfranchise the Negro, ending the fraud and the violence of previous elections by legally removing his political rights. A newspaper headline put it well: "White Supremacy—The One Idea of the Convention." Others called it the "Second Mississippi Plan."[47]

For most delegates, though, the key issue was not white supremacy but rather "*which whites* should be supreme." In simple terms, it pitted rich against poor, cotton planter against dirt farmer, the Delta against the hills. It was a clash of economic interests and of cultures. In the words of William Alexander Percy, the poor whites of Mississippi, known as "rednecks" and "peckerwoods," were an ignorant, mean-spirited rabble, simply aroused and easily misled. "The virus of poverty, malnutrition, and interbreeding has done its degenerative work," he wrote in *Lanterns on the Levee*, his brooding recollections of a planter's life. "The present breed is probably the most unprepossessing on the broad face of the ill-populated earth. . . . I can forgive them as the Lord God forgives, but admire them, trust them, love them, never."[48]

By 1890, these conflicts threatened to split both the Democratic party and its solid white facade. The small farmers, feeling squeezed and cheated, were demanding reform. At the constitutional convention, their delegates pressed for debt relief, railroad regulation, and an end to convict leasing, though not on humanitarian grounds. To their thinking, the forced labor of black prisoners had enriched a clique of arrogant planters and businessmen at the expense of everyone else. It had provided an unfair advantage to the people who deserved and needed it least.[49]

This combination of class anger and moral outrage carried the day. On September 5, 1890, the convention abolished convict leasing by an overwhelming vote. Article X of the new constitution stated, "No penitentiary convict shall ever be leased or hired to any person or corporation . . . after December the thirty-first, 1894." The delegates did not vote for immediate abolition because there was no place to put the prisoners, but they fully expected the state to solve this problem permanently by "establishing a prison farm" in the next several years.[50]

It did not quite happen that way. Convict leasing would linger in Mississippi, and the great prison farm known as Parchman would open a full decade later than planned. In the meantime, forgotten prisoners would continue to suffer and die, and critics would warn of God's wrath. "What an awful accounting there will be at the Great Day," said prison reformer J. F. Jones, "for the trail of horrors and of murders that this brutal system left behind in . . . Mississippi."[51]

And Mississippi was hardly alone.

✠

CHAPTER THREE

American Siberia

Before the war we owned the negroes. If a man had a good nigger, he could afford to take care of him; if he was sick get a doctor. He might even put gold plugs in his teeth. But these convicts: we don't own 'em. One dies, get another.

—A Southern employer explaining the benefits of convict leasing to reformer George Washington Cable in 1883

I

J. C. Powell was a very rough man. The captain of a convict camp in the Florida woods, he had lived a life that outsiders could barely imagine. Powell had flogged prisoners who "deserved" it and shot those who had "threatened" his life. He had tracked down runaways with bloodhounds and tied them to a fifty-pound ball and chain. He had buried the victims of overwork, accidents, escapes, disease, knife fights, and self-inflicted wounds. But his most vivid memory of convict life was his very first one: the sight of twenty-seven half-dead prisoners staggering from a freight train in the north Florida town of Live Oak in the fall of 1876.

The men had been leased to the St. Johns, Lake Eustis and Gulf

Railroad Company, which was adding a line through the tropical marshes and palmetto jungles of the inland wilderness. "There was no provision made for either shelter or supplies," Powell recalled. "Rude huts were built of whatever material came to hand. . . . The commissary department dwindled into nothing. I do not mean that there was some food or a little food, but that there was no food at all. In this extremity, the convicts were driven to live as the wild beasts, except that they were only allowed the briefest intervals from labor to scour the woods for food."

The ranks began to thin. Starvation, exposure, scurvy, dysentery, pneumonia, malaria—all took their toll. To maintain crumbling discipline, prisoners were tortured for minor infractions of the rules. Some were whipped to death; others, strung up by their thumbs, were left with hands "resembling the paws of certain apes." By the time the job ended, the land alongside the tracks was dotted with graves. Forty-five of the seventy-two convicts did not return. And the survivors—the young men who reached Live Oak on that fall day in 1876—were vermin covered, mostly naked, and wasted with disease. In Powell's words, "The sun never shone upon a more abject picture of misery and dilapidation."[1]

In truth, Powell was wrong: the sun shone daily on such pictures, and the misery widened over time. The suffering at Live Oak was but one scene in the epic drama of convict leasing, which would disgrace the South and shape its progress in fundamental ways. From its beginnings in Mississippi in the late 1860s until its abolition in Alabama in the late 1920s, convict leasing would serve to undermine legal equality, harden racial stereotypes, spur industrial development, intimidate free workers, and breed open contempt for the law. It would turn a few men into millionaires and crush thousands of ordinary lives.

For years, Southern opinion applauded the "benefits" of convict leasing, while ignoring its brutal underside. From a financial standpoint, the system turned a serious problem (the punishment of troublesome ex-slaves) into a remarkable gain. Across the South, leasing added millions in revenue to state and local coffers; it lowered the tax rate for average citizens and generated money for public projects like bridges, schools, and roads. But this was only part of the story—a rather small part—for the real profits of convict leasing went to the firms that hired out these prisoners and to the employers who worked them to exhaustion and beyond. By the 1870s, there was no more talk about leasing as a temporary response to the forces unleashed by emancipation and war. Now the talk had turned to leasing as a long-term asset, providing cheap, pliable labor to a devastated economy in the early stages of industrial growth.

There was more to this system, however, than the profits it generated and the development it spurred. Convict leasing would also serve a cultural need by strengthening the walls of white supremacy as the South moved from an era of racial bondage to one of racial caste. In a region where dark skin and forced labor went hand in hand, leasing would become a functional replacement for slavery, a human bridge between the Old South and the New.[2]

II

When the Civil War ended, Southern officials found their battered jails crowded with convicts who had never been in custody before. The great majority of them, said the Tennessee board of prison directors, were "ignorant" former slaves who had stolen items worth a few dollars or less. They "have no more idea of criminality . . . than a dumb beast that helps himself from his master's crib. It is plainly evident that a school of reformation or instruction is much more a fitting place for such uneducated unfortunates than a State Prison."[3]

But the Tennessee legislature thought otherwise. Railroad fever was sweeping the state, and unskilled labor was in short supply. After little debate and much bribery, the legislators turned over the entire prison system to a professional card gambler named Thomas O'Conner for $150,000 on a five-year lease. By 1871, state convicts were laying track and mining coal from Memphis to Knoxville. Each morning their urine was collected and sold to local tanneries by the barrel. When they died, their unclaimed bodies were purchased by the Medical School at Nashville for the students to practice on.[4]

The advantages of convict labor were quickly perceived. When the Cincinnati Southern Railroad decided to run a trunk line over the Cumberland Mountains to Chattanooga, it first hired gangs of Irish, Italian, and black workers at wages ranging from $1.25 to $3.50 a day. But free labor proved hard to manage, on and off the job. Some men, homesick and exhausted, wandered away. Others drank and brawled in the brothels and gambling dens that lined the mountain route.

So the railroad turned to convicts. Four hundred of them were leased from O'Conner at a daily rate of one dollar per man. Primitive log stockades were constructed, and local guards, sporting shotguns, were hired to mete out punishment and prevent escapes. The convicts worked sixteen-hour shifts with a short break for meals. Completed in a single year, the Cumberland line came in well under budget, and the high quality of the work led some to call it the "best railroad yet built in the United States."[5]

Convict leasing spread like wildfire. During the railroad boom of the 1870s and 1880s, convicts laid most of the 3,500 miles of new track in North Carolina. They were "mainly colored," a machinist recalled, and their crimes had been small. They would steal "two or three chickens," a jury would find them guilty, and the judge would sentence them to a few years in prison. Had they been white, he added, the maximum punishment would have been ninety days in the county jail.[6]

Railroad work was dangerous under any circumstances. The "Accident Record Book" of a small Southern line in a single year gives a clear sense of the peril to life and limb: "hand crushed, collision";

"killed, collision"; "struck by bridge and killed"; "fall from train . . . death"; "son of Rev. J. W. Miller killed"; "skull fractured, death resulted"; "negro boy run over and head cut off"; "leg run over necessitating amputation"; "wreck caused by broken wheel, killed."[7]

But the convict was more vulnerable than the free worker, and he paid a greater price. Despised, powerless, and expendable, he could be made to do any job, at any pace, in any location. "Why? Because he is a *convict*," a railroad official explained, "and if he dies it is a small loss, and we can make him work there, while we cannot get free men to do the same kind of labor for, say, six times as much as the convict costs."[8]

On many railroads, convicts were moved from job to job in a rolling iron cage, which also provided their lodging at the site. The cage—eight feet wide, fifteen feet long, and eight feet high—housed upwards of twenty men. It was similar "to those used for circus animals," wrote a prison official, except it "did not have the privacy which would be given to a respectable lion, tiger, or bear."

The prisoners slept side by side, shackled together, on narrow wooden slabs. They relieved themselves in a single bucket and bathed in the same filthy tub of water. With no screens on the cages, insects swarmed everywhere. It was like a small piece of hell, an observer noted—the stench, the chains, the sickness, and the heat. "They lie on their beds, their faces almost touching the bed above them. . . . On hot days . . . the sun streams down . . . and makes an oven of the place, and the human beings in it roast."[9]

Their lives were always in peril. A year or two on the Western North Carolina Railroad was akin to a death sentence; convicts regularly were blown to bits in tunnel explosions, buried in mountain landslides, and swept away in springtime floods. On the Great Northern Railroad, Texas convicts were starved, whipped, beaten with tree limbs, and hung naked in wooden stocks. At the prison camps of the Greenville and Augusta Railroad, convicts were used up faster than South Carolina authorities could supply them. Between 1877 and 1879, the G&A "lost" 128 of their 285 prisoners to gunshots, accidents, and disease (a death rate of 45 percent) and another thirty-nine to escapes. Scurvy was rampant among the survivors, whose bodies were covered with lesions from the vermin on their skin. The smell is "sickening to the uttermost extent," said a doctor who inspected the bare log pen that served as a "hospital" for these men. "The English language does not possess words sufficiently strong to express the stench that arose from [this] place."[10]

As the railroads expanded, new industries followed in their path. Southerners poured "enormous amounts of sweat and ambition, along with the relatively little money they had, into the products the world market would buy," wrote historian Edward Ayers. "They rushed to fill the only gaps in the national and international economies they could find: cheap iron, cheap coal, cheap lumber, turpentine, sugar, and tobacco products." In almost every one of these industries, convict labor played a crucial role.[11]

The South's economic development can be traced by the blood of its prisoners. In Texas, convicts worked in coal mines, lumber mills, and railroad camps across the state. The great bulk of them were shipped to the developing sugarcane plantations, where field work was exhausting and free labor scarce. Without convict leasing, the Texas sugar industry would have been hard pressed to survive. By the early 1900s more than half of the state's four thousand prisoners were on lease to outside farms at a monthly rate of $21 for a "first-class hand."[12]

Blacks in Texas made up one-fifth of the general population but almost three-fifths of the convicts. The typical state prisoner was a young, illiterate, male Negro serving a first-time sentence for burglary or theft. Typically his trial took place without a lawyer, in a matter of minutes, before an all-white jury prone to discount "nigger testimony" as a pack of lies.

American Siberia

On the farms, convicts rose before dawn, ate a quick, cold breakfast, and were marched to the field in chains. They labored until the last glimmer of daylight, "with only a few minutes to eat their dinner, which is hauled to them in a wagon and served on the ground." The fields were shadeless and sunstroke was a leading cause of death. Prisoners were beaten for breaking the rules, for falling behind in their work, or sometimes for the pleasure of the guards. In the 1870s, neighboring farmers complained that the groans and screams "of the convicts *at night* [are] often so absolutely heart rending as to prevent sleeping." Camp officials responded by gagging the prisoners to muffle their cries.[13]

Whipping was the punishment of choice. Though it had long been used against both races in the South, the belief persisted that discipline for blacks required a strong dose of physical force. During a major state prison investigation in 1913, camp managers begged the legislature not to abolish the lash. Nothing could replace it, they argued—not the wall chain, or the ankle spur, or the infamous dark cell, where a convict spent a week or more in isolation with almost no food. "The whip seems to scare the negroes, the very idea of it," said the manager of Retrieve Plantation. "They fear the chain, too, some, but it don't get the results."[14]

"As a rule," another legislative committee noted, "the life of a [Texas] convict is not as valuable in the eyes of the sergeants and guards and contractors as that of a dog." Almost routinely, it discovered, prisoners were "whipped into unconsciousness," "shot down upon the least provocation," and worked "until they drop dead in their tracks." In a typical year, forty or fifty convicts would be killed by gunfire, and dozens more would suffer "miscellaneous" wounds at the hands of poorly trained, heavily armed camp guards. Small wonder that the "average life of a convict" in Texas was about seven years.[15]

In 1910, a local chaplain caused a momentary sensation by relating the story of a black convict named Foster, who had been brought to the prison hospital at Huntsville after a savage beating at the hands of his guards. "Oh, they have nearly killed me. . . ," Foster told the chaplain. "I was too old and couldn't keep up . . . with the younger men and they stripped my britches . . . off and whipped me and then sprinkled sand on me and whipped me again and then made me climb a tree that was covered with ants and they got all over me . . . they bit me all over." Foster died the following week.[16]

Incidents like this tarnished convict leasing but failed to drag it down. For one thing, the major lessees in Texas were bank presidents and railroad builders, cattle barons and cotton planters, merchants and politicians—all competing for the labor of shackled men. The list included H. Cunningham, the state's largest grower and refiner of sugarcane; R. S. Willis, a founder of the Gulf, Colorado, and Santa Fe Railroad; T. S. Hendersen, long-time chairman of the University of Texas Board of Regents; and Albert S. Burleson, a U.S. congressman who served as postmaster-general under President Woodrow Wilson from 1913 to 1921.[17]

Convict leasing made money for the state while keeping taxes down. The people it brutalized had no voice, and little sympathy, in the world of respectable folk. Criminals were not "martyrs to cruel laws," a Texas newspaper fumed. They were loathsome creatures whose imprisonment must be an "object of horror" that "deterred" them, and others, from committing future crimes. In this widely held view, the lines between justice and vengeance, punishment and cruelty, were extremely thin. "We still act on the principle that the criminal has injured society and he must be injured in return," a Texan prison reformer confessed in 1903. "Surrounded night and day by the most vicious comrades and associates, removed from all the softening influences of [civilization], whipped and cursed and abused by brutal slave drivers, the convict serves out his time and returns to society a far more dangerous man than when he fell into the clutches of the state."[18]

III

The violent details of convict leasing varied from one location to another, but the larger themes of racial caste and cheap, steady labor were everywhere the same. In Alabama and Arkansas, Texas and Virginia, Florida and Georgia, North and South Carolina, Louisiana and Mississippi, the convict populations were overwhelmingly black. Of South Carolina's 431 state prisoners in 1880, only 25 were white; of Georgia's 1,200 state prisoners in that year, almost 1,100 were Negro. And the figures for Southern county convicts were roughly the same. In *Following the Colour Line,* journalist Ray Stannard Baker described his numerous visits to the local police courts of Georgia. "One thing impressed me especially," he wrote in 1908. "A [black man] brought in . . . was punished much more severely than a white man arrested for the same offense. The injustice which the weak everywhere suffer—North and South—is in the South visited upon the negro."[19]

The trends in Georgia mirrored prison changes throughout the South. Between 1870 and 1910, the convict population grew ten times faster than the general one. Prisoners became younger and blacker, and the length of their sentences soared. An investigation of Georgia's state convict population in 1882 showed "coloreds" serving "twice as long as whites for burglary and five times as long for larceny," the two most common crimes. Almost 50 percent of Georgia's convicts were under sentence of ten years or more, "although ten years," reformer George Washington Cable observed, "is the *utmost* length of time that a convict can be expected to remain alive in a Georgia penitentiary."[20]

Following Reconstruction, Georgia had leased its convicts to three different companies for the sum of $500,000 over twenty years. The lessees were powerful, well-placed men. What made Georgia distinctive, however, was the fact that political office-holding, as opposed to simple influence, became the prerequisite for winning a lease. The biggest winners were Joseph E. Brown, a former governor who served as chief justice of Georgia's Supreme Court; General John Brown Gordon, a former U.S. senator who founded Georgia's Ku Klux Klan; and Colonel James Monroe Smith, a powerful state legislator who ran perhaps the largest family-owned plantation in the postbellum South.[21]

Brown and Gordon comprised two-thirds of the "Bourbon triumvirate" that dominated Georgia politics between 1870 and 1895. Both men had deep roots in the Confederacy, and both had championed the New South's industrial path. Together, they leased a thousand prisoners at a time. Three hundred worked at Brown's Dade Coal Mines, for which the Georgia treasury received less than seven cents per convict per day. By 1880, Brown had become a millionaire, with profits from Dade alone reaching $100,000 a year. He had "turned a coal mine into a gold mine," a newspaper reported.[22]

There was some criticism. Free miners accused Brown and Gordon of taking away their jobs, and reformers compared the conditions at Dade to those at the infamous Confederate prison camp at Andersonville—a charge that Brown resented but did not wholeheartedly dispute. "We make some profit at the Dade Coal Mines, and there we use convict labor," he replied. "Is it a crime for a citizen to put his money into the development of mineral interests, especially if he should succeed in making money by his energy and enterprise?"[23]

One of Brown's convicts was a former slave named Lancaster LeConte. In a letter dated September 14, 1887, LeConte begged his old master, Joseph LeConte, to send him $65 to help get his sentence overturned. Working from dawn to dusk in ankle-deep water had left the convict barely able to move. "I am hear in prison for the turm of three years for rescving som stolen goods," he wrote, "and my helth is so bad that I donnt think I will to suav them out, so I thought I had done anougf for you in slavery time to ask you to please asist me now in my trubles." Lancaster LeConte was seventy-four years old.

The money never arrived. Yet LeConte continued his struggle for another seventeen months. The prison log read: "Lancaster LeConte; Receiving Stolen Goods; Colored; 75; Arrived June 3, 1887; Died February 13, 1889."[24]

Some ninety miles to the east, on the outskirts of Athens, Georgia, stood Smithonia, the plantation of James Monroe Smith. Described by his biographer as a "phenomenal" man whose career "has no parallel in Georgia history," Colonel Smith had spent a lifetime pursuing his oft-stated goal of acquiring "all the land that's next to mine." At his death in 1915, Smithonia covered thirty square miles—most of Oglethorpe County. Its five hundred buildings included six schools, a post office, a hotel, a sawmill, a slaughterhouse, a fertilizer plant, a general store (said to gross $100,000 per year), and a five-story ginhouse for "Colonel Jim's" cotton crop, the biggest in Georgia.[25]

Smith was a full-bearded, two-hundred-pound man with "hands like hams" and a "wen as big as a cabbage on his neck." He spent most of his day in a rocking chair on the front porch of his mansion, with hunting dogs at his feet and a "flock of negro boys" on call to fetch a cold drink or carry a message to the field. His two thousand workers included sharecroppers, day laborers, and leased convicts. The great bulk of them were black, and "Colonel Jim" prided himself on knowing each one by name.[26]

Smith described the Negro as a "tool," adding, "If you know how to use it, it will do you good service." At Smithonia, that service lasted from dawn to dark, six days a week. There seemed to be few "idlers" about—an impression that astonished those who viewed blacks as inherently lazy and slow. "What Colonel Smith doesn't know about the nigger is not worth learning," a neighbor gushed.

"He can take the most trifling vagabond . . . and make a good hand of him."[27]

How loyal were Smithonia's legions to the man they called "marse"? "They feared him, [and] they loved him, too," a friend of the colonel's recalled. "You couldn't drive those niggers away." But the "niggers" themselves described a system of entrenched peonage in which they were furnished with food and shelter at exorbitant rates that kept them in perpetual debt. "We never got cash money," a field hand remembered, "and there wasn't no way to get away except to run away, but Mr. Jim, he'd always ketch you."

When that happened, the colonel would gather everyone together for a public whipping. "He have a strop wide as your hand fastened to a leetle short stick er wood an' he grease the strop and then his overseer, he draw the strop long through the sand and git sand stuck all on it, and then he beat [the man] with that strop, and the sand make it cut wuss. Hit was turrible. I seen it."[28]

So, apparently, did many others. Though no one working at Smithonia dared to criticize "Colonel Jim," federal officials in Georgia received a steady stream of peonage complaints from those who had escaped. In the early 1900s, the U.S. attorney filed formal charges on behalf of fifty blacks who lived "in constant dread of being captured and taken back [to Smithonia] on some slight pretext." He claimed that conditions on Smith's plantation were worse than those described by Harriet Beecher Stowe in *Uncle Tom's Cabin*.[29]

The colonel dismissed his accusers as a bunch of "lazy . . . trifling . . . gambling . . . drinking . . . lying . . . thieving . . . all-around mean negroes." "I always made them do good and faithful work," he declared, and "I always paid the highest wages of any farmer [around]." Smith was never brought to trial. After all, it was his word against a few dozen black people, and his word in northeast Georgia was close to being the law.[30]

Smith was often short of labor, especially at picking time, so he leased about four hundred convicts each year, working most of them at Smithonia and subleasing the rest (at a sizable profit) to sawmills, railroad camps, and turpentine farms in a dozen locations. Having financed so many of the buildings and businesses in Ogelthorpe County, "Colonel Jim" seemed to look upon the justice system there as his own private preserve. "You had better send me some more niggers," he would joke to county officials, "or I will come down and take the courthouse away from you."[31]

Smith claimed to treat his convicts well. And in a comparative sense he probably did. The colonel prided himself on being a paternalist. He believed in taking care of "his" negroes if it did not cost too much. Convicts were neither starved at Smithonia nor beaten without "proper" cause. Working on a stable plantation allowed most to serve out their sentences and return home alive. Smithonia was safer than a coal mine or a railroad camp, a fact that allowed the colonel to strike an oddly humanitarian pose. But compassion did not come cheaply, he complained: "It has often been used against me that I [am] doing too much for the negro."[32]

IV

On Christmas Day, 1912, Governor George Donaghey of Arkansas pardoned 360 state prisoners in one fell swoop. His gesture made headlines across the nation, while surprising almost nobody at home. Donaghey had been trying to abolish the lease since his election in 1908, but a combination of forces—from cotton planters and coal mine operators to corrupt judges and worried taxpayers—had kept the system alive. Donaghey viewed leasing as a form of legalized murder that sentenced thousands of faceless victims to a "death by oppression" for often trivial acts. Under no other system, he believed, did the punishment so poorly fit the crime.[33]

Arkansas ran perhaps the most informal prison system in the country. The state's minimal records showed, among other things, that 105 of the 981 prisoners in 1895 were between the ages of twelve and fifteen, but no one knew for sure. Convicts worked at everything from brick making to tunnel blasting to domestic service in private homes. Their annual escape rate often reached 25 percent, while their mortality rate seemed too bothersome to measure. ("A graveyard near [one] penal camp testified to sixty or seventy deaths over which inquests had not been held as required by law.") Being imprisoned in Arkansas, an official admitted, was like entering a "revengeful hell."[34]

George Donaghey was not the first Arkansas governor to challenge the state's powerful lessees. The flamboyant Jeff Davis (1900–1908) had been battling them for years. Known as the "Wild Ass of the Ozarks," Davis had regularly targeted the "blood-suckers" and "high-collared aristocrats" who exploited prison labor for personal gain. And like so many other Southern demagogues of that era, he combined populist ideas with "nigger-baiting" in crude but powerfully effective ways.

In 1902, Davis had ignited a firestorm by claiming to have witnessed an unspeakable crime during a surprise visit to a convict camp in the Arkansas Delta. "The first sight that greeted my eyes," he said, "was a great, big, black negro with a pump gun guarding the white men and . . . saying, 'Hoe that cotton, damn you, or I will kill you.' " And then, according to Davis, a white convict had been knocked down, stripped of his clothing, and whipped on his bare back by negro guards until his flesh "puffed and curled like a bacon rind on a hot skillet."[35]

The story was probably a sham—Davis had a long history of bending the truth—but it put his opponents on the defensive and led to a predictable countercharge that Davis had coddled state prisoners, 90 percent of them black, by giving them fancy dinners at Christmas. As one mud-ball followed another, the spectacle became daily front-page news. Convict leasing in Arkansas could no longer be ignored.

American Siberia

Governor Donaghey had studied the system at some length. He knew that the local courts had become a conveyor belt for labor-starved employers throughout the state. And he listed the abuses for all to see:

Instance No. 1. In Phillips County . . . two negroes jointly forged nine orders for one quart of whiskey each. For this offense one of them was convicted for eighteen years and the other for thirty-six years. . . .

Instance No. 8. In Mississipppi County a negro was found serving a sentence of 180 days for disturbing the peace. . . .

Instance No. 10. In Miller County a negro convicted in a justice of the peace court was . . . sentenced [to] over three years for stealing a few articles of clothing off a clothes-line.

"These are only a few typical cases," the governor explained. "If they are not enough, an examination of my files will show many more."[36]

The lessons of Jeff Davis were still fresh in Donaghey's mind. He took pains to find white criminals who had been brutalized by the lease, and a search of the prison records turned up several cases. Donaghey noted that "white boy convicts, sentenced for minor offenses," had been whipped senseless with "a strap six feet long and four inches wide." One of them had dropped dead after being "compelled to work in the hot sun [with] a burning fever." Another had been shot through the chest and left to die by sadistic camp guards, "his blood trickling down the planks of the platform" where he lay. The message was simple if not exactly true: leasing was color-blind when it came to dishing out pain.[37]

Donaghey made his point. The state legislature abolished convict leasing in 1913, following months of protest by reformers, church groups, newspapers, and "hundreds" of letter-writing folk. ("Stick by your guns," a doctor told Donaghey. "The people are back of you.") Arkansas moved twelve hundred convicts to a penal farm owned and operated by the state. "It is difficult to conceive of a more ideal method of dealing with prisoners, especially negro prisoners, than this," wrote a leading prison reformer.

Arkansas had taken a major step forward—or so it seemed at the time.[38]

V

By 1915, convict leasing remained alive in only Florida and Alabama, where it served a need that free labor could not entirely meet. Florida's main industries were tied directly to the state's most exploitable natural resource, its twenty million acres of virgin longleaf pine. By the early 1900s, Florida had become the leading producer of naval stores (resin and turpentine) in the United States. But getting men to do dangerous and exhausting "turpentine labor" in desolate, disease-ridden forests was a difficult task.

Workers first drove "cups" and "gutters" into the trees to catch the resin that oozed from wounds opened by axe cuts through the bark. As the cups filled up, the resin was collected in fifty-gallon buckets, which were hand-carried from tree to tree. The men worked killing shifts in deep mud and thick underbrush. ("We go from can't to can't," explained one. "Can't see in the morning to can't see at night.") The pace was set by a mounted "woods rider," who controlled their lives as completely as the slave driver had in antebellum times. "It is little wonder," wrote one observer, "that turpentine workers were hard to find and even harder to keep in the forests during the long season."[39]

Forced labor filled part of this void. Florida had no state prison. Its twelve hundred convicts were leased to a single bidder—C. H. Barnes of Jacksonville—at an annual rate of about $200 each. Barnes never actually laid eyes upon these men. He simply subleased them, at double his cost, to the labor-starved employers of the north Florida woods. And these state prisoners were joined by thousands of county convicts, serving shorter sentences for lesser crimes—or, sometimes, no crime at all. In many Florida counties, employers worked hand-in-glove with local officials to keep their camps well stocked with able-bodied blacks.

A journalist in 1907 described an all-too-common arrangement between a local sheriff and a turpentine operator in desperate need of men. "Together," he wrote, "they made up a list of some eighty negroes known to both as good husky fellows, capable of a fair day's work." The sheriff was promised five dollars plus expenses for each negro he "landed." Within three weeks, he had arrested all eighty of them "on various petty charges—gambling, disorderly conduct, assault, and the like. The larger part of the list was gathered with a dragnet at Saturday-night shindies, and hailed to the local justice, who was in [on] the game."[40]

The most remarkable account of forced labor in the turpentine camps was "Captain" J. C. Powell's *American Siberia,* published in 1891.* Powell worked for one of Florida's largest lessees, a Northern firm that dealt in turpentine and resin. "We have little material for skilled labor among the criminals of the South," he observed. "The bulk of our convicts are negroes who could not by any possibility learn a trade, and how to employ them at anything save the simplest manual task is a problem not yet solved."[41]

Most were young men in their teens and early twenties, but the camp always included a number of black women and children who served as domestics, water boys, and prostitutes for both the workers

---

* *Captain* was a term routinely accorded white men who supervised blacks. Though turpentine labor has been aptly described as "outlaw work carried on by outlaws," it also attracted hundreds of free black workers with the lure of small cash advances, which took months, sometimes years, to pay off. As a result, the difference between forced labor and free labor in the turpentine camps was often marginal at best. Free workers lived in well-guarded compounds, surrounded by armed guards and barbed wire; they could not come and go as they pleased. And they bought their "necessities" on credit from the camp commissary at wildly inflated prices, a process that kept them in perpetual debt.

and the guards. One of Powell's favorite prisoners, a "negro named Cy Williams," had come there as a child. "He did not know his age," the captain recalled, "but when he was a mere pickaninny . . . he was arrested for stealing a horse. He was not large enough to mount the animal, and was caught in the act of leading it off by the halter, for which he was duly sentenced to twenty years imprisonment."[42]

Like most other men in his line of work, Powell greatly preferred black convicts to whites. In Florida, he admitted, "it was possible to send a negro to prison on almost any pretext but difficult to get a white there, unless he committed a very heinous crime." This meant that the few whites under Powell's supervision were more likely to be dangerous criminals who viewed their punishment as something fit for members of the "inferior" race. And they responded by assaulting guards, plotting escapes, attempting suicide, and mutilating their bodies in the hope of earning a hardship pardon.[43]

Powell knew prisoners who had chopped off fingers and toes. He recalled one man who had put a needle through his eye and another who had sawed open his throat with a box axe, "completely severing the windpipe and inflicting a horrible wound through which his tongue dropped." To Powell, such acts were a common (if marginally unpleasant) part of convict life. Take, for example, his description of James Peterson, a "professional thief" from Gainesville:

> He made up his mind not to work, and when sent into the woods to cut boxes, drove his axe through his foot. It was a very severe gash, but was healing and he was able to hobble about, when I sent him into the yard one day to split wood. He grumbled a good deal, and when he reached the woodpile placed his foot on a block and deliberately cut it again across the old wound. The blood spouted out in a perfect torrent and . . . for this act he paid a dear penalty. The wound . . . refused to heal; both foot and leg swelled to enormous size and finally gangrene set in. After lingering in great agony, he died.[44]

American Siberia

What most bothered Captain Powell were the numerous break-outs from his camp. To prevent escapes, the convicts wore leg irons, which limited their gait to very short steps. They were marched to and from the forest on a "squad-chain," surrounded by shotguns and dogs. The pace was so quick, and the work so exhausting, that some men had to be dragged through the dirt. A visitor to a turpentine camp in Osceola County saw a gang of convicts being trotted to work, eight miles away, in heavy chains. "They limped and scrambled along pitifully," he observed, "three guards with drawn guns bringing up the rear."[45]

Once back in camp, the convicts were counted, inspected, and fastened to a "building chain" that ran the length of the barracks. "This over," said Powell, "supper was served and eaten, and [soon] a bell rang for every man to lie down. That was the last thing in order for the night, and if any convict desired to move or change his position thereafter it was required that he first call to the night guard and obtain his permission."

Powell liked to experiment with new ways to stop escapes. One spring he brought in a special weapon: a guard dog so vicious that it had recently been "expelled" from Savannah, Georgia, for spreading "general terror in the city." Powell tied the brute to the cell house door. Escapes ended at once, but so, too, did normal life in the camp. The animal "had no other instinct than a ravenous desire to bite, rend, and tear anything that came within his reach." That included guards, convicts, livestock, alligators, and the captain himself. According to Powell, the "career of this monster, for he was nothing less, ended . . . one day when he suddenly . . . seized me by the hip, and I had a desperate fight to beat him off. I concluded that he had lived long enough and had him dispatched with an axe."[46]

In 1919, Florida ended the leasing of state prisoners to private concerns, but this new law did not seriously burden the turpentine operators because the number of county convicts was increased to cushion the loss. In Tallahassee, for example, Leon County officials made a deal to lease all of their convicts to the Putnam Lumber Company, a Wisconsin-based producer of resin and turpentine, at a monthly rate of twenty dollars per man.

The result was predictable. A minor "crime wave" hit Leon County. Vagrancy arrests shot up by almost 800 percent in the seven months following the Putnam Lumber deal—from 20 to 154. "Men charged with vagrancy were brought before the county judge and instructed by the sheriff and his deputies to plead guilty," said a source familiar with the scam. Many of these trials took place at night before "inebriated court officers."[47]

Among those arrested was a young white man from North Dakota named Martin Tabert. Bored with farm work, Tabert, age twenty-two, had left home "to see the world." Reaching Florida in the fall of 1921, he made the mistake of "stealing a ride" on a freight train as it wound through the isolated panhandle on its way to Tallahassee. Tabert was arrested, found guilty of vagrancy, and sentenced to ninety days at the Putnam Lumber camp.[48]

Two months later, the Tabert family received a letter of condolence from a Putnam official. "This is to advise you," it began,

> that Martin Tabert . . . died in our camp on February 1, 1922, of [malarial] fever and other complications. This company has all convicts from [Leon] County [and] is the reason he came to be here. . . .
>
> For your information, the boy was given a Christian burial in a cemetery near here and had a minister officiate in same. We regret that the boy was so unfortunate, and please accept our sympathy in your bereavement.[49]

The Taberts did not suspect foul play until two convicts who had served time with their son at the camp said much the same thing: Martin had been overworked, underfed, beaten senseless, and left to die. Before long, Tabert's killing became front-page news across the country. His story riveted national attention upon a system that had been slaughtering Southern blacks for decades with scandalous ease.

In 1923, the Florida legislature voted to investigate Tabert's death. It found that Tabert had been put to work in a poison swamp, shoveling mud in hip-deep water for fifteen hours a day. When he could no longer keep up the pace, he had been flogged with a seven-pound strap until his back "was all scabs and cuts from his shoulders to his knees."

Tabert died after one of these beatings. The camp's "whipping boss," Walter Higginbotham, had called him out of line on a moonless evening and given him "about thirty-five to fifty licks" by the light of a bonfire. After each stroke, Higginbotham carefully dragged the strap "through sugar and sand" to increase its sting and weight. "Martin begged to be let loose," a witness recalled, "but his speech was not distinct and it seemed he was so weak he could not talk plain." Tabert died two days later. He was buried without ceremony in some old clothes belonging to a "nigger escapee."[50]

Florida ended the leasing of county prisoners a few months later. Powerful interests had emerged to challenge the system on economic as well as humanitarian grounds. Boycotts of Florida products were growing in the North, and the state's emerging image as a tourist mecca was suffering as well. Convict leasing "is making Florida synonymous with Russian Bolshevism," warned a local mayor whose fears were echoed by citrus growers, hotel owners, and land speculators throughout the state.[51]

Yet the abolition of convict leasing did little to disturb the brutal turpentine culture of the north Florida woods. And nothing demonstrated this fact better than the subsequent career of Walter Higginbotham, the man who had beaten Martin Tabert to death. Higginbotham was tried for murder in 1924, found guilty, and sentenced to twenty years in prison. But his conviction was set aside on a technicality, and a new trial was ordered by the state supreme court. In 1926, Higginbotham was acquitted of all charges by twelve of his Leon County peers.

Six months later, he killed again. His victim this time was a black turpentine worker named Lewis "Peanut" Barker. Higginbotham never stood trial for the murder; an automobile accident left him "physically unable to appear in court." Yet he remained healthy enough to continue his work as an armed guard at the Putnam Lumber camp in neighboring Dixie County, where convicts and free workers were locked up together behind barbed wire fences. Martin Taber may have died a martyr's death in 1923, but the conditions that killed him would remain in place until the end of World War II, "when the extraction of turpentine gum ceased to be a major industry in Florida."[52]

VI

To the northwest, in Alabama, convict leasing was synonymous with coal. As the demand for fossil fuels exploded and railroads penetrated the rich mineral belt around Birmingham, the recruitment of miners became a regional obsession. Between 1875 and 1900, Alabama's coal production leaped from 67,000 to 8.4 million tons. By 1910, it was the sixth largest coal producer in the nation.[53]

Convict leasing was essential to this growth. More than one-quarter of all miners in the rich Birmingham district were state or county prisoners, and more than one-half of all miners in Alabama had learned their trade in chains. State convicts were leased en masse to the Tennessee Coal and Iron Company (TCI), the South's largest corporation. County prisoners were spread widely among TCI's major competitors: Sloss-Sheffield, Pratt Consolidated, and the Red Feather Coal Company. In Alabama, the apprenticeship system for miners began at the courthouse door.[54]

Convicts came from all parts of the state, and their condition was shocking to ordinary eyes. A visitor to Alabama described their "re-volting" appearance aboard a railroad train in 1885: "In filthy rags, with vile odors and the clanking of shackles . . . , nine penitentiary convicts chained to one chain, and ten more chained to one another, dragged laboriously into the compartment of the car. . . . The keeper of the convicts told me he should take them . . . two hundred miles that night. They were going to the mines."[55]

Their numbers ebbed and flowed according to the labor needs of the coal companies and the revenue needs of the counties and the state. When times were tight, local police would sweep the streets for vagrants, drunks, and thieves. Hundreds of blacks would be arrested, put on trial, found guilty, sentenced to sixty or ninety days plus court costs, and then delivered to a "hard labor agent," who leased them to the mines. In an average year, 97 percent of Alabama's county convicts (serving two years or less for misdemeanor crimes) had "colored" written next to their names.[56]

By nightfall, these convicts would be hard at work pulling twelve-to sixteen-hour shifts. A visitor to Pratt's infamous Banner Mine met a prisoner who had been fined $1 dollar for his crime—and $75 more for "costs." The convict pleaded with the visitor for help: "I'll work for you as long as you say. Do buy me out, Sah, please do."[57]

This was not an exceptional case. Court costs were a leading source of revenue for county officials throughout the South. The figure, which could range from $15 to $100, was used to cover the "fees" of judges, jurors, lawyers, sheriffs, jailers, and other interested folk. The convict paid off these "costs" by serving additional "jail time" at the rate of 30 to 40 cents a day. Thus, a person sentenced to six months plus $50 in costs could expect to spend a full year at hard labor—and sometimes more.[58]

Employers routinely worked county convicts beyond their scheduled release dates because public officials had no incentive—beyond common decency—to intervene. The files of Southern governors of this era are filled with letters from the relatives of county convicts seeking the whereabouts of their kin. A Mrs. Jane Childes inquired about her son Walter: "He rote to me that his time would be out in May and then he would come home. I have not heard a word from him since. have ritten to him and cannot get enney anseer. Please rite to me if he is alive or dead and when his time is out and how he it geting along."[59]

The Banner Mine blew up in 1911, killing 128 convicts. Next to the names of the dead, the local newspapers listed the crimes that had led them to their awful fate: gambling, vagrancy, weapons violations, and bootlegging. "Several negroes from this section ... were caught in the Banner mine explosion," a rural newspaper reported. "That is a pretty tight penalty to pay for selling booze."[60]

No one should have been surprised. Convict leasing was not about justice, equal treatment, or making the punishment fit the crime. Convict leasing was about profits, brutality, and racist ideas. Alabamans knew this better than others because their system was an open book. Their prisoners were not hidden away in remote railroad camps or on isolated farms; most of them dug coal on the outskirts of Alabama's emerging towns and cities, often with free miners near their side. It was hardly a secret that convicts worked whole shifts without a break in ankle-deep pools of water, eating fistfuls of spoiled meat and cornbread that had been stuffed into their clothes. In 1882, Alabama's new warden described his prisoners as worn-out, battered men who lived like animals in disgusting quarters, where they "breathed and drank their bodily exhalation and excrement." The system, he wrote, "is a disgrace to the State [and] a reproach to the civilization."[61]

A few years later, a literate black convict recalled the life he had endured at the Eureka Prison Mines in northern Alabama. The men had slept in chains, covered with "filth and vermin," he began.

American Siberia

[We used] powder cans for slops whitch would fill up and run over our beds and we could not move out of the way. . . . We would leave the cells at 3 oclock AM & return at 8 oclock PM going the distance of three miles through rain and snow . . . we go to cell wet, go to bed wet and arise wet the following morning and every guard knocking beating yelling . . . & Every Day Some one of us were carried to our last Resting, the grave. Day after day we looked death in the face & was afraid to speak.[62]

Prisoners were whipped for failing to meet their daily quotas and tortured for various infractions, a practice that would continue well into the twentieth century. They were hung from makeshift crucifixes, stretched on wooden racks, and placed in coffin-sized sweatboxes for hours at a time. "Generally made of wood or tin," explained a student of the Alabama prisons, the sweatbox "is completely closed except for a [small] hole at nose level. When placed under the blistering Southern sun the temperature inside becomes unbearable. In a few hours a man's body swells and occasionally bleeds."[63]

In 1870, Alabama prison officials reported that more than 40 percent of their convicts had died, prompting a doctor to warn that if the trend continued, the entire convict population would be wiped out within three years. Although the death rate dropped significantly in the 1880s, it did not include the hundreds of broken-down convicts who were cut loose after suffering from black lung or dysentery or who had been hideously crippled in the mines.[64]

By 1890, the convict lease in Alabama had become a huge operation, supplying bodies like the slave trade of old. Black males, age twelve and older, went directly to the mines; black women, black children, and "cripples" were leased to lumber companies and to farms. White men usually remained in the penitentiary or in local jails. White women and children (a minuscule number) were kept in special facilities.

The categories were precise. TCI paid the state of $18.50 per month for "first-class men," who mined four tons of coal a day; $13.50 for "second-class men," who mined three tons; $9.00 for "third-class men," who mined two tons; and "simple maintenance" for "fourth-class men" (or "dead-heads"), who mined a ton or less. Convict leasing generated about 6 percent of the state's total revenue in these years, giving Alabama the most profitable prison system in the country.[65]

There were problems, of course. Most of these convicts were first-time offenders who had never mined coal before. They were unskilled, often undisciplined, and no doubt overwhelmed by their surroundings. Escape attempts were common, prisoner violence was rampant, machines were misused or sabotaged, and work quotas were sometimes "filled" by loading rocks and slate into the coal cars. "The demand for labor and fees has become so great that most convicts who go to the mines are unfit for such work," complained a member of the Alabama Prison Board in 1904. "They drag out a miserable existence and die. . . . If the State wishes to kill its convicts it should do so directly."[66]

Yet the benefits of leasing clearly outweighed these liabilities. The system provided employers with a regularity that free labor could never match.* Convicts did not skip work for picnics, holidays, fu-

---

* A recent study of convict coal mining in the late nineteenth century showed that convicts produced far less coal per man than free miners. This is not surprising, given the skill level required of miners, the short terms and rural backgrounds of many prisoners, and their understandable resistance to an enforced task. The great natural benefit of convict mining was its constancy in an industry where the free work force was always on the move, looking for better pay and conditions. "Three hundred [convicts] go to bed at night," wrote one observer, "and three hundred men go to work in the morning, for 310 days of the year." A song from the convict mines of Georgia expressed it well:

> The captain hollers hurry,
> Goin' to take my time.
> Say captain holler hurry.
> Goin' to take my time.
> Say he makin' money,
> I'm trying to make time.
> Say he can lose his job.
> But I can't lose mine.[67]

nerals, and excursions. Nor did they disappear on drunken binges, leave town in search of better wages, or go out on strike. "Convict labor is desirable by firms or corporations for the reason that it can be depended on—always ready for work," boasted one prison official. "Contracts for the output can be made with the knowledge that the goods can be delivered."[68]

And often at a lower price. In 1894, TCI's chief engineer told Henry Clay Frick, the Pittsburgh industrialist, that "convicts mined the cheapest coal ever produced by the Company." He was not merely boasting. "It is an indisputable fact," said a mining superintendent for three of Birmingham's biggest producers, that "coal cannot be produced by free labor within 20 cents per ton of what it can be produced by convicts."[69]

The system also gave employers tremendous leverage over the rest of their workforce. Throughout the South, free miners viewed convict labor "as a Sword of Damocles dangling above their heads." They understood that if they pressed too hard for higher wages or better working conditions, they could easily be replaced. They knew that if they walked off their jobs in protest, they might never get them back. The beauty of convict leasing, explained Arthur Colyar, TCI's former president, was its unspoken power to intimidate workers and undermine their confidence in each other. "We were right," he said, "in calculating that the free laborers would be loath to enter upon strikes when they saw that the company was amply provided with convict labor."[70]

Colyar made his remark in 1892, at the very moment free miners were organizing labor unions in the coal fields of Alabama and Tennessee. He believed that convict labor would be TCI's best weapon in a showdown with its workers, and in Alabama, at least, his weapon won the day. But something happened in Tennessee—something almost unimaginable to the mine owners and politicians of that state. When the companies tried to intimidate their workers by bringing in convict labor to take over their jobs, the workers responded by storming the stockades, freeing the prisoners, and loading them onto freight trains bound for Nashville and Knoxville and places far away.

What began as an isolated protest in the company town of Coal Creek spread quickly across the Cumberlands to engulf most of eastern Tennessee. Thousands of miners took part in these uprisings, and thousands of armed state guardsmen were sent to face them down. The Tennessee convict war was one of the largest insurrections in American working-class history. And yet, unfolding at exactly the same time as the more publicized labor wars in Homestead, Pennsylvania, and Coeur d'Alene, Idaho, it was largely ignored.

Unlike Homestead and Coeur d'Alene, however, the Tennessee insurrection ended in a partial victory for the workers. Tennessee abolished the convict lease in 1896. The system had become an economic liability, a drain on public coffers. The cost of keeping troops in the field far exceeded the $100,000 per year that mine owners were paying to lease the state's sixteen hundred prisoners. Stripped of its profit-making magic, the system quickly died out.[71]

But the end of convict leasing in Tennessee did not mean a new beginning for the prisoners who had suffered under it. Instead of mining coal for a private corporation, the bulk of them were shipped to Brushy Mountain and forced to mine coal for the state. Conditions were better there, though stories of brutal discipline were common. By 1904, state profits from convict labor had grown to almost $200,000 per year, but the convict population stayed much the same as it had been since Reconstruction, with "able bodied young colored men" filling the vast majority of cells. In Tennessee, as elsewhere, the link between race and crime remained firmly in place.

VII

How could leasing be rationalized in the face of so much suffering and death? The answer lay partly in the powerlessness of its victims and in the stereotypes that dogged their daily lives. It was almost an article of faith among Southern whites that the Negro would not exert himself unless compelled to do so by hunger or force. "None of them feels that work *per se* is good; it is only a means to idleness," argued William Alexander Percy, the voice of planter paternalism in Mississippi. "The theory of the white man, no matter what his practice, is the reverse; he feels that work is good, and idleness, being agreeable, must be evil."[72]

It followed, therefore, that the Negro did not hold the appropriate view of prison as a humiliating deprivation of liberty. Quite the opposite: he seemed to welcome the jail cell as a refuge from hard work, a place to lounge about with other loafers, free from the cares of the world. Governor Robert Patton of Alabama spoke for many whites when he claimed that the Negro needed different penalties because he simply did "not regard confinement as punishment." And no penalty would serve him better, Patton believed, than the "hardships of labor in [our] mines."[73]

Even the regional opponents of convict leasing agreed that blacks could not be punished by traditional means. At virtually every national prison convention, a Southerner would rise in obvious frustration to lecture outsiders about the "unique" problems of convict life below the Mason-Dixon line, where 90 percent of the nation's black population resided. "We must not be held to too strict an accountability," a Southern penologist complained. "We have a large alien population, an inferior race. . . . How we are going to reform that race we do not yet know."[74]

In the meantime, convict leasing filled the void. And its more positive aspects, some argued, had been purposely ignored. Alabama prison officials claimed that a poor black sentenced to the coal mines had a higher standard of living than a poor black who remained free. The convict not only received better food, clothing, and medical care; he also got the chance to shed some of his old "nigger" habits by learning a valuable skill. A good convict could leave prison as a trained miner, accustomed to "rigid discipline" and "regular hours."[75]

After Slavery, Before Parchman

Of course, the convict had to survive in order to profit. And that raised the inevitable question: Why did so many of these prisoners die? The answer, quite naturally, was linked to race. Texas officials described the average black convict as a moral degenerate who entered prison with the "seeds of disease" already in his system. The convict appeared normal until he was "put to hard labor"—at which time the seeds flowered and the poor fellow dropped dead. Florida's chief prison doctor concluded that an array of "debasing habits" (led by "lust and passion") had produced the high mortality rate among Negro convicts. Alabama officials insisted that blacks fared poorly in the coal mines because of their "physical inferiority." The tougher the job and the more dangerous the conditions, the worse they did in comparison to whites.[76]

This logic was preposterous, as the mine owners well knew. Black convicts had a higher mortality rate because they mined coal under appalling conditions, while most white convicts were tucked safely behind prison walls. Furthermore, blacks comprised about 40 percent the free coal miners in Alabama, and no employer ever accused *them* of being physically inferior to whites. At that very moment, in fact, the prestigious *Manufacturers' Record* was insisting that the "negro has no equal for patient industry and mule-like endurance."[77]

But logic hardly mattered when the issue was race. Blacks had to be punished for their crimes, and that meant hard labor. Don't blame us, said the mine owners. We are innocent brokers, caught between the inferiority of the Negro and the criminal code of Alabama. "What reproach is it that we cannot alter a law of nature and keep his death rate down to the white basis?"

In Mississippi, a solution was slowly emerging. After numerous delays, the legislature was making plans for a vast penal plantation in the Yazoo Delta. The driving force was a "redneck radical" who would help to revolutionize politics, race relations, and prison development in Mississippi and the larger South.

✠

CHAPTER FOUR

The White Chief

Never before in the history of this Commonwealth were its white people confronted with so grave a problem as that which confronts it today.

—Governor James Kimble Vardaman of Mississippi describing the increase of "Negro crime" in 1904

I

To the poor whites of Mississippi he was part showman and part messiah: a huge man with shoulder-length hair and a limp right arm that had been mangled years before in a corn sheller. Thousands flocked to greet him at barbecues, county fairs, and church suppers, traveling for miles in ox-drawn wagons over rutted country roads. Dressed in a white linen suit and a black broad-brimmed hat, he would stand atop a makeshift platform, often a cotton bale, and speak for hours until exhaustion set in. He "has come and gone," a newspaper reported, "and the fire of his Robesperien oratory was heard last night by one of the largest gatherings seen in [this town] since the last hanging."[1]

His name was James Kimble Vardaman, but his followers called him the White Chief. Born in dirt-poor Yalobusha County in 1861, the son of a common Confederate soldier, Vardaman had left the Mississippi hills as a young man to board with prosperous relatives near Greenwood, a booming cotton center on the edge of the Yazoo Delta. "Hour upon hour he spent engrossed reading the volumes of law, history, political theory, and literature found in the family's library," wrote a Vardaman biographer. "Three years later, in 1882, he passed the state bar examination, a feat that required only the barest acquaintance with law, but one that gave him a sense of achievement."[2]

In short order, Vardaman married a wealthy widow and bought a failing newspaper, the *Greenwood Enterprise,* which became a sounding board for his endless grudges and vaguely populist views. His crusade against local corruption led to a wild gun battle that left one opponent dead, another wounded, and the fortunate Vardaman with only a bullet hole in his coat. The shootout defined him, quite literally, as an "editor who would stand by his work."[3]

In the 1890s, Vardaman moved beyond local affairs. His main target became the Delta patricians who ruled Mississippi with the arrogance of feudal lords. In an era of national depression and seething discontent, he blamed these planters—and their legions of "field niggers"—for an economic slide that had turned the majority of white farmers into landless tenants, buried hopelessly in debt. By 1900, Mississippi had become the nation's poorest state. Thousands of whites found themselves falling into a labor system—sharecropping—designed for free Negroes, a system that mocked the white man's claim to membership in a superior race. Vardaman blamed the wealthy. "Capital has no conscience," he declared. "I don't believe a man ever made a million honestly."[4]

Vardaman sought a way to channel the fears and anxieties of poor whites into the political system. His opportunity came in 1902, with the passage of an "open primary" law that allowed Mississippi's eligible voters—meaning white men who paid a poll tax—to choose the candidates for statewide office. The result was dramatic. Almost any white man could enter politics now, and his chances of winning depended on his ability to arouse mass support.[5]

In 1903, Vardaman campaigned for governor as the champion of common whites. He promised to tax the planters, regulate the railroads, and provide services to the poor. Be proud of the "honest sweat" on your faces, he told the huge crowds, and be certain of your enemies. According to Wilbur J. Cash, a Vardaman-type rally was far more than a political event. "It swept back the loneliness of the land, it brought men together under torches, it filled them with the contagious power of the crowd, it unleashed emotion and set it to leaping and dancing."[6]

The main emotion was fear—the fear of losing one's land, of slipping deeper into despair. But Vardaman added a racial dimension that gave his message a special jolt. Unlike the Delta patricians, who routinely described "their" Negroes as docile and content, Vardaman sketched a more ominous portrait in which blacks were demanding social equality, pursuing white women, and committing awful crimes. The Negro, he asserted, "is a lazy, lying, lustful animal" whose behavior "resembles the hog's."[7]

II

Vardaman's campaign was helped by national events. In 1901, President Theodore Roosevelt invited Booker T. Washington, the prominent black leader, to dine with him at the White House. Appalled by this breach of racial etiquette, Vardaman accused Roosevelt of coddling a "nigger bastard" for political advantage. A year later, when the president announced plans to vacation in Mississippi, Vardaman placed a mock advertisement in his Greenwood newspaper: "WANTED, sixteen, big, fat mellow, rancid 'coons' to sleep with Roosevelt when he comes down to go bear hunting." After the president left, Vardaman celebrated his departure in verse:

Teddy has come and Teddy has gone,
And the lick spittle spittled
and the fawning did fawn.
The coons smelt as loud as a musk rat's nest,
And Teddy licked his chops
and said it smelt the best.[8]

During the 1903 campaign, Vardaman blasted Roosevelt for allowing blacks to hold federal appointments in Mississippi. The president, he charged, was a "coon-flavored miscegenationist" bent on "filling the head of the nigger" with dangerous ideas. As an example, Vardaman singled out Minnie M. Cox, a middle-class, college-educated black woman who ran the post office at Indianola, the seat of Sunflower County, deep in the Yazoo Delta.

Her patrons, black and white, described Mrs. Cox as a "model of efficiency, tidiness, and good service." Yet Indianola had begun to experience severe racial friction in this era as the cotton economy sagged. Some whites took out their frustrations on the "uppity niggers"—those who owned their own land or belonged to the Delta's tiny black middle class. In the fall of 1902, word spread that a black customer had been "discourteous" to a white salesgirl at the "Jew dry goods store" on Main Street. The "offending negro" was "banished" from Indianola along with the local black doctor, whose only offense may have been his thriving medical practice.[9]

Mrs. Cox would be next. Her success had made her too visible, despite consciously humble ways. When Vardaman campaigned in Indianola, he chided the white crowds for "receiving mail from the hands of a coon." The issue was simple, he said: "We are not going to let niggers hold office in Mississippi!"[10]

The white citizens of Indianola agreed. At an angry public meeting, they accused Mrs. Cox of permitting "crap-shooting darkies" to congregate in the post office lobby "where white women and children had to pass." Mrs. Cox offered to resign. ("It is my opinion that if I don't there will be trouble," she wrote her superiors in Washington.) But Roosevelt refused to accept her gesture, closing the Indianola post office instead. As the stalemate dragged on, local whites hired an "old negro" to transport their mail to and from a nearby delta town.[11]

Vardaman blamed the trouble on a "Yankee conspiracy" of "nigger-loving" Republicans in Washington. And he warned that his own defeat in the governor's race would be viewed by local blacks as an "endorsement of Roosevelt's criminal policy of social and political equality." This was particularly dangerous, Vardaman explained, because the "evidence" showed that blacks became more aggressive when their dreams of equality were encouraged by misguided whites. As governor, he promised, he would handle the "coon problem" by abolishing negro education and repealing "frivolous safeguards" relating to race. These included the Fifteenth Amendment, which protected the voting rights of black men, and the Declaration of Independence, which, in Vardaman's view, did not apply to "wild animals and niggers."[12]

In truth, Mississippi spent next to nothing on Negro education. Black children, comprising three-fifths of the state's school-aged population in 1900, received less than one-fifth of the school funds. Yet Vardaman opposed all such spending on the grounds that it undermined the Negro's God-given role as a servant to whites. "The only effect of educating him," he sneered, "is to spoil a good field hand and make an insolent cook."[13]

As Vardaman saw it, schooling frustrated the Negro by raising false hopes about his limited future. It made him yearn for things he could never achieve or obtain, and it led him to ponder such forbidden topics as social equality and interracial sex. The result, Vardaman insisted, was an explosion of crime. The average black became less law abiding as his level of education increased—a phenomenon "unique to the negro."[14]

For the White Chief, one crime stood above the rest. It was a rare Vardaman speech that did not contain some reference to rape, with a "black fiend" on the prowl. It hardly mattered that such assaults were extremely rare. Vardaman was a demagogue, not a logician. But he did believe, along with most other white men of his time and place, that the essence of honorable behavior lay in defending the "superlative qualities of Southern women," and, that the threat to their virtue lurked in every Negro cabin, on every country road. As one Mississippian put it: "I never heard of but one case of attempted assault by a negro on a white woman. That negro was taken out and hanged. I said that we never had any trouble with negroes, but it's because we never take our eyes off the gun. You may wager that I never leave my wife and daughter at home without a man in the house after ten o'clock at night—because I am afraid."[15]

Vardaman knew that white fears about social equality grew stronger in rough economic times, and he sensed that for poor white men, the ability to protect one's wife and daughter from the "black beast" had become a vital substitute—a compensation of sorts—for the inability to shield them from the ravages of hunger and debt. The White Chief's campaign banner said: "A VOTE FOR VARDAMAN IS A VOTE FOR WHITE SUPREMACY, THE SAFETY OF THE HOME, AND THE PROTECTION OF OUR WOMEN AND CHILDREN."[16]

Not since the 1870s had a political campaign in Mississippi been mired in so much hate. At one point, Vardaman defended the lynching of a black rape suspect who had been horribly tortured and then burned alive at the stake. "I sometimes think that one could look upon a scene of that kind," he mused, "and suffer no more moral deterioration than he would by looking upon the burning of an Orangoutang that had stolen a baby or a viper that had stung an unsuspecting child to death." At another point, Vardaman spoke approvingly of "local mob rule," adding: "If I were the sheriff and a

Negro fiend fell into my hands I would run him out of the county. If I were governor and asked for troops to protect him I would send them. But if I were a private citizen I would head the mob to string the brute up, and I haven't much respect for a white man who wouldn't."[17]

These statements did not go unchallenged. A fair number of merchants, professionals, and planters—the so-called better whites—portrayed Vardaman as a "vain demagogue" and a "top-notch medicine man." "He has done more to arouse a spirit of lawlessness and mob rule throughout the state," said one critic, "than all other causes combined."

Yet much of this sentiment was rooted in barren soil. The large planters seemed less concerned about the morality of lynching than about the danger it posed to their black labor supply. By endlessly inciting the mob, they believed, Vardaman was encouraging terrified field hands to flee the state. "[Is any home] threatened with social equality with the negro?" sneered an anti-Vardaman newspaper. Of course not; the issue was a fraud, "conjured up by its agitator . . . to ride into office." It was clear that the Negro had long ago accepted his inferior status—and equally clear that Mississippi, for better or worse, could not long survive without him.[18]

But Vardaman carried the day. His margin of victory in the governor's race came largely from the hill country, where the fear of "race leveling" was most intense. For many people, a vote for Vardaman meant that a white man, however humble, could always consider himself superior to the Negro. As one newspaper gloated, "a nigger is [still] a nigger" in Mississippi, and even President Roosevelt "could make him nothing more."

Vardaman boasted that his victory had been a blessing to both races because the white man remained on top and the Negro remained alive. Had he lost, Vardaman said, "we would have had to kill more negroes in the next twelve months in Mississippi than we had to kill in the last twenty years."[19]

III

Shortly after taking office in 1905, Governor Vardaman sent an urgent message to the "law officers" of Mississippi. The vast increase in "criminal negroes," he wrote, had become a "peril to the peace of the community and a menace to the safety of the white man's home." Vardaman urged police and prosecutors to crack down hard. "Let there begin a most vigorous campaign against the Vagrant—the vicious Idler and the Keeper of Dives of Infamy. Let the rendezvous of the Rapist, the Murderer, the Crap-Shooter, and the Blind Tiger, be closed!" Unless this was done, he warned, "the mob will usurp the function which you should perform, but which you have betrayed."

His logic was familiar. Freedom, he said, had been a disaster for the Negro. It had failed to make him more honest or responsible or to teach him self-restraint. "He is a barbarian still," the White Chief asserted, with a "thin veneering of civilization" and an "increased capacity for crime."[20]

Vardaman's message had wide public support. For years, white Southerners had been complaining about the behavior of young blacks, born after the Civil War ended, who had never experienced the "civilizing" effects of slavery. In 1895, a Louisiana newspaper observed that "the [new] generation of negro bucks and wenches have lost that wholesome respect for the white man, without which two races, one inferior, cannot live in peace and harmony together." Although the newspaper was referring to certain breaches of racial etiquette, a larger message came through: the faithful slaves of yesteryear had been replaced by a more dangerous breed. White Southerners could no longer count on the deference and loyalty of younger blacks because emancipation had placed them beyond the traditional orbit of white control.[21]

Free Negroes, wrote Philip A. Bruce, a distinguished Virginia historian, were "fast reverting" to the "physical type" and "original morals" of their "primitive" African roots. Slavery had "provided restraints on their character," Bruce explained in *The Plantation Negro as a Freeman*. It had kept their "criminal habits" and "ardent sexual appetites" under tight control. But "the new generation, in being less accustomed to restraint than the old, are more inclined to act upon their natural impulses. They are more headstrong than their immediate ancestors, and to that degree, have a more decided tendency to retrograde."[22]

This theory of racial regression seemed well suited to the apprehensive white South. By stressing the "destructive" consequences of emancipation, it linked the "inferiority" of Negroes to the need for racial subordination and control. "The factors of ruin among the black people are making steady progress," warned Mississippi educator Charles H. Otken in *The Ills of the South*. "Licentiousness, lying, thieving, drunkenness, gambling, and perjury have made alarming gains. . . . Homicides are common. . . . The boys are street loafers. . . . The girls . . . wish no honorable employment."[23]

Otken's views were repeated endlessly in the following years. Dunbar Rowland, a Mississippi historian, claimed that emancipation had unleashed the "defective moral nature of the negro." The sad result "is a rapid increase in crime and lawlessness among blacks under forty years of age." Even Dr. H. B. Frissel, the white superintendent at Virginia's all-black Hampton Institute, believed that slavery had served a useful purpose in this respect:

While it kept negroes from being educated, it also kept them from being criminal. . . . When emancipation came, the naturally depraved and criminal class of negroes were let loose and deprived of this restraining influence of the slavery system. Such men began, naturally, to confound license with liberty, and they have instinctively degenerated since slavery days.[24]

After Slavery, Before Parchman

These writers provided a measure of respectability to politicians of the Vardaman stripe. Some, like Bruce and Otken, emphasized the dangers of emancipation to a free but obviously "inferior" race. Others, including doctors and scientists, examined the biological "weaknesses" of blacks, particularly their "simple minds" and "primitive urges." Writing about the "smaller brain" of Negroes in 1906, Dr. Robert Bean took note of their "deficient judgment" and "lack of self-control" in sexual matters. Dr. William Bevis said much the same thing in the prestigious *American Journal of Psychiatry*. Early in adolescence, "around puberty," he explained, blacks experience a surge of sexual passion and a corresponding decline in "mental development." From that point forward, "promiscuous sex relations, gambling petty thievery, drinking, and loafing consumed [their] time." Without "proper guidance," Bevis added, the Negro would make a "complete wreck of his physical and mental life."[25]

And the lives of white women as well. According to a Maryland researcher, the Negro's "intense sexual passions" (developed over centuries to offset a high African "death rate") had created chaos in the post–Civil War South. More than 90 percent of both sexes were "unchaste," the doctor estimated, although the male Negro, "son of a wild and tropical race," posed a much greater threat.[26]

No one—not even the White Chief himself—described this threat more graphically than Dr. Robert W. Shufeldt, a Southern army officer, in *The Negro: A Menace to Civilization*, published in 1907. Black men and women, he wrote, "are almost wholly subservient to the sexual instinct. They copulate solely for the gratification of the passion—for the erotic pleasure it affords them. In other words, negroes are purely animal."

Shufeldt believed that blacks had a deep yearning for white flesh and that no punishment—not even lynching—could fully check their "savage lust." In Shufeldt's world, all white females, including children, were at terrible risk; the black rapist might even "increase the size of

the genital fissure by an ugly outward rip of his knife, a common practice among negroes when they assault little white girls."

Shufeldt saw no chance for improvement, no hope for change.
Blacks were "deteriorating morally every day," he claimed, and there
was nothing the white man could do. "It is their nature, and they
cannot possibly rid themselves of that, any more than skunks and
polecats can cast away their abominable scent glands and the outrageous odor they emit."[27]

These sentiments were not limited to the South. Theories about
brain size, sexual urges, and arrested development were part of a
larger movement, known as scientific racism, that had a strong following nationwide. By 1900, dozens of physicians and psychologists,
historians and social workers, criminologists and statisticians were
discovering a dangerous "new" Negro, menacing to whites. Many of
them relied on public documents, including those of the U.S. Cen-
sus, to chart the growth of Negro crime. In 1890, blacks comprised
12 percent of the national population and 25 percent of the prison
population. By 1910, the figures stood, respectively, at 11 percent
and 34 percent. The problem, moreover, was not unique to the
South. In every region, sociologist Charles McCord concluded, "the
percentage of colored prisoners is in excess of the percentage that
the colored formed of the total population."[28]

McCord provided a "social explanation": the black defendant—
"ignorant, without money, and without influence"—faced very long
odds. A combination of prejudice and poverty increased his conviction rate, lengthened his sentence, and lessened his chances for a pardon or parole. Yet McCord did not stop here. Genetics came next.

Blacks belonged to a "child race," McCord observed in *The
American Negro as a Dependent, Defective, and Delinquent.* "Shiftless"
and "impulsive," they lacked the "independence of character" to
overcome their hostile surroundings. And their moral lapses made
them a danger to whites as well as to themselves. The "horror and
menace of rape in the South cannot be exaggerated . . . ," he wrote.

"Things sometimes happen that cannot be told even in a book like this."[29]

Walter Wilcox, a Cornell statistics professor, went further than McCord, insisting that high black crime rates were a constant in American life: they did not change much from one region or environment to another. And Frederick Hoffman, chief statistician for the Prudential Insurance Company, went still further. His *Race Traits and Tendencies of the American Negro*, published by the prestigious American Economic Association in 1896, described blacks as hopeless degenerates, unable to care for themselves or to respect the "lives and property of others." Hoffman viewed Negro education as futile, blamed lynchings on the victims, and predicted the ultimate extinction of all blacks in the United States. The "colored population," he explained, "is gradually parting with the virtues . . . developed under the regime of slavery."[30]

These theories of racial regression would have a profound impact on the treatment of black criminals. As convict leasing died out, the idea of "socializing" wayward Negroes, of returning them to a "natural environment"—a plantation-like setting—seemed a safe and natural choice. "To confine the negro [in jail] is to doom him to death," a prominent journalist declared. "To reform his character is an almost hopeless task. . . . The Negro is a Negro. We must deal with him as he is."[31]

IV

"Do Negroes constitute a Race of Criminals?" Ida Joyce Jackson did not think so. The very question was insulting to black Americans, she declared, and it badly missed the point. After listing the "real" causes of crime among Negroes—from the "immoral" legacy of slavery to the "lack of justice" in American courtrooms—Mrs. Jackson turned the question upside down. "The dominant race of this country," she wrote in 1907, "is largely responsible for whatever criminal tendencies the colored race has inherited."[32]

Mrs. Jackson was not alone. As president of the Colored Federation of Woman's Clubs, she represented the thinking of numerous black scholars and professionals who were alarmed by the apparent rise of Negro crime, as well as the hostile white response to it. They now faced the unenviable task of providing logical explanations for the sort of behavior that they themselves despised. In the words of William S. Scarborough, a black professor of classics at Wilberforce College, "The criminal negro is one of the heaviest burdens that the race has to carry today."

This was understandable. As a man of obvious accomplishment, Scarborough resented the racial theories and attitudes that lumped all blacks together at the bottom of the human pile. "There are *negroes* and *negroes,*" he complained. "Crude, cultured, shiftless, thrifty, grotesque, urbane; immoral and grossly debased; clean and living the life of the spirit. The Vardamans of the world know no distinctions, make no discriminations, brand us all alike as a lower order of creation. Therefore Negro criminality cannot be ignored by us."

By 1900, black writers were covering this issue with mounting interest and concern. Their articles appeared regularly in the "colored" press, bearing such titles as "The Negro Criminal—How Best Reached," "Degeneration and Crime," and "Some of the Evils Which Are Producing Desperadoes and Murderers among the Negroes, and the Remedies." Like Professor Scarborough, the majority of them taught at black colleges such as Howard, Atlanta, Tuskegee, and Fisk. What they all had in common, aside from their elite status, was the belief that Negro crime had become a serious problem in the United States but that white oppression was largely to blame.[33]

Not surprisingly, these writers rejected scientific racism as an affront to serious scholarship, and to human dignity as well. Howard's Kelly Miller, a prominent mathematician and philosopher, debunked the approach of white researchers who "sifted mercilessly for ugly and uninviting information" about Negroes. What could be more unfair, he asked, than to judge an entire people by the weaknesses of their "most submerged members"?[34]

Miller did not deny that black crime had shot up after emancipation. "Slavery suppressed wrongdoing, but did not implant the corrective principle," he reasoned, "so that when the physical restraint was removed, there was no moral restraint to take its place." For many ex-slaves, freedom meant license and trouble; for some, it still did. Yet the Negro was improving, not regressing, he believed, despite enormous obstacles in his path.

Tuskegee's Monroe Work thought much the same thing. Trained as a sociologist at the University of Chicago, he viewed criminal activity among Negroes as a natural response to the "confusion" and "disorder" that had accompanied emancipation in the South. Yet for many blacks, he admitted, crime had become a depressing way of life, encouraged by a legal system that controlled and exploited Negroes rather than protecting them from abuse. The inevitable result was a growing disrespect for the law. "At present," Work noted, the Negro "looks upon courts as places were punishment is meted out rather than where justice is dispensed."[35]

In 1904, W. E. B. Du Bois hosted a conference at Atlanta University, where he worked, on the subject of "Negro Crime." A brilliant historian and sociologist with advanced degress from Harvard and the University of Berlin, Du Bois had chronicled the African-American experience in bold patterns and meticulous detail. His thoughts about race and crime had already appeared in a host of national magazines, including the *Independent,* which described him as the "leading writer among the colored people of this country on social questions affecting his race." Like Professors Miller and Work, Du Bois argued that a high crime rate among Negroes after emancipation was inevitable. "It is impossible for such a social revolution to take place," he wrote, "without giving rise to a class of men, who, in the new stress of life, under new responsibilities, would lack the will and power to make a way, and would consequently sink into vagrancy, poverty and crime."[36]

Du Bois was a harsh judge of character. His work was frank, often unforgiving, with a rigid moral tone. The Atlanta Conference's Final Report, which he helped to write and edit, had the ring of a strait-laced Calvinist tract. A key section on the causes of crime listed ten "faults" of the modern Negro:

1. Abuse of their new freedom. . . .
2. Loose ideas of property, petty pilfering.
3. Unreliability, lying and deception.
4. Exaggerated ideas of personal rights. . . .
5. Sexual looseness, weak family life, and poor training of children. . . .
6. Lack of proper self-respect. . . .
7. Poverty, low wages. . . .
8. Lack of thrift and prevalence of the gambling spirit.
9. Waywardness of the "second generation."
10. The use of liquor and drugs.

What made this report so revealing was the ambivalence—and frustration—of the black scholars who composed it. All of them blamed Negro crime on the "wrong social conditions" of a "deeply racist culture." Yet most believed that crime had reached crisis proportions in the black community, that not enough was being done internally to combat it, and that the problem had soiled the Negro's reputation in the larger white world. "This is a dangerous and threatening phenomenon," the scholars agreed. "It means large numbers of the freedmen's sons have not yet learned to be law-abiding citizens or steady workers, and until they do, the progress of the race, of the South, and of the nation will be retarded."[37]

V

Whether Governor Vardaman served to ignite a racial explosion or simply to exploit one for political ends is a matter of some dispute. What is certain, though, is that the years surrounding his election in 1904 were among the bloodiest in Mississippi's turbulent history. As the campaign heated up, white terrorist groups came alive in areas where black farmers had experienced modest success. Calling themselves "whitecaps," these nightriders beat and tortured Negroes, burned their barns, trampled their crops, and shot into their homes. According to conservative accounts, about a dozen blacks were murdered and hundreds more driven from their land.[38]

Vardaman's Mississippi also led the nation in lynchings, with an average of twenty reported each year. (The actual number was much higher.) During Reconstruction, lynching had helped to overthrow Radical Republican rule. By 1900, it had evolved into the region's most popular form of vigilante justice. The main victims were young black men who appeared to challenge the racial boundaries that had seemed virtually impregnable only a generation before.

"You don't understand how we feel down here," a white Mississippian told a visitor in 1908. "When there is a row, we feel like killing a nigger whether he has done anything or not." Whites liked to believe that their mobs were punishing real crimes by dangerous Negroes. If they happened to lynch the wrong person—well, that too served a purpose by reminding other "niggers" of their place. This particular lesson was brought home to the blacks of Rocky Ford, Mississippi, when a Negro field hand named J. P. Ivy was chained to a wood pile, doused with gasoline, and roasted to death before a crowd of six hundred jeering people. A local newspaper reported his apparent crime: "She was not sure, but thought he looked like the [Negro] who attacked her."[39]

Whites claimed that "sexual assaults" by black men—which included everything from a violent attack to an innocent nudge, from a careless remark to an accidental glance—were the leading cause of lynching. When Vardaman proclaimed that white men "would be justified in slaughtering every Ethiop on the earth to preserve the honor of one Caucasian home," his reference to "honor" went far beyond any legal definition of rape. And when he announced that certain crimes demanded a punishment more painful and humiliating than a legal execution, there were few (if any) in his audience who did not know exactly what he meant. "I only regret the brute [does] not have ten thousand lives to pay for his atrocious deed," Vardaman declared after a black man had been lynched for "violating" a white woman. "An eternity in hell will not be adequate punishment for it."[40]

By the early 1900s, lynchings in Mississippi had taken a ghoulish turn. The mobs grew larger, often including women and children, and a ritual of torture often prevailed. In October 1902, the *Jackson Clarion-Ledger* carried a banner headline about a lynching at Corinth, in the Mississippi hills: "BURNED AT THE STAKE: Five Thousand Persons Saw a Negro Pay Penalty for His Crimes—Killed a [White] Woman." In a carnival-like atmosphere, the suspect was brought back to the scene of the murder, where he made a full confession to the crowd, which included the victim's family. "Reserved seats were placed for the women who might desire them," the newspaper reported, "and a number were there. Special trains were run to the scene and hundreds took advantage of the opportunity. The brother of the murdered woman lighted the fire."[41]

In the midst of the 1903 campaign, two black men were lynched in separate incidents in Sunflower County. A few newspapers blamed Vardaman, who had recently traveled there to stir up local whites against their "negro wench postmaster" Minnie M. Cox. The following year, a black sharecropper named Luther Holbert was suspected of murdering a white plantation owner near the Sunflower County town of Doddsville. Holbert tried to escape with his wife, but the two were captured by a posse and tied to a tree. More than a thousand spectators were on hand, eating hard-boiled eggs, sipping lemonade, and swigging whiskey, as the Holberts were subjected to "fiendish tortures" before being burned alive:

> [They] were forced to hold out their hands while one finger at a time was chopped off [and] distributed as souvenirs. [Their] ears were cut off. Holbert was beaten severely, his skull was fractured, and one of his eyes, knocked with a stick, hung by a shred from the socket. . . . The most excruciating form of punishment consisted in the use of a large corkscrew in the hands of some of the mob. This instrument was bored into the flesh of the man and woman, in the arms, legs, and body, and then pulled out, the spirals tearing out big pieces of raw, quivering flesh every time it was withdrawn.[42]

Many lynching victims died like the Holberts, in what one newspaper called "Negro barbeques." Others were drowned, whipped, branded with hot irons, and seared with blowtorches. In one case, a black suspect was "tied alive behind an automobile and dragged around the town until dead." In another, a fifteen-year-old Negro accused of entering the bedroom of a white girl was "shot to pieces" by a mob near Philadelphia, Mississippi. "Our women must and will be protected," warned the local newspaper. In Indianola, blacks were horrified to learn that the cadaver of a Negro victim had been shipped to a nearby college laboratory, where the "flesh was stripped from the bones, and the skeleton arranged and used as an anatomical exhibit."[43]

It became an article of faith among the "better" whites of Mississippi—the Delta's David Cohn, Hodding Carter, and William A. Percy, among them—that lynchings were "low-class affairs" led by sullen, slack-jawed rednecks in faded overalls and sweat-stained hats. According to Cohn, poor whites needed to hurt and humiliate the Negro in order to reinforce their meager claims of social superiority. "A white man ain't a-goin' to be able to live in this country if we let niggers start gittin' biggity," a mob member told Cohn. "I wish they'd lemme have him. I'd cut off his balls and th'ow em to the hawgs."[44]

The White Chief

To many blacks, this portrait of redneck rage seemed painfully authentic. "We never had no trouble out of the upper class whites, those that had made something of themselves," a Negro woman recalled. "The trashy whites were harder on [us] than the better to do ones," said another. Whenever something went wrong, a black farmer complained, the "poor white went out and got him up a crowd of his own kind of people and went and took care of the Negro. The white man with money had no control when the poor man had something on the Negro to go after him for."[45]

There surely was truth to this. Yet recent studies of lynching have noted that the composition of these mobs varied widely from place to place and depended on a number of different factors, such as the crime itself, the reputation of the white victim, or a specific need to reaffirm white supremacy and racial control. Mass mobs included all sorts of participants, one study concluded, although the "family, friends and neighbors of an alleged criminal's victim often took part and assumed a prominent role."[46]

This particular scenario, so common to Mississippi, was described in chilling detail by James Howell Street, a popular journalist born and raised in rural Jones County, a bastion of Vardaman support. Street witnessed his first lynching at fourteen. The victim, a black hotel porter named John, had been suspected of raping a white woman on a summer evening in 1917. "Her men-folks didn't call the sheriff," Street recalled:

They called the neighbors. They pulled pistols from oiled rags in bureaus, lifted shotguns from pegs over the mantels. They needed dogs. Bob Gant's were the best in the state. Three men piled into an automobile and thundered into the night—ninety miles over rough roads to Bob's house. They returned after midnight.

The dogs "flushed the negro" at Sandersville, the posse caught him at Hot Coffee, and "the bunch started to Ellisville for a lynching bee." Young Street was surprised to see so many familiar faces. His father had told him that only "white trash" lynched Negroes, yet the whole county was on hand: "Farmers had come from miles around. Their wives and children and dogs were along. Many brought lunches—big six-layer cakes and fried chicken. They ate their picnic on the courthouse lawn, under the Confederate monument."

John was dragged to the scene of the crime. "You'se got the right niggah, white folks. I'se sorry," he told the growing crowd. Cries of, "Let's burn him, let's stomp him," erupted as people rushed forward to kick the Negro unconscious. "A rope was thrown over the first branch of [a] sycamore and John's body was jerked into the air. Pine needles and boughs were piled around the tree. A volley of shots was fired at the body." Then the tinder was lit, the rope was severed, and John's lifeless corpse tumbled down into the flames. That evening, an old Negro servant complained to Street that the mob had gone too far. "Dey didn't have no right to burn that niggah," she said. "Only de Lawd has de right to burn folks."[47]

VI

Blacks accused of assaulting white women in Mississippi were rarely afforded the luxury of a trial. Some fled the mob and escaped; others, like John, were tracked down and killed. As late as 1931, the *Jackson Clarion-Ledger* reported, with grim satisfaction, that a black youth named Tom Carraway was actually being tried for this crime in a local courtroom. It hardly mattered that Carraway's lawyer put up no defense as an angry mob gathered outside. What did count was the trial itself—the fact the Carraway was "one of the first [such] negroes in Mississippi" to be spared a lynching "at the hands of indignant white citizens."[48]

This was a mild exaggeration. Between 1880 and 1930, ten men—all Negroes—were legally executed for rape in Mississippi, and at least two dozen more were sentenced to life imprisonment.

The White Chief

Their stories were roughly the same. The sheriff had captured them quickly, a judge had tried them instantly, and the governor had sent troops to protect them from the mob. One such case occurred in the town of Brandon in 1909. The local headline read: "Will Mack Publicly Hanged: Vast Crowd Sees the Brute Pay the Penalty of a Horrible Crime—His Last Word was 'Guilty.' "[49]

If Mack's trial showed anything, it was the small gap that separated a lynching from an execution. Mack was indicted, tried, convicted, and sentenced in a courthouse ringed by state militia. The whole process took just six hours, the shortest criminal proceeding in the history of Rankin County. More than three thousand people assembled for Mack's execution, snacking on ice cream and watermelon, in the broiling summer sun. "Some ladies were present," the *Brandon News* observed. "A few were nursing infants who tugged at the mother's breasts, while the mother kept her eyes on the gallows. She didn't want to lose any part of the program she had come miles to see, and to tell to the neighbors at home."

Will Mack reached the platform at high noon. He seemed completely at ease (a "common trait" of the "negro fiend") as he once more admitted his guilt. "On being asked if he desired to warn other negroes [about] committing such crimes, Mack replied, 'Yes, sir; please tell them that for me.' " Then a hood was placed over his head, the trap door sprang open, and the spectators roared. It had cost the state almost $3,000 to execute him, which seemed to many in the crowd a needless expense. But all grasped the larger lesson that had little to do with the law. "Whatever the cost in money, time, or blood," said the *Brandon News,* "the negro rapist must die."

What made mob violence so terrifying in Jim Crow Mississippi was the virtual absence of opposition. Local sheriffs often encouraged it, grand juries never brought indictments, and coroners simply reported "death at the hands of parties unknown." White ministers avoided the subject because it made their congregations "uncomfortable." Most newspapers either ignored mob killings or hid them on the bottom of an inside page ("Four Negroes Lynched in Grenada; Also Another in Oxford"). But others supported lynchings ("Speedy Justice to Negro Fiend"), advertised them in advance ("John Hartfield Will Be Lynched by Ellisville Mob at 5 o'clock This Afternoon"), or even forecast them like the weather ("Prospects Good for a Lynching, and Indications Are That When It Comes It Will Be Wholesale").[50]

In fact, not a single white editor in Mississippi found the courage to condemn lynching without qualification in the years between 1900 and World War I. Printed opinion ranged from the *Raymond Gazette,* which endorsed the lynching of "insane" Negroes who became public nuisances, to the *Jackson Clarion-Ledger,* which described lynching as "horrible" but "excusable" for "certain heinous crimes." "Here in the South," it explained, "are thousands of defenseless white women, exposed constantly to a sensual race . . . with the most fiendish passions."[51]

The White Chief could not have said it better himself.

✠

PART TWO

The Parchman Era

CHAPTER FIVE

The Birth and the Birthplace

The cardinal characteristic of crime in the Delta is that it is crime of violence.

—David Cohn, *Where I Was Born and Raised*, 1935

I

By the time James K. Vardaman became governor in 1904, the state legislature had purchased more than twenty thousand acres for the construction of several prison farms. The biggest tract was in the Yazoo-Mississippi Delta, ninety miles south of Memphis, at a dilapidated railroad spur known as Gordon Station. Local people called it the Parchman place, after the Sunflower County family that had owned it for years. Under Vardaman's personal supervision, the land was drained and cleared, and a sawmill was built to cut timber for prison buildings. Cotton was planted on several thousand acres, along with crops to feed the convicts, the mules, the hogs, and a dairy herd. In 1905, less than one year later, Parchman had turned a profit of $185,000.[1]

Profit, however, was not the White Chief's main objective. Vardaman had a long-standing interest in penal reform. As a representative of poor whites, he had opposed convict leasing on the grounds that it enriched big planters and railroad barons at the public's expense. As a private citizen, he had condemned the system because it oppressed those least able to defend themselves. Vardaman would spend a lifetime fighting to deny blacks political rights and social equality. Yet he also believed that Negroes who accepted their lowly place in the human order should be protected from abuse.[2]

That included convicts. To Vardaman's thinking, a good prison, like an efficient slave plantation, could serve to "socialize" young blacks within the limits of their God-given abilities. It would not raise their intelligence or their morality, but it could teach them proper discipline, strong work habits, and respect for white authority. "You cannot create something when there is nothing to build on," he surmised, "but they can be well trained, and that is the best that can be done with the genuine negro."[3]

Vardaman took personal charge of this process. Viewing a plantation environment as both a humane and sensible response to Negro crime, he moved virtually all state convicts to Sunflower County during his years as governor and created the post of superintendent to oversee the ever-expanding prison operation. Parchman would become a monument to Mississippi's White Chief—a huge penal farm in the Delta for blacks who had "lost" their way.*

---

* Vardaman's personal dealings with black convicts said much about his views on paternalism and race. As a newspaper editor in the 1890s, he had printed numerous articles against the convict lease, including one in which a black prisoner was chained up without medical attention after his frostbitten fingers had been cut off at the joints. As governor, Vardaman made a point to personally inspect Parchman and the county penal farms. One of his favorite activities was to lead a mounted posse, complete with prison bloodhounds, on a mock hunt of a convict who was given a morning's head start. After tracking him down, the group would enjoy a picnic lunch, with the convict eating off to the side. In 1906, Vardaman made headlines by "throttling" a convict-servant named Hezekiah Planer, who worked at the governor's mansion in Jackson. Planer left his post one evening, got drunk in a downtown tavern, and was arrested. Even worse, he apparently "sassed" Vardaman upon his return, leading the governor to kick him to the floor and crack a broom over his head. Returned to the Oakley prison farm, Planer did not expect to see Vardaman again. But their paths crossed a year later, when the governor rushed to Oakley to help quell a bloody riot. Boldly confronting the ring leader, Vardaman might have been killed had not Planer jumped in to disarm the man. In gratitude, Vardaman took Planer back to Jackson and quickly pardoned him.

II

"I think I was the very first white woman to cross Sunflower River," wrote Mary Hamilton in her haunting autobiography, *Trials of the Earth*, and "I know I am the first white woman that ever came through what is now Parchman." As the wife of a frontier lumberman, Mrs. Hamilton was no stranger to hardship and struggle. Yet the land she explored—and settled—in 1897 was like nothing she had seen before. The tangled swamps and swollen rivers were filled with alligators and poisonous snakes. The forests were so dense that "a man couldn't get through . . . without a compass in one hand and a cane axe in the other to blaze every foot of the way." Bears and wildcats roamed the chest-high sage grass at the edge of the woods. "I could never get used to hearing a panther scream, nor wolves howl," she recalled, "though it was an every-night occurrence."[4]

The land that Mary Hamilton described was the central Yazoo-Mississippi Delta, an inland wilderness soon to become the Cotton Kingdom of the South. The Delta runs for two hundred miles along the Mississippi River, from Memphis down to Vicksburg, and for seventy-five miles east to the Chickasaw Ridge. For thousands of years, until huge earthen levees were built, the Mississippi had over-flowed her banks each spring, dumping a rich new film of sediment upon this flat alluvial plain. The Delta's thick brown topsoil, known as buckshot, is often fifty feet deep. "Nature knows not how to com-pound a richer mixture," one geologist marveled. "Every square foot of it riots in vegetable life."[5]

The Delta had always been partial to large planters, those with the resources to clear and drain the land. Its western edge, near the high bluffs and port towns of the Mississippi River, had been settled be-fore the Civil War. In 1860, four Delta counties were listed among the thirty-six wealthiest in the United States, and slaves outnum-bered whites by a margin of six to one. Yet it was not until the 1880s, with the emergence of inland transportation and serious flood control, that the Delta really took off. Planters and railroad gangs, timber crews and levee workers, all pushed back the region's once-impenetrable frontier. Cotton production soared as new railroads linked isolated plantations to the world's expanding market economy. By 1890, the Delta was generating almost 30 percent of the state's cotton sales on less than 12 percent of its cultivated land.[6]

Workers poured into the region from every side. Some were convicts from the state's expanding criminal class. Others were refugees from the depleted soils of the older cotton South. Virtually all of them were black, and together they brought wealth and change to the Delta, but at a frightful human cost. The Negro laid every mile of track, a planter observed.

> These forest lands have been cultivated by him into fertile fields. . . . The levees upon which the Delta depends for protection from floods have been erected mainly by the Negro, and the daily labor in field and town, in planting and building, in operating gins and compresses and oil mills, in moving trains, in handling the great staple of the country—all, in fact, that makes the life behind these earthen ramparts—is but the Negro's daily toil."[7]

The Delta became a slaughterhouse for thousands of them. In 1878, an epidemic of yellow fever swept through the region, killing four hundred people in the cotton town of Greenville, population twenty-three hundred. Criers went through the streets, shouting, "Bring out your dead," as the burial wagons passed by. The fever always "struck without warning," a Deltan recalled. "First, the flushed yellow face, the drunken look, the chills and fever. . . . Then the delirium, black vomit, hemorrhage—and miraculous recovery or merciful death."[8]

Hookworm, pellagra, smallpox, tuberculosis: all took their toll. But the worst affliction by far was "swamp fever," or malaria, a disease that would ravage the Delta until the 1940s, when screened houses and powerful insecticides finally brought it under control.

Carried by the anopheles mosquito, malaria hit perhaps one-third of the region's people in any given year. The telltale rhythm of chills and fever, chattering teeth and burning faces, became a fixture of everyday Delta life. In Sunflower County, a planter buried six successive wives from malaria before his seventh wife buried him. During a particularly severe outbreak, a Delta man might propose to a woman by asking, "Miss Lucy, may I have the honor of buying your coffin?"[9]

Delta people, it was said, were not afraid to look death in the face. They had too much practice with it to turn meekly away. "The Delta," wrote David Cohn, a native son, "was founded and wrought in pain." Its early settlers endured floods and fevers, pursued violent pleasures, and worked at murderous tasks. Seeking a fresh start or simple adventure, only the strong and fortunate among them survived.

The cheapness of human life was often recalled by those who damned the rivers, drained the swamplands, and chopped down the trees. If a worker happened to stumble and fall into a pit along the levees, an old-timer remembered, "why, they just dump the next dirt on him and leave him there—cover him up and forget him—I've seen that happen." Indeed, the key to survival in the levee camps was brutally clear: "You can kill anybody you like, so long as you can work better than him. But, for God's sake, don't kill anybody who can work better than you, or they'll put you under the jail."[10]

In this world of casual violence, no one was immune. A young levee engineer described his own vulnerability in chilling terms. "Everybody carries a gun . . . ," he wrote to his family in 1905. "The way these levee niggers shoot one another is something fearful. One got shot in a crap game in camp here. It didn't even stop the game. . . .

"If one of the white foremen shoots a couple of niggers," he continued, "the work is not stopped. They are buried at night and that's all there is to it. Just look a moment at the conditions and you will understand. . . . Think of one white foreman, miles from anywhere, working a hundred and fifty of the most reckless niggers in the world. It's a plain case of which you'd rather do, shoot or get shot. . . ."[11]

Mary Hamilton provided a similar portrait of early Delta life. She knew that the loggers drank and gambled and brawled—that each man carried a gun, a loaf of bread, and a pint of whiskey to his job. And she had been told that killings and lynchings were common in the camps as a form of entertainment on Saturday nights. "I took it as a joke," she said—but not for long. A few months later, while treating a lumberjack whose foot had been split open with an axe, Hamilton "smelled a strong odor" coming from the man's pocket. When she reached in, a "Negro's finger" dropped into her hand.

"I was trembling all over," she recalled. The foreman quickly apologized, explaining that his men had just lynched a "nigger" accused of raping a white woman and then cut him up for "souvenirs." "That is all right. I approve of that part," Hamilton replied, "but if you have any fingers or toes about you don't bring them in the house."[12]

III

By the early 1900s, the Delta frontier had largely disappeared. With the levees up, the best land cleared, and the railroads in place, King Cotton found its perfect Southern home. In no other region did nature provide such lush inducements for success. "To speak of agriculture here means one thing: cotton," wrote anthropologist Hortense Powdermaker. Yet cotton meant more to Delta people than agriculture alone. Cotton fueled the economy, determined the class structure, and dominated race relations. "It is because of cotton that slaves were brought here, because of cotton that Negroes [far] outnumber whites, because of cotton that the plantation system developed under slavery has been modified to continue 'after freedom.' "[13]

As land prices exploded in the Delta, poor white farmers lost all hope of settling here. They remained in the hill country to the east, despised by class-conscious planters, feared by local Negroes, often ridiculed by both. Hodding Carter described them as a miserable lot, who "provide William Faulkner and Erskine Caldwell with characters from life, the Association for the Advancement of Colored People with lynching statistics, and [upper class whites] with a feeling of impending doom." A popular black verse, sung in careful privacy, went:

> My name is Sam, I was raised in the sand
> I'd rather be a nigger than a poor white man.[14]

The Delta became the realm of the planter and the tenant—one white and powerful, mixing modern business techniques with antebellum dreams; the other black and vulnerable, tending the rich man's cotton for a fraction of the take. In 1900, the percentage of Negro population stood at 12 percent in the United States, 58 percent in Mississippi, and 89 percent in the Delta. There were more blacks in Bolivar County than in all of Massachusetts, more blacks in Sharkey County than in all of Minnesota. One writer joked that the 377 blacks living in North Dakota would make a disappointing turnout at "the funeral of a Delta Negro preacher."

Plantation owners viewed the Negro as stronger, less demanding, and more deferential than the poor white. He didn't vote, rarely complained, and could easily be cheated. "He is a pain and a grief to live with," William Alexander Percy declared, "a solace and a delight. There are seven to eight of them to every one of us and he is the better breeder. Ours is surely the black belt."[15]

By 1910, more than ninety percent of the Delta's farmland was being worked by tenants, 95 percent of whom were Negroes. The plantations were enormous, covering ten thousand acres and more. As self-contained units, they provided services normally reserved for the local towns, such as schools, stores, churches, a post office, medical help, and graveyards. Everything about them revolved around the cotton crop and the labor force it required. The unpainted plantation cabins—without lights, plumbing, or insulation—lined the flat dirt roads that led to the fields. Children attended ramshackle one-room schools in the "off-times" between spring planting and fall picking, when their labor was not needed. Workers were often forced to shop in over-priced plantation commissaries because their credit was extended in scrip or coupons rather than cash. (Some tenants, as late as the 1950s, had never seen a dollar bill.) "The Delta is cotton-obsessed, Negro obsessed, and flood ridden," a scholar remarked. "It is the deepest South, the heart of Dixie, America's super-plantation belt."[16]

The arrangement between tenant and landlord varied from place to place. On most plantations, sharecropping was the rule. In return for a cabin, water, firewood, a mule team, farm tools, and cotton seed, the tenant gave the landlord a fixed portion—usually 50 percent—of his crop. Families worked as a unit, from first light to last. Their day began at 4:30 A.M., with a breakfast of fried okra, salt pork, and tomato gravy. "By five o'clock they are all in the field. The blistering heat sends them in about eleven, and dinner is cooked—turnip greens, cornbread, [more] salt pork, and sometimes pie. They lie around and rest until about 1:30, then return to the field until sundown. Supper consists of the left-overs from dinner."[17]

March 1 was Limit Day in the Delta, when the first credit (or "furnish") was extended at the plantation store. Each family could charge from ten to twenty dollars per month in supplies, depending on the acreage it farmed. The prices were considerably higher than those in town, and the interest rates often reached 25 percent. But planters neatly defended the furnish as a protection for their tenants—a way of getting them to purchase necessities instead of squandering their money on whiskey, gambling, and sex. "The besetting sin of the Delta Negro," said one straight-faced apologist, "is his uncurbed, headlong extravagance."[18]

In the early spring, the tenant prepared the ground and planted his crop. In April and May, he thinned the cotton stalks and chopped the vines and grasses that grew along the rows. In late June, the tight green bolls appeared, and the crop was "laid-by." July and August brought some relaxation, as the cotton swelled and matured in the scorching summer heat. In September, the bolls burst open, and the Delta turned white. This was the cotton season, or harvesttime, and almost everyone took part. The local towns emptied and the jails were unlocked, as Negroes of all ages and both sexes poured into the fields. "Along the rows the pickers bent, trailing six- or nine-foot long white cotton sacks behind them, strapped over a shoulder, the open end at waist level on the left. Using both hands, they reached into the hard-shelled brown bolls, avoiding if possible the sharp edges, pulling out the white lint with seed. A man averaged up to three hundred pounds a day. Sometimes a woman could beat him."[19]

Then came the ginning, the bailing, and the sale. The year officially ended on Settlement Day, when cropper and landlord sat down to figure their split. The opportunities for cheating were endless. Few tenants had the ability to read their furnish statements or to add up the numbers, and fewer still were bold enough to question the planter's final count. "He not gonna show me the book," a cropper recalled. "He egvance me food and some clothes, but I don't know how much he charged me for um. I gotta take his word that I owe what he say. If I don't, then I get on his bad side and I got to move."[20]

The planter, of course, took a more benevolent view. No other system, said one, was as good to the Negroes. "Their houses are guaranteed to them. They get medical attention and clothing and an ample supply of food and tobacco. . . . At the end of the year, if crops and prices are bad, their accounts at the plantation store are frequently canceled and they start with a clean slate. No wonder they are care-free, light-hearted people."[21]

Another planter described sharecropping as the most "humane, just, self-representing, and cheerful a method of earning a living as human beings are likely to devise." Indeed, he went on, "I watch [these] limber-jointed, oily-black, well-fed, decently clothed peasants . . . and I feel sorry for the telephone girls, the clerks in chain stores, the office help, the unskilled laborers everywhere—not only for their poor and fixed wage, but for their slave routine, their joyless habits of work, and their insecurity."[22]

There was one drawback, this planter admitted: sharecropping gave men like himself "an unusual opportunity" to swindle these peasants "without detection or punishment." But this was rather uncommon, he thought; and it spoke to a failure in human nature, not in the system itself. Most planters were fair and affectionate with their Negroes, and poverty, where it existed, was the result of "inferior racial traits."

Some observers disagreed. Hortense Powdermaker estimated that "not more than twenty-five or thirty percent" of the Delta sharecroppers got an honest count on Settlement Day." The rest "either broke even or were left in debt to the landlord." In *The Yazoo River*, Congressman Frank E. Smith recounted the story of a shrewd tenant who is told on Settlement Day that his cotton proceeds had *exactly* equaled his debts:

Tenant. Then I don't owe you nuthin, Cap'm?

Planter. No, you don't owe me a cent.

Tenant. An' you don't owe me nuthin?

Planter. You saw the books.

Tenant. Then what's I gonna do with them two bales I ain't done hauled in yet?

Planter. Well, what do you know! Just look at that! Here's two pages stuck together. I'll have to add this whole account up again.[23]

To some, the furnish was worse than crooked. It resembled an old-fashioned dole, a series of enervating handouts, although the tenants had earned their money through backbreaking work. According to psychologist John Dollard, the furnish produced a deep dependence on the landlord and a passive expectation of rewards. "One can think of the lower-class Negroes as bribed and drugged by this system," he noted. "The effect of the social set-up seems . . . to grant them . . . freedom from responsibility, and also to exercise the autocratic control over them which is the prerogative of the patriarchal father."[24]

Those who felt cheated often moved away. In December and January, the Delta roads were "filled with wagons piled high with household goods, the families perched on top. They are hoping to find something better, but they seldom do." For thousands of tenants, migration was an act of power: a way of expressing their resentment, exerting their independence, and protecting their meager rights. In some cases, a tenant moved on because a white overseer had beaten him or demanded sex with his wife. Others wandered about for reasons known only to themselves. The planters called them floaters and blamed their "Negro blood."[25]

Some tenants were encouraged to leave. Those who could read and write and keep track of things were seen as bad examples. One cropper recalled the case of Bernie Morris, who worked on a plantation where the landlord had never opened his books. When Morris showed up on Settlement Day with his own set of figures, he caused quite a stir. "It wuzn't on'y what he wuz keepin' dem from stealin' from *him*," the cropper explained, "it wuz dat he wuz showin' de uthuh nigguhs de wrong idea, see? Cordin' to de white man, he wuz spoilin' his nigguhs!"

Morris was evicted. "Dey tole [him], 'Well Bernie . . . You got de wrong attitude. You bettuh go somewheah wheah you kin use yo' pencil.'" Of course, it was like that almost everywhere, the cropper said:

Nought to nought, an' figguh to figguh—
All fuh de white man an' none fuh de nigguh!"[26]

For every tenant who was forced to leave the plantation, there were dozens more who were forced to stay on. Until well into the twentieth century, some planters used the furnish as a means to control the labor supply by keeping their workers perpetually in debt. According to Mississippi law, it was illegal for a tenant to break his contract after taking an advance, no matter how small it might be. As a result, debt servitude—a form of latter-day slavery—flourished throughout Mississippi and other parts of the South.

In 1907, an investigator claimed that at least one-third of the large planters in the cotton belt were holding their Negro workers to a "condition of peonage." That same year, journalist Ray Stannard Baker described a not uncommon episode in which a Mississippi tenant, deeply in debt, had been "sold" by one planter to another, along with his entire family. When the tenant balked, he was whipped and beaten to a pulp. "[His] children removed him to his home," Baker reported, "but the white men returned the next day, produced a rope and threatened to hang him unless he consented to go to the purchaser of the debt. The case came into court but the white men were never punished. [The tenant] was in Jackson, Miss., when I was there; he still showed the awful effects of his beating."[27]

The persistence and brutality of peonage can be gleaned from the correspondence of Mississippi governor Earl Brewer, a former district attorney from the Delta. In the spring of 1915, Brewer wrote the sheriff of Tallahatchie County to complain about the "mistreatment of negroes by planters." The problem was serious, Brewer warned. Specific complaints—beatings, shootings, and lynchings—had been reported to federal authorities in Jackson.

"There is going to be an effort to indict certain planters in that section for peonage," he said, "and unless they mend their ways it ought to be done."[28]

The sheriff was not particularly helpful. He had investigated the killings, and a grand jury had returned its usual verdict: "death at the hands of unknown parties." "I am ready and willing to enforce the law," he replied, "but you know as well as I that unless an officer is backed up by at least some of the people, his efforts are worth very little."[29]

Brewer also wrote to one of the culprits, his good friend Selwyn Jones. "At first I treated this matter lightly," he began, "and presumed it was some negroes . . . that [were] trying to run off and leave their crop without provocation after they had been [furnished] by the planter." But this was serious business, he said, and the violence had to stop. "You will find a tremendous number of negroes down in Jackson that bear upon their bodies the physical evidence of having been whipped and beaten up, and they stand here as a barrier against labor going into the Delta again."[30]

One of the more damaging complaints, Brewer told Jones, had been lodged by a "negro woman on your place" named Eva Blackburn. Claiming to have been whipped and held against her will, she had escaped to Jackson without her two young girls, eight-year-old Flossie and six-year-old Birdie, who were left behind at the Jones plantation. "I would want to suggest to you as a friend," Brewer wrote, "that I would have those children sent down here to their mother at once."[31]

Jones did not delay. Two days later, Flossie and Birdie were sent to Jackson by railroad, along with their mother's meager household goods. "The negro children came in today," Governor Brewer advised the nervous planter, "and I hope this will be settled in a way to avoid any controversy about in the Federal Court." No charges were ever filed.

IV

In the segregated world of the South, racial etiquette played a crucial role. It was the "very essence of caste," wrote the distinguished sociologist Robert Ezra Park, "since the prestige of a superior always involves the respect of an inferior." In the Mississippi Delta, where blacks far outnumbered whites, racial etiquette was both self-enforcing and intuitively understood. Its meticulous customs defined and regulated all aspects of daily life.[32]

In 1941, Professor Charles S. Johnson of Fisk University published *Growing Up in the Black Belt*, a powerful account of Negro youth throughout the rural South. Of the regions he studied, the Delta stood alone. "It has the most exacting restrictions of [all]," Johnson noted. "The limitations of life . . . generate bitter hopeless attitudes. . . . A common belief in Negro communities outside Mississippi is that it is the worst place in the entire country for Negroes."[33]

Johnson listed some of the Delta's racial codes. They included the obvious taboos against intermarriage and interdancing, as well as the unwritten rules that Negroes "must give whites the right-of-way on the sidewalks" and "cannot touch a white man without his resenting it." Though interracial sex was publicly deplored, relations between white men and black women were frequent (and often exploitative), as they had been since slave times. "Some white men fool around with Negro women and nigger men are too scared to do anything," a black tenant told Johnson. " 'Course once in a while niggers kill em up. Then they got to take to the bushes [and hide]. There used to be big mobs hunting for a nigger, but now you just hear about some nigger found hanging off a bridge."[34]

Racial etiquette in the Delta left little to chance. Since no gesture implying social equality could be tolerated, whites withheld common courtesies as a matter of course. They never tipped their hats to blacks, never addressed them as "Mr. or "Mrs.," and never stood up when they entered a room. "Colored people and white people do not as a rule shake hands in public," Hortense Powdermaker learned. "If a white educator addresses a group of Negro teachers, he might shake hands with them after his speech. On such occasions refreshments might be served, but it would be lap service, with no question of sitting at the same table."[35]

Blacks were forced to follow their own strict set of rules. They always tipped their hats to whites, always stood in their presence unless told to sit, and always addressed them with some title of respect ("Boss," "Sir," and "Ma'am" were the most common). When driving an automobile, a Negro did not pass a white person's car on a dusty road. When shopping at a local store, a Negro waited patiently until each white customer had been served. When approaching a white family's home, a Negro never entered through the front door. The power of this particular custom was so strong in the Delta that many whites locked only the back door against thieves. "They assume that no colored person would go in the front way," a visitor noted, "and, apparently, that no white person would steal."[36]

Few dared to challenge these customs because the risks were too great. Yet what most impressed Professor Johnson, after interviewing hundreds of young Southern blacks, was their smoldering indignation at the caste system: their private feelings of anger, resentment, self-loathing, and racial pride. On the surface, blacks appeared to get along "fine" with whites. ("You got to treat them like they a silk handkerchief on a barbed wire fence.") But a clear majority described the whites they knew as "mean" and "stingy" and preferred to avoid them.

These feelings were strongest in the Delta, where the planters still professed their deep affection and responsibility for local Negroes. In Bolivar County, north of Vicksburg, more than 30 percent of the blacks in Johnson's study claimed to "hate" white people. "Mississippi is awful," said one. "All the important things Negroes can't do. This is the last state in the world. Ought not to be in the Union."[37]

Racial caste and custom also pervaded the legal system. There were four kinds of law in Mississippi, whites liked to say: statute law, plantation law, lynch law, and Negro law. According to S. F. Davis, a prominent Delta attorney and self-described scholar: "The judges, lawyers, and jurors all know that some of our laws are to be enforced against everyone, while others of our laws are to be enforced only against the white people, and others . . . only against the Negroes, and they are enforced accordingly."[38]

Davis was correct. Though the criminal statutes of Mississippi did not discriminate by race, the decision to arrest, prosecute, and sentence depended in large part on a person's skin color, as did the workings of the trial itself. The logic of "Negro law" was simple: blacks should not be held to white standards of justice for reasons beyond their biological control. To judge one race like the other was pointless; to punish both equally was unfair. The Negro had to be treated like a *Negro*—with patience and discipline, with flexibility and intuition, which the white Southerner did best.

In truth, Negro law placed the clear majority of Mississippians beyond the protection of formal statutes and written guarantees. It allowed whites to exploit blacks without legal limit, to withhold the most basic rights and safeguards while claiming to be indulgent, paternalistic, and fair. Worse, perhaps, it turned the criminal justice system into a corrupt and capricious entity, utterly undeserving of respect.

It was unusual for a Negro to be arrested for adultery or bigamy, since he was not expected to obey the legal sanctions of marriage, and rare for a black man to be prosecuted for raping a black woman, because, in white parlance, "all niggers want sex." The frivolous legal response to such charges is apparent from a story told by one Delta judge about a "sex case" he handled involving a black woman named Lilie Mae. "How much underwear did you have on?" he asked. "I was wearin' a pair of drawers an' a pair of teddies," Lilie Mae replied.

"Did this man here tear your underwear?" "Naw, suh, he didn't tear it," she said. "He was fixin' to tear it, so I pulled em down [myself]."[39]

The same held true for prostitution, a common crime. White women were thought to be victims of circumstance, black women to be prisoners of lust. A convicted white prostitute did not normally serve jail time for her misdemeanor, because that meant "nigger work" on the road gang or the county farm. But a black prostitute was often sent away, particularly if her clients were known to be white. In a typical case, Jane Jackson, "colored," was sentenced to 90 days, a ten dollar fine, and court costs of $14. When her jail term expired, she still faced an additional 240 days on the road gang to work off her twenty-four dollar debt. After three more "brutal months," a white patron helped win Jackson a pardon by claiming, among other things, that a Negro could not be expected to control her sexual drive. "I submit that she has suffered sufficiently," he said, "in view of the tropical origin of her race."[40]

Crimes of theft and violence were also viewed through a racial lens. It was an article of faith among whites that the Negro lacked both the conscience for honest living and the capacity for remorse. If his crime occurred on a plantation, it rarely reached the courts. All good planters were expected to maintain order on their land—to settle family quarrels, arbitrate tenant disputes, punish the wayward, and protect the weak. "It would require a fat volume to record all the crimes which were committed on my plantation during the nine years I managed it," a planter recalled. "All the thieving of corn and gasoline, of gear and supplies, of hay and merchandise, the making and selling of whiskey, the adultery and bigamy, the cuttings, lambastings, and shootings."[41]

In most instances, these matters were either ignored or settled privately, often with a strap. "When a minor controversy arises between a white man and any negro working for him," a Delta judge explained, the white man "generally gives the negro an ex-parte hearing in the barn or gin-house, at which time and place he impresses his theory of the case on the negro with a piece of gin belting, or a [buggy whip], which is usually very effective, and the hearing is then adjourned sine die."[42]

The largest plantations often employed their own police force. At the Delta and Pineland operation, covering 38,000 acres, criminal matters were handled from within. "When a tenant got out of line," the manager noted, "he was expelled from the plantation, certainly a disgrace. We just put his household belongings in the road and let some other planter who needed labor hire him. I have seen tenants who *repented* and asked to come back. These we usually accepted, with the warning that they must be on their good behavior."[43]

When a serious crime occurred, and an example had to be made, the planter might call in the law. And when a tenant or some "favorite" Negro found trouble in town, the planter usually intervened. The diary of William Alexander Percy gives a clear picture of this role:

10:30 P.M.—Knock at door. Negro friend in tears. Displays lacerated arm which he says wife has bitten from shoulder to elbow in a fit of unwarranted exasperation. Question submitted: should he kill her or call the law? I give him a dollar and advise him to spend the night away from home."

11 P.M.—Go to bed. Phone. Negro friend after receiving dollar and advice went home, gave wife terrific beating, threw neighborhood into uproar, and is now in jail. Will I go his bond? I will.

Midnight—Phone. Same Negro on being released again went home and visited even more memorable chastisement on his consort. Again in jail. Will I bail him out? I will not."[44]

But others did—again and again. By all accounts, plantation workers came to depend on this intervention when they broke the law, and employers spent a great deal of time and money keeping them out of jail. "I know that every Negro got to have his white man, his boss, to look after him when he got in trouble with the white world," a tenant explained. Indeed, the Negroes on "Mister Bud" Doggett's Delta plantation composed this ballad about him when he died:

> They'll arrest you and put you
> In the Coahoma County jail,
> Then you'll want bad Mister Doggett
> To go your bail.
> But since he's dead
> And can't bail you out,
> Those cold iron bunks
> Will wear your black ass out.[45]

This sort of feudal protection plagued the Delta for years. The result, in fact, was to lower the arrest and conviction rates while permitting criminal activity to flourish, and law breakers to go free. Furthermore, because the great bulk of this crime was black on black, the Negro community suffered most of all. As one white man noted: "We have very little crime. Of course, Negroes knife each other . . . but there is little *real* crime. I mean Negroes against whites or whites against each other."[46]

This comment was instructive, if not exactly true. Criminal violence in Mississippi, black and white, had always been severe. The heritage of slavery and frontier life, the codes of honor and vengeance, the effects of poverty, ignorance, and isolation had all left their bloody mark. Mississippians earned less, killed more, and died younger than other Americans. They were five times more likely to be illiterate than a Pennsylvanian and ten times more likely to take another person's life.[47]

For blacks, the problem was worse. Both races seemed to agree that crime was rampant, brutal, and rising among Negroes at this time. But white concerns were muted by race prejudice (the Negro was a born criminal) and a measured distance from the mayhem (the victims also were Negro). When black lawlessness was confined to black enclaves, many whites saw no real crime. In the rare instances when racial boundaries were crossed, the reaction was intense.

Black Mississippians shot, stabbed, bludgeoned, and killed one another with monotonous ease. In an average year between 1900 and 1930, close to five hundred murders were reported in the state, making Mississippi a leader in white homicides (around 9 per 100,000), black homicides (33 per 100,000), and total homicides (25 per 100,000). The real figures were probably higher; black murders did not arouse much attention, and inquests were rare. "We had the usual number of [Negro] killings during the week just closed," a state newspaper casually reported in 1904. "Aside from the dozen or so reported in the press, several homicides occurred which the county correspondents did not deem sufficient to be chronicled in the dispatches."[48]

According to available statistics, blacks comprised about 67 percent of the killers in Mississippi and 80 percent of the victims. Most of the murders involved liquor, gambling, and personal disputes. And many of them occurred in the juke joints and "blind tigers" where young, unattached Negroes came to feast on catfish, drink moonshine whiskey, swap stories, listen to music, find sexual partners, role the dice, and relax. Saturday nights were a violent time in the Delta, and the great bluesmen had the scars and prison records to prove it. A jealous husband poisoned Robert Johnson with some "bad whiskey" at a roadhouse near Greenwood. He died a few days later, at age twenty-seven. Charley Patton had a "long, wicked knife" plunged into his back at a dance hall in Merigold. He barely survived. Eddie "Son" House and Washington "Bukka" White both served time at Parchman for shootings committed at drunken "Negro frolics." James "Cairo" Thomas remembered a wild Saturday night gun battle that began, as so many others did, with sexual banter between intoxicated, snuff-dipping dancers. "Lots of people got killed like that," he said. Lee Kizart used to keep his automobile parked by the side door of the juke joint so he could make a quick getaway when the shooting started: "I got in my car and when I cranked it up, I like to drove over I don't know how many folks up under my old racer."[49]

Charley Patton's family lived on Dockery Farms in Coahoma County, a magnet for musicians like young McKinley Morganfield (known later as "Muddy Waters") and the place where the blues supposedly began. Planter Joe Rice Dockery described a typical Delta Saturday this way:

> The crap games started about noon . . . and then the niggers would start getting drunk. I've seen niggers stumbling all over this place on a Saturday afternoon. And then they'd have frettin' and fightin' scrapes that night and all the next day. . . . And of course some of them would end up in jail.
>
> There's a story about a psychologist from the North who comes down here and asks this big buck, this bachelor, "Why do you work hard all week long and then get drunk and throw your money away and have a scrap and get put in jail? Why do you do that?" And he says, "Boss, has you ever been a nigger on Saturday night?"[50]

Dockery's description is similar to many others. In 1940, the *Delta Leader*, a black newspaper popular among the region's tiny Negro middle class, complained that most "colored farm workers" lacked ambition and drive. "Tomorrow doesn't interest them," it said. "This 80 percent of Negroes look forward . . . to driving to the nearest store in some nearby town where they can brawl all Saturday night." A few weeks later, in response to a string of shootings around Greenville, the newspaper called on white plantation owners to "end wild Saturday night frolics."[51]

Dockery lived a few miles from Clarksdale, one of the Delta's larger towns. To scan but a single month of its daily newspaper in the late 1920s, the era that Dockery described, is to grasp the intense linkage between blackness and crime. Each Monday, the *Press-Register* carried the full docket of the police (or misdemeanor) court under the mocking title, "Good Mawnin' Judge." The cases for October 23, 1928, included: "Eugene Eddy, negro, $100 for trespass; Garfield Price, negro, $10 and costs for assault and battery; Ben Scott, negro, $10 and costs for drunkenness; Clarence Herrin, negro, $5 and costs for disturbing the peace; and Elmer Jones, negro, $25 and costs for trespass."

White lawbreakers seemed not to exist. On October 27, a "negro murderer" was apprehended. On October 29, a black woman was "sent to the pen." On November 1, a Negro was "robbed and beaten to death." The following day, a "posse" went looking for a "negro criminal." (He had made "indecent advances toward a white woman.") On November 3, a Negro was "shot by his wife." On November 5, a black man was "killed at Hillhouse."

The newspaper's crime stories noted, almost in passing, the force used by local police. Over this four-week period, in a town of ten thousand people, at least two violent run-ins were reported. In one case, police officers cornered "negro murder suspect" Richard Johnson and "beat him to the draw." Johnson was killed. In the other, "Officer Dennis was called to Fourth and Issaquena Streets to arrest Price Lyles for being drunk and disorderly, and the negro, who bears a bad reputation in the community, assaulted him. The negro is now in the hospital with two .38 calibre bullets in his back."[52]

V

No one who examined the Delta at close range ever doubted the enormous volume, or violent nature, of Negro crime. Yet two scholars who offered thoughtful explanations of this problem dismissed the so-called biological weaknesses of blacks. In his 1937 study, *Caste and Class in a Southern Town,* psychologist John Dollard portrayed black violent crime as a natural outgrowth of stifling racial caste. "The usual human response to frustration is aggression against the frustrating object," he explained. "In this case, the frustrating object is the American white caste system which maintains its dominance over the Negro caste in various ways. Our problem then becomes: what happens to the aggression which is inevitably germinated in this situation?"[53]

The answer, said Dollard, was disastrous for Delta blacks. Unable to vent their anger against the all-powerful white oppressor, they turned their aggression inward, upon themselves. Since the "hostility of Negroes against whites is violently and effectively suppressed, we have a boiling point of aggressive effect within the Negro group." The result was black-on-black crime of enormous scope and brutality, which served to confirm white attitudes about the "savage" Negro race.

Anthropologist Hortense Powdermaker took a rather different view. In *After Freedom,* published in 1939, she blamed Negro crime and violence on a number of factors, including the arbitrary and complacent workings of the law. "While the high percentage of black assaults may not be attributable solely to white policy and attitudes," she wrote, "some connection can hardly be denied. The courts punish with drastic severity Negro violence against whites. But they function in a way that serves as an inducement to the Negro to take the law into his own hands when his difficulties involve other Negroes. Since he can hope for no justice and no defense from [the] legal institutions, he must settle his own difficulties, and often he knows only one way."[54]

The Negro, then, lived largely outside the law. He played no role in making it, enforcing it, or judging those who broke it. The law did not protect him from white oppressors or from black criminals. It did not treat him justly in the courtroom or sentence him consistently for his offense. As a result, the Negro saw little reason to respect the law or to look down upon those who were punished and sent to jail.

Powdermaker used homicide as an example. In 1933, she noted, the vast majority of black-on-black murder trials ended in acquittal. Of those convicted, only 3 percent were sentenced to death, and 1 percent were executed. "That intra-white killings are not so lightly regarded is a point which does not call for proof. When a white man kills a Negro, it is hardly considered murder. When a Negro kills a white man, conviction is assured, provided the case is not settled immediately by lynch law."[55]

Her point was well taken. The circuit courts of Mississippi, which tried felony cases, were composed of white prosecutors, judges, and juries who meted out justice to black defendants on the basis of how they believed a Negro should and did behave. The great bulk of "nigger killings" were disposed of quickly, and often leniently, on the grounds that blacks were "bound to do some shooting and cutting" because they could not help themselves. A harsh sentence had particular meaning: that the killing had been barbaric, the victim was a "good" Negro, or racial anxieties had been aroused. On occasion, wrote one observer, "the white caste becomes conscious of a 'crime wave' among the Negroes. There has been an unusually large number of fights, resulting in injuries or killings. . . . When that point is reached, the attitude of the juries and courts begins to shift, the penalties become heavier, and the first murder is likely to bring a death sentence."[56]

Some whites did in fact lament the capricious treatment of blacks in the Mississippi courts. Yet their concerns usually ignored the issues of equal rights and fair trial procedure while focusing on the senseless punishments that judges sometimes imposed. A rather chilling example was provided by editor Hodding Carter, a leading Southern progressive, in the pages of his Greenville newspaper, the *Delta Democrat-Times*. Furious at the sentences that blacks were receiving in local courtrooms, Carter penned an editorial about two cases decided the same day. He titled it "One Life Equals One Pair of Shoes."[57]

In the first case, a Negro was found guilty of stealing a $2.98 pair of brogans from a rooming house. "He got a year in the state penitentiary," wrote Carter, "which is no bed of roses and which he probably deserved." The second case involved a Negro murder. The sentence: one year. "How can a such situation come about? "Well, the Delta, unfortunately, has never considered the killing of one negro by another seriously." Until it did, the slaughter would go on.

Carter wanted tougher sentences for such crimes—a long stretch at hard field labor would do just fine. Though his words were meant to shake up one Delta custom, his solution meshed with another. An old-time politician put it well: "If a man had two fine mules running loose in a lot and one went mad and kicked and killed the other he certainly would not take out his gun and shot the other mule, but would work it. Therefore, I believe that when one negro kills another he should be put in the penitentiary and made to work for the state."

In Mississippi, that meant Parchman Farm.

✠

CHAPTER SIX

Parchman Farm

Judge gave me life this morning:
down on Parchman Farm.
I wouldn't hate it so bad:
but I left my wife and my home.
Oh goodbye wife:
all you have done gone.
But I hope some day:
you will hear my lonesome song.

—"Parchman Farm Blues," recorded by former
inmate Washington "Bukka" White in 1940

I

Every month or so, the legendary figure known as Long-Chain Charlie would make his appointed rounds. As traveling sergeant of the Mississippi State Penitentiary, his job was to escort new convicts from the county lockups to the sprawling Parchman Farm. A witness in the 1930s—a white Southern writer of some distinction—recalled the sergeant's appearance at a rundown Delta jail. "The names of those who were to leave were called by the sheriff. His voice rang through the steel corridors.

"Manny Sutton!" he yelled.

"Yas, suh, white folks . . . ,"

"Abe Jones!"

"Comin' up, boss."

"Will Jordan!"

"Got my travelin' clothes on . . ."

"Aleck Ball!"

"I heahs you, Cap'n."

Finally all the prisoners were assembled: There were twelve Negro men, three white men, and two Negro girls. One of them could not restrain her giggling. I asked her what she thought about going to prison for two years. She smiled widely. "It ain't no diffunce, white folks," she replied. "I'm got to work wherever I'm is."[1]

This story may have been apocryphal. White Southerners liked to believe that blacks did not much mind going to prison—that there was no shame to it, no loss of status, no fear of what lay ahead. Not surprisingly, this writer viewed Parchman as a smooth and simple extension of normal black life: "They do the same work, eat the same food, sing the same songs, play the same games of dice and cards, fraternize with their fellows, attend religious services on Sunday mornings and receive visitors on Sunday afternoons."[2]

The black convicts took a rather different view. Their prison songs in Mississippi and Tennessee portrayed Long-Chain Charlie as an evil man who stole their freedom and brought them despair:

I looked out the window,
saw the long-chain man (*twice*)
Oh, he's comin' to call us boys, name by name . . .

I got a letter from home,
reckon how it read? (*twice*)
It read, "Son, come home to your mama,
she's sick and nearly dead."

I sat down and I cried,
and I screamed and squalled (*twice*)
Said, "How can I come home, mama,
I'm behind these walls . . ."

'Cause the judge he sentenced me boys
from "Five to Ten" (*twice*)
I get out I'm go to that woman,
I'll be right back again.[3]

By the early 1900s, the great bulk of Mississippi's convicted felons had been delivered to Parchman Farm. According to the state penitentiary report of 1917, blacks comprised about 90 percent of the prison population. Most were illiterate young farm workers or laborers serving long sentences for violent crimes (murder, 35 percent; manslaughter, 17 percent; assault and battery, 8 percent; rape or attempted rape, 5 percent) against other blacks. Thirty-eight percent of the Negro inmates had received life terms, and 58 percent ten years or more.[4]

The convicts who reached Parchman with Long-Chain Charlie must have been surprised by what they saw—and what they did not see: no walls or guard towers, no cell blocks or stockades. From the outside, it looked like a typical Delta plantation, with cattle barns, vegetable gardens, mules dotting the landscape, and cotton rows stretching for miles. "Only a few strands of barbed wire marked the boundary between the Parchman State Penitentiary and the so-called free world," wrote folklorist Alan Lomax in *The Land Where the Blues Began*. Yet "every Delta black knew how easily he could find himself on the wrong side of that fence."[5]

Parchman's twenty thousand acres covered forty-six square miles. Just inside the main gate was Front camp, which contained a crude infirmary, a post office, and an administration building where new convicts were processed and issued their prison garb. The men got "ring-arounds," shirts and pants with horizontal black and white stripes; the women wore "up-and-downs," baggy dresses with vertical stripes. The long-time Parchman registrar, Mrs. O. M. Strickland, recorded the physical characteristics of each convict in meticulous detail. Her hand-written "description books" contained entries such as:

PITTMAN, WILL

Age, 38 years; height 5 feet, 8 inches; weight, 139 lbs; nativity, Tennessee; complexion, mulatto; hair, black, eyes, brown; mole on stomach; narrow face; narrow head; black mole on cheek near nose; has deep scowl between eyes. Sentenced from Chickasaw County, October 29, 1913; crime manslaughter; term, ten years.

And:

PRICE, JIM

Age, 19 years; height, 5 feet, 5 ins.; weight, _____ pounds; nativity, Mississippi; complexion, mulatto; hair, black; eyes, brown; scar on left elbow; two scars on back; scar right shoulder blade; tattoo on right wrist—heart. Sentenced from Wayne County, January 14, 1909; term, life; crime, murder.[6]

The plantation was divided into fifteen field camps, each surrounded by barbed wire and positioned at least a half-mile apart. The camps were segregated only by race and sex. First offenders were caged with incorrigibles, and adults with juveniles, some as young as twelve and thirteen. "Feeble-minded" convicts were everywhere. Parchman housed prisoners like John Brady, an ax-murderer with the mental age of a five-year-old, because Mississippi did not recognize "idiocy" and "imbecility" as special categories in its criminal code. The result was a brutal, predatory culture made worse by the prison's vast and isolated expanse.[7]

Each field camp had a "cage"—a long wooden barracks with barred windows where the inmates ate and slept. The cage had two dormitories—one for regular convicts, another for trusties—separated by a dining area in the middle. Both rooms had bunks stacked side by side along the walls, with two or three feet in between. Like everything else at Parchman, these barracks helped to keep down costs; individual cells were more expensive to build and maintain.

By 1915, Parchman already was a self-sufficient operation. It contained a sawmill, a brick yard, a slaughterhouse, a vegetable canning plant, and two cotton gins. In design, it resembled an antebellum plantation with convicts in place of slaves. Both systems used captive labor to grow the same crops in identical ways. Both relied on a small staff of rural, lower-class whites to supervise the black labor gangs. And both staffs mixed physical punishment with paternalistic rewards in order to motivate their workers. What this meant, in simple terms, was the ability "to drive and handle niggers."[8]

The Parchman superintendent was akin to the master. He lived at Front Camp in a Victorian mansion, complete with spindles, gables and a wrap-around porch. A small army of convict servants attended to his every personal need. The superintendent was not expected to be a professional penologist. The state wanted an "experienced farmer" for this position, and that is exactly what the law required. The superintendent's job was to make a good crop. "His annual report to the legislature is not of salvaged lives," a newspaper remarked. "It is a profit and loss statement, with the accent on the profit."[9]

Each field camp was directed by a sergeant, or overseer, who lived on the grounds. It was his responsibility to fix the work schedules, discipline the convicts, inspect the crops, and set the daily routine. Under him were two assistant sergeants, or "drivers," known as "cap'n" to the men. One driver worked the convicts in the fields; the other, a nightwatchman, ran the barracks where they lived.

The sergeant's job was usually a lifetime occupation, passed down from father to son. The same families staffed this position over the years. The pay was poor, even by Delta standards, but the benefits included a small wood cottage, fresh meat and vegetables, and the use of convict servants—all at no cost. One study described these men as "short on formal education and grasp of penological principles, but long on [knowledge] of the rural southern subculture." For sergeants, it stressed, the "folk wisdom accumulated from years of experience . . . is an essential element of every decision regarding inmates."[10]

The sergeant's word was law. He based his decisions on how best to control his convicts and keep their productivity high. "I had all kinds of sergeants," recalled a long-time inmate. "Some of them was whuppers, beat you all the time. Some would treat you good." In one camp, the food might be fresh and plentiful; in another, it was rancid and scarce. In one camp, the inmates would be locked up after work; in another, they could fish or garden or lounge outside. "It all depended on the boss man," the inmate added. "Your life could be all right, or he could make you wish for hell."[11]

The sergeant and his drivers supervised more than a hundred inmates in each camp, an arrangement made possible by the fact that the prisoners guarded themselves. Throughout its history, Parchman used the trusty system, in which selected inmates, called trusty-shooters, watched over the regular convicts (known as gunmen, because they toiled under the guns of the trusties). Comprising about 20 percent of the prison population, the trusty-shooters lived apart from the gunmen, wore vertical stripes instead of horizontal ones, and carried .30-.30 Winchesters on the job.[12]

There were no written criteria for selecting trusties. The sergeant made his choice by instinct and observation, as he did everything else. Most trusties were serving long sentences at Parchman, usually for murder. They were picked for their ability to intimidate other convicts, and their willingness to use force. Once chosen, a trusty became an unpaid member of the prison staff. He got better food and quarters than the regular convicts, and did not have to stoop all day in the fields. He could move freely about the camp, hunt and fish in his spare hours, and spend some extra time with his wife, a lover, or a prostitute brought in from a nearby town.

In their new role, the trusties isolated themselves from the other convicts, severing social ties. Their allegiance lay solely with the sergeant who had promoted them. If they trusties did their job well, a pardon might follow; if they misbehaved, the sergeant could demote them back to gunman, a dangerous move given their former status as guard. The trustees lived a privileged yet tenuous life at Parchman: determined to please the white men above them, feared and hated by the black men below them. Their situation was similar to that of the plantation slave drivers, described by historian Eugene Genovese in *Roll, Jordan, Roll.* "To keep their position and their privileges, they had to do the masters' bidding," Genovese explained. Yet "they too were black slaves and knew that no accomplishment would change their station—the constraints of being black inexorably prevailed."[13]

The sergeant's trust in his shooters was essential. They were his complete security staff: the men who guarded the cage and the fields, the men who protected his home and his family. "As his own life and well-being depended on his judgment," a Parchman study reported "the sergeant rarely made an error in selection."[14]

This was not exactly true. Shooters escaped more often than regular convicts because their opportunities were better, and stories of their quick tempers and questionable killings became the stuff of legend throughout the South. The arming of dangerous men left everybody vulnerable, gunmen and staffers alike. Indeed, the lynching of Charley Shepherd in 1929—considered by some to be the "most revolting" public spectacle in the history of Mississippi—involved a black shooter gone mad.*

---

* It is impossible to know the number of such incidents, since prison officials did not publicize them. In 1921, a black trusty named Louis Wimberly "brutally assaulted" the wife of a sergeant and "mutilated" her two children before escaping. After being captured and handed over to Long-Chain Charlie, Wimberly was set upon by a mob of "unknown men" a quarter mile from the penitentiary gate and lynched. In 1936, a white trusty named John Hartfield, serving a life term for murdering his wife, stabbed and killed a man in a dance hall in Jackson. Hartfield had been one of the white trusties used as "drivers" for Parchman officials, taking them to meetings throughout the state. In 1947, a black trusty named Edmund Perryman, also serving a life term for murder, "ran amuk," wounding three people "before killing himself with a bullet."[15]

Shepherd, a convicted murderer, had "razored" a fellow in a brawl near Vicksburg. Like many other trusty-shooters, he was illiterate, mentally retarded, and terrifying to the men. On December 28, 1928, Shepherd killed his sergeant, J. D. Duvall, by slitting his throat. Then Shepherd kidnapped Duvall's teenage daughter and took her to the woods. As word of the incident spread, local whites went "plumb wild." "It was one of the two man hunts I ever saw," a witness recalled, "in which half-way law-abiding folks took the law unto themselves. In nine out of ten lynchings, the recruits come from the pool rooms and log cabins. But [this one] rated pursuers from the big-porched houses in normally quiet little towns."[16]

Three separate posses tracked Shepherd across the Delta, beating local Negroes along the way. Five thousand men—on horseback, in pick-ups, with bloodhounds—were involved in the hunt. When he could run no longer, Shepherd surrendered to a white woman in return for her promise to protect him from the mob—a promise, it was reported, she "vainly sought to keep." On December 31, Shepherd was captured, hogtied, and driven from place to place like a carnival exhibit. Then he was taken to an open field where, according to one newspaper, "the enraged farmers and townspeople of the Delta went about their work of torturing" the convict for seven straight hours.

Shepherd was placed on a funeral pyre doused with gasoline. He was beaten and stabbed, and his ears cut off for souvenirs. When the burning began, Shepherd's nose and mouth were filled with dirt in order to prevent his inhaling gas fumes—and instant death. The crowd roared its approval as the charred legs and feet of the convict fell from his body into the fire. "It was 45 minutes before the powerfully built negro finally quit his convulsive twitching and agonized fighting at the ropes and flames."

By sheer coincidence, Governor Theodore Bilbo happened to be visiting Parchman when the lynching occurred. The next day, after casually inspecting the remains of Charley Shepherd, whose "smoking skull" had been found in a roadside ditch, Bilbo dismissed the

Parchman Farm

idea that he—or the state of Mississippi—become involved in the search for Shepherd's killers. "I have neither the time nor the money to investigate 2,000 people," he said—and left it at that.[17]

II

The gunman's day began at 4:30 A.M., when the steam whistle sounded and a trusty-shooter roused him from bed. After a breakfast of biscuits, syrup, and coffee, he was marched to the fields in close formation, starting his labor by dawn. Each convict belonged to a work gang, and each had a daily quota to meet. In the fall months, that meant picking 200 pounds of cotton as part of the "long line"—an easy load for an experienced sharecropper. "Some of us could pick twice that amount," an inmate recalled. "I was a high roller, used to picking 500 clean pounds a day. I had to slow down sometimes to keep the line together. The hard part was staying out there so long."[18]

The heat was often unbearable, and there was no escape from the sun. "We worked from before you could see until you couldn't see," a convict told prison investigators in 1914. "Right in the hottest part of the Summer—in June."

Q. "How was your food prepared?

A. Well, it wasn't prepared. . . . It was just fixed up and sent out there to you. . . .

Q. You had to eat that out on the farm at noon?

A. Yes, sir; if we were out in the field . . . dinner was always sent out to you; ate it right there where you were.

Q. Were you allowed to go to the shade?

A. If you were near the shade you would go; if you were a quarter of a mile away you wouldn't; you would lose too much time. . . . We were given about thirty minutes for dinner; took that time to eat and rest in. A man could eat what we were getting in three minutes, and if you wanted to you could rest all the time; I usually rested. I ate enough for breakfast to run me until supper."[19]

The noon meal was larger, consisting of beans, peas, sweet potatoes, a cold drink, and some salted meat. "I called it 'weevil food,' " a convict said. "The stuff was full of bugs and worms. The only way I could eat it was to crumple my corn bread on top so I wouldn't see those things crawling around."[20]

For an inmate who had never done field work in the Delta—and there were many—the long line was a perilous ordeal. In the 1930s, Mrs. W. A. Montgomery, president of the state prison board, charged that convicts routinely collapsed from sunstroke and overwork. As an example, she cited Parchman inmate 5157, whose cause of death, a "blocked artery," seemed innocent enough. "His stay was so short," she said, "that we did not remember his name. He told the sergeant he was sick. . . . He could not keep up with the gang in the drive for 200 pounds of cotton each day. All night long he moaned and groaned. The next morning . . . he begged to be spared, he just could not make it. He was forced to go. Along about 10 o'clock he died in the cotton field with a cotton sack around his neck."[21]

Violence sometimes flared in the fields. The heat, the long hours, and the tight formations led to squabbles that were settled with fists. When tensions ran high, the driver would pull two men out of line and yell "ten minutes," allowing the pair to slug it out. "The fights could be nasty," a convict recalled. "There wasn't no such thing as backing down. You had to defend yourself because some of those guys would whack you till you dropped."[22]

The work quotas were enforced by the driver, who rode the fields on a mule. "He is the one who says how fast you can go and how much work you can do and cannot," a Parchman official explained. "The [shooters] aren't even permitted to talk with those prisoners. The man on the mule is the man who . . . does the driving."[23]

Parchman Farm

But the pace of work was set by a caller, chosen from the ranks. Work chants were part of the common culture of West Africa and the slave South, and they remained alive on the penal farms where gang labor, as opposed to sharecropping, was still used in the fields. The men worked to the caller's chanting tempo, the whole line moving as one. The caller would sing his verse; a mighty chorus would respond. The power of that sound, said a visitor to Parchman, "could almost take you off your feet."[24]

The callers had nicknames describing their looks, their whereabouts, and the crimes that had put them away. There were "Fat Head" and "Bootmouth," "Bama" and "Cleveland," "Red Worm" (killed a man over fish-bait), "Burndown" (an arsonist), and "22" (serving twenty-two years). A good caller created the proper tempo, even-paced and not too fast. The gang did not want quick chanters or lazy gunmen, both of whom added to their burden. A good caller knew how to improvise, adding his own verses and rhymes. But above all, as Bama himself explained, "it take the man with the most understandin to make the best leader in anything. If you bring a brand-new man in here, if he had a voice where he could sing just like Peter could preach, and he didn't know what to sing about, well, he wouldn't do no good."[25]

The callers sang about the day-to-day life at Parchman, and the world they left behind. Their verses drew knowing laughter.

Oh wasn't I lucky when I got my time,
Babe, I didn't git a hundred, got a ninety-nine.

And shouts of approval:

Take this hammer,
take it to the sergeant
tell him I'm gone.

And sometimes sullen nods:

> I'm choppin in the bottom wid a hundred years,
> Tree fall on me, I don bit mo care.[26]

In the heat of the day, the callers sang to the sun, begging "her" to move faster:

> Been a great long time since Hannah went down
> Oh, Hannah, go down;
> Been a great long time since Hannah went down,
> Oh, Hannah, go down!

But mostly the callers sang about women: about Roxie and Alberta, Mollie and Dollar Mamie; and about Rosie, the queen of Parchman Farm:

> I seen little Rosie in my midnight dreams (*three times*)
> O Lord, in my midnight dreams,
> O Lord in my midnight dreams.
>
> CHORUS:
> Ho, Rosie!
> Hey-a hey-a!
> Ho, Rosie!
> Ho, Lord gal!
>
> You told a promise when you first met me (*three times*)
> Well, now, you wasn't gonna marry, till-uh
> I go free.[27]

There were endless verses to Rosie, added over the years. Some were sexually playful:

> Big-Leg Rosie, with her big-leg drawers
> Got me wearen these striped overalls.

The road to Parchman Farm was a long one. From Emancipation to the swiftly imposed Black Codes and burgeoning jails, and then to convict leasing and labor, Parchman's reinvention of the old plantation system followed decades of forced black labor. Spread over 20,000 acres in the heart of the Yazoo-Mississippi Delta, Parchman contained fifteen work camps, surrounded by barbed wire and positioned at least a half-mile apart. Even today Parchman remains an isolated, distant expanse, largely hidden from public view.

Jones S. Hamilton. A former county sheriff, state senator, and Confederate cavalry officer, Hamilton was the primary lessee of the Mississippi state penitentiary in the late 1870s and 1880s. He was known as a reckless, quick-tempered adventurer, and he became a millionaire by subleasing hundreds of convicts to labor-starved railroad builders and plantation owners. Without state supervision, these prisoners were worked to exhaustion and beyond. One official claimed that convict leasing in Mississippi had produced an "epidemic death rate without the epidemic." Furious at public criticism of his leasing empire, Hamilton shot and killed a leading newspaper editor in a duel.

James Kimble Vardaman. Known as the "White Chief," Vardaman won the race for governor in 1903 by promising to regulate the railroads, end the remains of convict leasing, and provide services to the poor whites of Mississippi. A virulent racist, Vardaman believed that a good prison, like an efficient slave plantation, could serve to "socialize" young black criminals by teaching them proper discipline, strong work habits, and respect for white authority. As governor he transferred state convicts to the new penitentiary in the Yazoo-Mississippi Delta. Parchman would become a monument to the White Chief—a huge penal farm for blacks who had "lost" their way.

Sharecropping, about 1940. Black tenants and field workers made up the vast majority of Parchman inmates. Many had worked on the huge Delta plantations near the penitentiary, where sharecropping was the rule. In return for lodging, water, firewood, farm implements, and cottonseed, the cropper gave the landlord a fixed portion—usually fifty percent—of the crop. Families worked as a unit, from dawn to dusk. Their unpainted cabins, without lights, plumbing, or insulation, lined the flat dirt roads that led to the cottonfields, as shown here. Children attended ramshackle, one-room schools in the "off-times" between spring planting and fall picking, when their labor was not needed. Workers were often forced to shop in overpriced plantation stores because their credit was extended in scrip, or coupons, rather than cash. "The Delta is cotton-obsessed, Negro-obsessed, and floodridden," a scholar remarked in the 1920s. "It is the deepest South, the heart of Dixie, America's super plantation belt."

In December and January, wrote one observer, the Delta roads "[are] filled with wagons piled high with household goods, the families perched on top. They are hoping to find something better, but they seldom do" (above). For thousands of tenants, migration was an act of power: a way of expressing their resentment, exerting their independence, and protecting their meager rights. The most famous migration path followed Route 49, shown below with a cotton truck heading from a plantation to a warehouse.

The year officially ended on Settlement Day, when the cropper and the landlord sat down to figure their split. The opportunities for deception were endless, because most tenants were illiterate and the landlord kept the books. This photo shows a standard Saturday payday for cotton pickers.

Juke joint. Every town and hamlet in the Delta—from Sledge to Alligator to Itta Bena—had at least one juke joint, a place where local blacks came after work on Saturday to relax, feast on catfish, drink whiskey, swap stories, roll the dice, dance, and listen to the blues. Jokes and music "flow together in small rooms filled with smoke and the smell of alcohol," wrote one observer, "as couples talk, slow-drag, and sing with the performer. On summer nights their sound travels throughout Delta neighborhoods like Kent's Alley, Black Dog, and the Brickyard."

Highway 49, after cutting through many Delta cotton fields, passes the main gate of Parchman Farm, shown here in its modern version (above) and with a still-surviving sign from decades ago (below).

Field work. The typical convict was called a gunman because he toiled under the gun of the trusty-shooter. The gunman wore "ring-arounds," shirts and pants with horizontal black and white stripes. His day began at 4:30 A.M., when the steam whistle sounded and a trusty-shooter roused him from bed. After a breakfast of biscuits, syrup, and coffee, he marched to the fields in close formation, starting his labor by dawn. During spring plowing season, he rode his mule (above). Each gunman belonged to a work gang, and each had a daily quota to meet as part of the "long line" (below). The quotas were enforced by a white assistant sergeant, known as the driver, who rode the fields on a mule. But the pace was set by a caller, chosen from the ranks. The men worked to the caller's chanting tempo, the whole line moving as one. The caller would sing his verse; a mighty chorus would respond. The power of that sound, said a visitor to Parchman, "could almost take you off your feet."

The men ate their lunch in the hot, shadeless fields. They were serviced by a water boy "on a crazy cart containing a whiskey barrel of water" (above). At the edge of the field stood the trusty-shooters, with their "gun line" drawn crudely in the dirt. Armed with high-powered rifles, they stood ready to shoot convicts who tried to escape. When a man had to relieve himself, he would yell, "Getting out, shoot," and wait for an "OK." "The shooters did not permit the gunmen to approach closer than 20 feet," said one observer, "and crowding a shooter, even accidentally, could be fatal. A long-line of 100 inmates required at least six shooters for effective custody."

  Parchman had no walls and few fences. The illusion of escape was ever present, the reality something else. Parchman bloodhounds, bred and trained by trusty "dog boys" (below), were the finest in the South. The recapture rate was exceptional because the prison was isolated and the dogs could "follow a scent without difficulty on a five-hour lead." Also, Parchman provided an incentive for recapture unheard of in the South, or anywhere else. If a trusty-shooter killed or wounded a gunman trying to escape, he usually was pardoned by the governor of Mississippi, no questions asked.

The Parchman system in its entirety relied on a strict division of labor and careful planning to turn a profit. Here, gunmen dressed in horizontal stripes and seated on mules fill the foreground. Gunmen on foot are immediately behind, from the right; a single trusty is on horseback in the left middle ground, and more gunmen are on foot in the rear, both sides.

Superintendent's house, ca. 1915. The superintendent ran Parchman like a slavemaster from antebellum times. He lived in this Victorian-style mansion at Front Camp, the administration center, where a small army of convict servants attended to his every need. The superintendent was appointed by the governor, who frequently used the position to reward a loyal friend or a campaign contributor. The superintendent was not expected to be a professional penologist. The state wanted an "experienced farmer," since the main task was to bring in a profitable crop, not to rehabilitate the convicts.

Each field camp had a "cage"—a long wooden barracks with barred windows, where the inmates ate and slept. The cage had two dormitories—one for regular convicts, another for trusties—separated by a dining area in the middle. (Camp for white boys, above.) Both rooms had bunks stacked in tiers along the walls, with two or three feet in between. "I don't know if you can imagine what that place was like," a visitor recalled in the 1930s. "Long shed-like buildings. . . . Bunks stacked high, rows after rows. In the runways between the buildings were guards, sometimes dogs, always guns." (Modern unstacked bunks, below).

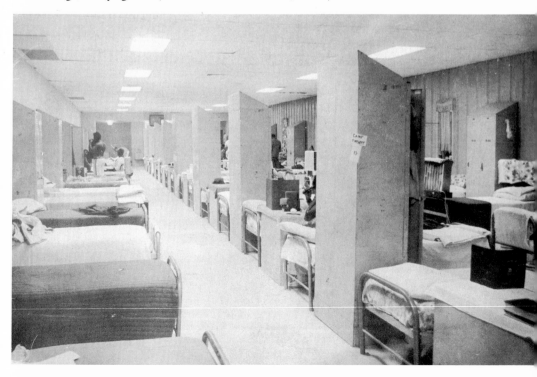

Each camp was largely self-sufficient, with prisoners taking care of their own needs. They grew their food, cooked their meals, repaired their implements, did their laundry. There was a timelessness about Parchman, an environment almost frozen in place. In his report to the state legislature in 1949, the superintendent complained, "[We] now have a population of approximately 2500 inmates, employees and their families. I know of no other institution comparable in size that is forced to use the old wash-tub method of laundering." (Laundry day, above).

On Sunday the convicts rested. Some attended morning religious services guarded by trusty-shooters. Others played baseball (above), with most camps fielding a team.

On Sundays and holidays a special meal might be served, with ham and pork, fresh vegetables, milk, tea, bread, and pies. (Outdoor meal, above; camp dining hall, below.) Sunday brought families to Parchman, and conjugal visits with wives, lovers, and prostitutes from nearby Delta towns. Parchman was the first American prison to permit conjugal visitation—a system that continues to this day.

Women were a distinct minority at Parchman. They committed fewer crimes than men, and their offenses tended to be minor ones, such as prostitution and petty theft, punishable by a month or two in the local jail. At no time did women comprise more than five percent of the state prison population. Their numbers remained low, and their color never changed. Virtually all women sent to Parchman were black.

Women wore "up-and-downs," baggy dresses with vertical stripes. They slept in a large dormitory and toiled from dawn to dusk, much like the men. They canned vegetables and worked in the fields during "cotton-picking time" in the fall. But their main task was to make clothes, bedding, and mattresses for the entire farm in a sweat-filled sewing room (above; mail call, below). One of their work songs ended:

You talkin bout trouble
You don't know what trouble means (repeat)
What I call trouble
Is a Singer Sewing Machine.

Booker T. Washington "Bukka" White was one of several bluesmen to serve time at Parchman. A former prizefighter and minor league baseball player, he was convicted for shooting a jealous rival in 1937. "Well, I had a '38 Colt . . . and I let it loose," he recalled. At Parchman, White escaped much of the heavy field work by performing for the inmates and trusties. He even taught the camp sergeant's son to play guitar. Released in 1939, he moved to Chicago and recorded two original songs about his prison experience: "When Can I Change My Clothes," which describes the stripes he had to wear; and the legendary "Parchman Farm Blues." His experience "reflected the obsessions of the men . . . locked behind the lines of barbed wire in the Parchman enclosure," wrote one music critic, "They worried about their families, about their women, they built elaborate fantasies about their lives outside of prison, they even dreamed of their own deaths."

Between 1882 and 1930, Mississippi experienced more deaths by lynching (463) than any other state. Indeed, Mississippi led the nation in every imaginable kind of mob atrocity: most multiple lynchings, most lynchings of women, most lynchings without an arrest, most lynchings of a suspect in police custody, and most public support for the process itself. The main victims were young black men suspected of assaulting whites or challenging the boundaries of racial caste. "You don't understand how we feel down here," a white Mississippian told a visitor in 1908. "When there is a row, we feel like killing a nigger whether he has done anything or not."

Portable electric chair. In the 1930s, a series of gruesome public hangings in Mississippi led to calls for change. The result was a portable electric chair, which allowed the executions to take place in the county where the crime had been committed. Seventy-three people were put to death in this contraption between 1940 and 1954. Though these executions usually occurred inside the county jail to avoid the spectacles of the past, local residents sometimes surrounded the building in a festive mood. Author Florence Mars recalled the electrocution of a convicted killer in her hometown of Philadelphia, Mississippi: "A crowd gathered late at night on the courthouse square with their chairs, crackers, and children, waiting for the current to be turned on and the streetlights to dim."

Maximum security unit. Constructed in 1954 to house dangerous and incorrigible inmates in individual cells, the MSU also contained the "black hole" for solitary confinement, Death Row, and the gas chamber. "Everything went at MSU," a convict recalled. "It got the meanest sergeants and the worst trusties on the farm. We called it 'Little Alcatraz.' Nobody left there without bumps and busted bones." In the 1990s, Parchman opened a new maximum security unit, a "state-of-the-art" facility where more than a thousand inmates spend twenty-three hours a day in their individual cells without television or radio. Though Death Row has been moved to the new MSU, the gas chamber is still housed in the old one, along with a lethal injection room.

When she walks, she reels and rocks behind,
Ain't that enough to worry a po convict's mind?[28]

Others were painfully sad:

Well you won't write me, you won't come and see.
Say you won't write me, you won't send no word.
Said I get my news from the mocking bird.
Said I get my news from the mocking bird.[29]

At their best, these songs provided some inner relief and distance from a world the convict was powerless to change. At the least, they relieved his boredom and made the time pass. "When you listenin how the song run, the day just go by mo faster," said one, "and befo you know it, the sergeant or the driver is hollerin dinnertime."[30]

III

At the edge of the field stood the trusty-shooters, with their "gun line" drawn crudely in the dirt. "Armed with high-powered rifles and shotguns, they formed a floating, flexible barrier between the gunmen and the free world. They were also the driver's protection as he [rode] among the gunmen giving orders or forcing them on to greater efforts." When a man had to relieve himself, he'd yell, "Getting out," and wait for an "O.K." If he crossed the gun line without permission, he was warned with a shout. If he kept moving, shots were fired. "The shooters did not permit the gunmen to approach closer than 20 feet, and crowding a shooter, even accidentally, could be fatal. A long-line of 100 inmates, required at least six shooters for effective custody."[31]

In the 1920s, a Northern penologist visited Parchman to study its organization. His unpublished notes are revealing. "Their cotton is very profitable," he wrote, "but that profit is secured by reducing the men to a condition of abject slavery." What most disturbed him was the use of inmate guards. "I saw 65 convicts working in a cotton field at Parchman," he went on. "There were two [mounted] overseers who carried whips but displayed no arms. There were four convict guards, two of whom were armed with shotguns and two with rifles. Their orders were if a convict tried to run away the guard with the shotgun was to shoot him in the legs. If he failed to stop him then the guard with the rifle was to shoot to kill him, and if he killed the prisoner he got a pardon."[32]

At a meeting of the American Prison Association in 1925, a Mississippi official explained the trusty system to a rather incredulous audience of his peers. "You *arm* the convict guards?" a Northern delegate asked. "Yes," came the reply. "And if [our prisoners] undertake to run, we have two ways of stopping them: order them to halt, and if they don't, our trusties have a shotgun for short range to shoot in their lower limbs, and if they get out of reach, they use a high powered rifle."

A Texas delegate broke in. "We have a great many negroes like you have," he said. "Do you have negro guards over the negroes?"

"Yes."

"Negro trustees?"

"Yes."

"And you give them the inducement, if a man tries to run and he shoots him down, you will pardon him?"

"That goes to his credit in addition to his other good conduct."[33]

At dusk, the men were marched back to the cage. As they reached the yard, the field driver turned them over to the nightwatchman, who had each convict frisked. Inside the barracks, the trusties took control. Two "shack-shooters" guarded the doors, while a pair of "night-shooters" prowled the flood-lit grounds. The gunmen were counted every hour by a "cage boss," who marked his tally on a blackboard. "I don't know if you can imagine what that place was like," a visitor recalled. "Long shedlike buildings. . . . Bunks stacked high, rows after rows. In the runways between the buildings were guards, sometimes dogs, always guns."[34]

There was more. The true symbol of authority and discipline at Parchman was a leather strap, three feet long and six inches wide, known as "Black Annie," which hung from the driver's belt. Whipping had a long history in the South, of course, and not only on the slave plantations. It had been legally, often publicly, employed against white criminals for a host of minor crimes, and it had survived long after other forms of corporal punishment, such as branding and ear cropping, had been abolished.[35]

Yet whipping had strong racial overtones because it had been used so frequently against slaves. "Punishment on the plantation was, essentially, *physical* punishment," wrote one historian. And the lash "was the correctional instrument of all purpose." When ex-slaves recalled their experiences, whipping was rarely overlooked. "Ole Marse was good, but when yo' made him mad he wud hav' yo' whupped," a Mississippi freedman recalled. "He would come out in the mornin' an' want to whup everything he seen," said another. One ex-slave remembered the whipping of his mother and the retribution he had planned: "I sed to myself 'iffen I eber get free I wus gwine to whup dat overseer. His name wus Silas Jacobs. But he died not long afte' de war an' I neber got to whup him."[36]

By 1900, corporal punishment for prisoners had been abandoned—in law, if not in practice—by most states outside the South. (The glaring exception was Delaware, a border state, where thousands of public whippings were inflicted upon lawbreakers well into the 1950s.) Arkansas, Texas, Florida, and Louisiana all used the lash on their convicts without serious public opposition. It was part of the regional culture, and most prisoners were black.[37]

At Parchman, formal punishment meant a whipping in front of the men. It was done by the sergeant, with the victim stripped to the waist and spread-eagled on the floor. What convicts most remembered were the sounds of Black Annie: the "whistlin' " air, the crack on bare flesh, the convict's painful grunt.

> J.S. They whupped us with big wide strops. They didn't whup no clothes. They whupped your naked butt. And they had two men to hold you.
>
> W.B. Four!
>
> J.S. As many as they need . . .
>
> A.L. Did they ever injure anybody that way?
>
> J.S. Wooo!
>
> W.B. Yeah!
>
> J.S. Kill um! Kill um!
> W.B. They'd kill um like that."[38]

The most common offenses—fighting, stealing, "disrespect" to an officer, and failure to meet work quotas—were punishable by five to fifteen lashes. Escape attempts carried an unspeakable penalty: a whipping without limits. One superintendent recalled a mass break-out in the 1930s in which a trusty-shooter was killed. "To get confessions," he said, "I had whippings given to the eight we caught who weren't wounded. Before the young ringleader confessed, I had him lashed on the buttocks, calves, and palms, then gave him fifteen lashes on the soles of his feet. This cleared his mind."[39]

The number and severity of whippings depended on the sergeant in charge. "Book rules" meant little in the field camps, which were fiefdoms unto themselves. The sergeants worked in relative isolation. Some of them were alcoholics; a few were sadists. "They beat hell out of you for any reason or no reason," an inmate remarked. "It's the greatest pleasure of their lives." Above all, the sergeants were under pressure to make a good crop, and that meant pushing the men. "What can you expect in the way of judgment at fifty dollars a month?" asked one prison official. "What kind of foreman on the

Parchman Farm

outside [is] employed at fifty dollars a month?" They usually pay foremen more than anybody else, the man who works the men, but that's what they pay here—fifty dollars a month!"[40]

There were sergeants who saved the lash for serious infractions, and sergeants who whipped all the time. There was little supervision, despite the pompous claims of the superintendents, because whippings were viewed as the best way to keep the men working—and afraid. It was not unusual for a convict to be lashed for breaking his shovel in the fields, or for several dozen convicts to be whipped for the theft of a single postage stamp. "There is no telling what punishment will be used in this prison," said a gunman in the 1930s, "It all depends on how mad the sergeant is, as to whether you get 15 or fifty lashes."[41]

When asked to defend Black Annie, Parchman officials did so with pride. The lash was effective punishment, they insisted, and it did not keep men from the fields. "You spank a fellow right," claimed a superintendent, "and he'll be able to work on." Most of all, Black Annie seemed the perfect instrument of discipline in a prison populated by the wayward children of former slaves. There simply was no better way "of punishing [this] class of criminals," said Dr. A. M. M'Callum, Parchman's first physician, "and keeping them at the labor required of them."[42]

Public opinion in Mississippi strongly supported the lash. Prison officials and sheriffs, politicians and judges, church groups and newspapers—most seemed to favor its use. "The whip makes no appeal to hidden virtue," said the *Jackson Clarion-Ledger*, "but it is a sure and effective means of planting fear . . . in the hearts of [criminals]. It is retribution, and retribution hurts."[43]

No one knew this better than the convicts who had felt Black Annie's clout. Their fear and pain were heard across the fields.

Ridin' in a hurry.
Great Godamighty!

Ridin' like he's angry.
Great Godamighty!
Well, I wonder whut's de matter?
Great Godamighty!
Bull whip in one han', cowhide in de udder.
Great Godamighty!
Well, de Cap'n went to talkin',
Great Godamighty!
'Well, come on here an' hol' him!'
Great Godamighty!
'Cap'n let me off, suh!'
Great Godamighty!
'Woncha 'low me a chance, suh?'
Great Godamighty!
'Bully, low' down yo' britches!'
Great Godamighty!
De Bully went to pleadin',
Great Godamighty!
De Bully went to hollerin',
Great Godamighty!

IV

On Sunday the convicts rested. Morning services were led by itinerant preachers or by the convicts themselves. Parchman had no chapel because the state did not see the need for a frivolous "nigger building" when blacks seemed "perfectly content" to worship outside. This attitude led one superintendent to recommend the construction of a "good church" for Parchman's white prisoners. But the state turned him down on the grounds that the blacks would then demand a church of their own. So praying continued in the open fields, and mass baptisms were performed in the muddy cattle ponds.

"There is no church or chapel, and guards stand by with guns," a convict noted in 1946, "but the spirit of the service is good."[45]

For most inmates, however, the Sabbath's blessing had little to do with the Lord. Parchman was the first American prison to allow conjugal visitation. No one knows exactly when or how it began; the system was always informal, without any written rules. In the early days, these visits were limited to Negro men, married and single alike, who were serviced by black prostitutes from the neighboring delta towns. As one prison official recalled: "I never saw it, but I heard tell of truckloads of whores bein' sent up from Cleveland at dusk. The cons who had a good day got to get 'em right there between the rows. In my day we got civilized—put 'em up in little houses and told everybody that them whores was wives. That kept the Baptists off our backs."[46]

By the 1930s, conjugal visitation had widened its scope to include white male inmates (though not women, who might become pregnant). In each field camp, a crude wooden shack, nicknamed the "red house" or the "tonk," was constructed to accommodate these Sunday afternoon interludes. The shacks had five or six spartan rooms, maintained by the convicts themselves. The inmate and his partner were given remarkable privacy. "The attitude of the penitentiary staff," wrote a sociologist who examined sexual behavior at Parchman, was "simply to leave [them] alone."[47]

Prison officials praised these visits for keeping marriages alive, which likely was true, and for reducing homosexuality and sexual assaults, which probably was false. According to one study, about half the convicts at Parchman engaged in homosexual activity, a standard percentage for penal institutions. But some field sergeants believed that sexual assaults were worse at Parchman because the living quarters were wide open, and the weak (juveniles and first offenders) lived side by side with the strong. "That's the ones you have to look out for," said a sergeant of the "wolves" who took so-called teenage gal-boys. "They never even think of a woman. They think a boy looks better than a real woman. That's what makes me mad—when some freak tries to bust a young boy. I won't put up with that."[48]

Conjugal visitation would be viewed as Parchman's singular contribution to the annals of penal reform. Yet the motivating forces behind this system were the same ones that dominated all other aspects of the Parchman operation: profit and race. Conjugal visitation came about because prison officials wanted as much work as possible from their Negro convicts, whom they believed to have greater sexual needs than whites. "You gotta understand," said a long-time sergeant, "that back in them days niggers were pretty simple creatures. Give 'em some pork, some greens, some cornbread, and some poontang every now and then and they would work for you."[49]

These feelings persisted. In the late 1960s, a sergeant in one of the Negro camps was asked whether conjugal visits helped his men. "Oh, yeah, they are better workers," he claimed. "If you let a nigger have some on Sunday, he will really go out and do some work for you on Monday."[50]

V

And work they did. In his penitentiary report of 1917, Superintendent E. J. O'Keefe noted that 6,977 bales of cotton had been produced at Parchman that year, despite awful weather conditions and the "advent of the boll weevil." His report gave ample, if indirect, evidence of how hard the convicts there toiled. "Our crop was regularly planted during the first week of April," he wrote. "Continued rains retarded a stand and some replanting was necessary. [Then] on May 3, a violent hail storm swept the plantation, with a result which at first seemed staggering. Acre after acre of the young plant was actually whipped out of the ground. Replanting on a gigantic scale at once began, and inside of twelve days nearly 5,000 acres were re-planted."[51]

In spite of these setbacks, the penitentiary made a handsome profit in 1917. Unlike other prison systems, which drained public coffers at an ever-expanding rate, this one poured almost a million dollars into the state treasury through the sale of cotton and cotton seed. The figure was so astounding—it totaled almost half of Mississippi's entire budget for public education in 1917—that politicians and editors were soon calling Parchman the "best prison" in America, as fertile and productive as the "Valley of the Nile."[52]

In less than a decade, Parchman had become a giant money machine: profitable, self-sufficient, and secure. For Southerners of both races, it represented something familiar as well. Parchman was a powerful link to the past—a place of racial discipline where blacks in striped clothing worked the cotton fields for the enrichment of others. And it would remain this way for another half-century, until the civil rights movement methodically swept it away.

✠

CHAPTER SEVEN

The Other Parchman:
White Men, Black Women

Since I been in prison
My friends all throw me down.
I motherless an fatherless
an sister and brotherless.
With a twenty year sentence
hanging over my head.

—"I'm in Prison Now," by Parchman
inmate Wilma B. Young, 1936

I

On a blistering August day in 1895, Dabney Marshall and three associates shot and killed a young businessman named R. F. Dinkins at the railroad depot in Brandon, Mississippi, just east of Jackson. The murder made front-page news because Marshall and Dinkins belonged to the state's rather inbred upper class. Marshall, a Vicksburg attorney, was well known for his romantic poetry, magnificent flower garden, and eccentric musings about life. He had recently published a book entitled, *Everything, Nothing, and Other Things: Being Reflections on Politics,*

Love, Literature, Girls, Kisses, and Good Eating. A Jackson newspaper described Marshall as the "scion of one of the oldest and most influential families in Warren County." Of R. F. Dinkins, it said: "He is of as noble birth and as highly connected as any man in the State."[1]

The killing had more to it than distinguished blood. Two weeks before, Marshall and Dinkins had roomed together at a hotel near Jackson. According to Dinkins, Marshall made a sexual advance. (The local newspaper described it, rather delicately, as an offense "similar to the one for which Oscar Wilde is now serving a term in the English prison.") Dinkins related the incident to a friend "in confidence," and within days, it was "the talk of the county." When Marshall found out, he placed a note in the *Jackson Clarion-Ledger* denouncing the story as a lie. Then he sent a "second"—his law partner, W. J. Vollor—to demand an official retraction from the offending party.

But Dinkins stood firm, telling Vollor that the "story was true." Marshall saw no alternative: his accuser must die. The end came on August 9 when Marshall and his group confronted Dinkins at the railroad depot and fired a "veritable fusillade of shots" into his body at point-blank range. As Dinkins lay unconscious, Marshall put a final bullet between his eyes. Their work done, the men sat down to await the sheriff's arrival. One of them was W. J. Vollor, who had come unarmed "in the capacity of an attorney."

The public was outraged. It "is the universal sentiment," a newspaper reported, "that the four men who did the killing are in a mighty bad fix." Marshall had acted like a coward, not a gentleman, people believed. He had ambushed his opponent two weeks after the insult instead of confronting him instantly in a truly fair fight. "The time for Marshall to kill Dinkins was on that day . . . when the charges were first made," the newspaper declared. "Had he defended his honor then, his course would have been endorsed."[2]

Instead, the four men were charged with murder. And a deal was quickly struck.* Three of them pleaded guilty and got life in prison, while Vollor went free. This was the most that could be expected. There had not been a multiple hanging of whites in Mississippi since 1804, and these defendants had the benefit of good breeding, political contacts, and the best lawyers money could buy. Dinkins's family did not object. "I have been on personally intimate terms with all the defendants," said the victim's brother, "and our relations were very friendly."[3]

Though Marshall apologized for the murder at his sentencing, he actually felt little remorse. "You simply cannot understand my feelings . . ." he wrote a female relative from prison. "I had done all that an honorable man, that a law-abiding man could do. . . . There are certain insults and wrongs that only can be washed away in blood."[4]

The case of Dabney Marshall said much about the white Southern attitude toward crime and punishment in this era. Marshall himself had gone beyond the law to settle a personal dispute. His "honor" had demanded no less. He might have escaped prosecution altogether had he confronted his accuser in a more equitable way. Marshall belonged to a culture in which violence and extralegal justice went hand in hand—a culture in which a perceived insult demanded a physical response, and a fair fight between adversaries was no business of the law.

It was a culture, too, in which state power was viewed with suspicion. Whites did not usually send fellow whites to prison without a good reason, and when they did, it was not for very long. (Marshall would receive a full pardon from the governor in 1901.) To deny a white man his liberty was to treat him like a slave. As historian J. F.

---

* Marshall appears to have accepted the deal for two reasons. First, a white man of his standing would not spend more than a few years in prison in Mississippi, regardless of the sentence. Second, Marshall probably feared his exposure as a homosexual at a public trial. As the *Clarion-Ledger* noted: "[We are] not prepared to affirm or refute these sensational charges but will state that . . . those who knew Dinkins do not doubt he spoke the truth. Furthermore the prosecution declared they would have been able to prove by half a dozen witnesses, had the case ever come to trial, that Marshall had been guilty of this revolting performance on previous occasions."

H. Claiborne noted in 1880, the state courts of Mississippi operated under the guideline set forth by Sir William Blackstone: "It is better that ninety-nine guilty men should escape, than that one innocent man should suffer." This guideline was unwritten, of course, and it applied only to whites.[5]

II

Marshall was sent to Oakley Farm, a 2,700-acre tract for white state convicts in Hinds County, south of Jackson. As an educated man, he became the prison's commissary clerk, a rather easy job. "I have abundant time to read my German books and to study them *ad infinitum*," he wrote a friend. Marshall well understood the cultural gulf that separated him from the other convicts. They were "mostly country boys," he claimed, and "among the vilest of the earth." Yet his correspondence offered a rare glimpse into a world that few people saw, and fewer still could put clearly into words. "Those on the outside think they know trouble," he mused, "but they do not even catch a glimpse of the real dark sorrow that life can hold."[6]

Oakley was the white forerunner of Parchman Farm. Its population was divided into two classes: trusties and gunmen. "The trusties are men ... who have shown themselves willing and obedient," Marshall explained. Their main job was to watch over the gunmen "day time or night time, waking or sleeping," to keep them "always within range of a shotgun or rifle."

Each morning, the white gunmen were marched to the fields, four abreast, with armed trusties on all sides:

> Immediately in front of them rides a beefy man, called a foreman or driver, armed with a heavy handled bull whip. . . . Behind the gunmen comes the "dog sergeant," that is a semi-trusty leading two leashed blood hounds. Still further behind comes the trusty water boy on a crazy cart containing a whiskey barrel of water.

The Other Parchman

What most impressed Marshall was the meticulous organization in the fields. The men hoed and plowed in rhythm as the trusties kept close watch. The bloodhounds moved down one line, the water cart up another. The driver seemed to be everywhere, "directing, scolding, encouraging, or whacking across the shoulders with the whip." Under him were special trusties, known as "strikers," who forced the "weaklings" and "sicklings" to keep up with the gang. "Does it not make you *shudder* to read of this?" Marshall wondered. "What must it do then to witness or endure it?"

Yet Marshall knew better than to complain. "I myself am made as comfortable as I can be made in an uncomfortable place," he said, "and have been fortunate in misfortune." Others suffered from overwork, from the intense heat, and from the malarial fever that sapped them to the bone. "I truly trust that I will not get sick here," Marshall wrote, "for the very thought of sickness in a convict camp in the country is appalling. And yet there are men here so inured to suffering of all kinds, that they do not mind so much the pain of the sickness as they fear the loss of time from the crops and the . . . displeasure of the sergeant."

The convicts Marshall described were sullen and humiliated, resenting their confinement and their toil. Some men "went crazy" at Oakley, while others "teetered on the very gulf of madness." Suicide attempts were common though not always successful. "Last Wednesday, one poor fellow beat up and swallowed [some] glass, but [his] nerve failed him, and he told the sergeant, and the doctor was summoned, and he was brought back to the life he loathed."

Marshall ended one letter with a warning: "I hope you won't say anything about what I have written in regard to the treatment of the prisoners, for should any adverse criticism . . . be traced [to] me, it would result greatly to my harm. In the penitentiary we walk on the edge of a Vesuvian crater, and the least imprudence, the slightest misstep, will throw you into the deeps below."[7]

III

By 1915, the great bulk of white convicts had been moved to Parchman, where they lived in separate field camps, segregated by race. Comprising about 10 percent of the prison population, they performed the same tasks as the Negro convicts, and had much the same routine. Those with particularly useful skills sometimes escaped the "nigger work" in the fields. At Parchman, the most trusted blacks were used as cooks and servants in the homes of prison officials, while the whites hoped for jobs as carpenters, mechanics, truck drivers, maintenance men, or "dog boys" who trained the hounds. Anything beat picking cotton all day in the Mississippi sun. As Dabney Marshall admitted: "Work in the fields would kill me."[8]

In 1925, the Parchman superintendent reported that the white population was growing "by leaps and bounds." "We had 149 white prisoners in 1917," he wrote, "we have 280 today." Though he didn't bother to explain this increase, the reason was clear: prohibition. The United States had gone dry in 1919, with Mississippi leading the way. Its legislature had been the first to ratify the Eighteenth Amendment, and public opinion forced some sheriffs to crack down hard. Prohibition had criminalized one of the South's most popular habits. Of the 280 white prisoners at Parchman in 1925, 87 were serving time for alcohol-related crimes, such as "manufacturing liquor" and "possessing a still."[9]

Typical of the new convicts at Parchman was a white bootlegger named Jessie Rials. For most of his life, Rials had been an obnoxious presence in his community—cursing, brawling, and selling moonshine whiskey. "He ran over a friend of mine," a neighbor recalled. "He drug him underneath the car . . . and then deliberately ran away." When prohibition came, Rials's luck ran out. He was convicted of manslaughter and liquor violations for the kind of offense he had been getting away with for years. While transporting moonshine "under the influence of whiskey," his lawyer admitted, Jessie "ran over his uncle in the public road . . . resulting in his death."[10]

The Other Parchman

The percentage of white convicts continued to rise in the 1930s, despite the repeal of prohibition on 1933. This was hardly a surprise. For one thing, the black population in Mississippi had begun a steady decline in relation to the white population. The coming of the boll weevil, the lure of better-paying Northern factory jobs, the chance to escape sweltering racial oppression—all contributed to the huge "Black Exodus" that started around 1915.[11]

In the next five years, as the United States entered World War I and the demand for industrial workers shot up, more than half a million rural blacks left the South for northern cities, 100,000 from Mississippi alone. The migration was so intense—the Northern reaction, at times, so severe—that Mayor "Big Bill" Thompson of Chicago actually sent a telegram to Governor Theodore Bilbo in 1920, asking him to take some Mississippi Negroes "back home." Bilbo's response was instructive: "[We] have all the room in the world for what we know as N-I-G-G-E-R-S, but none whatever for 'colored ladies and gentlemen.' If these Negroes have been contaminated with northern social and political dreams of equality, we can not use them, nor do we want them. The Negro who understands his proper relation to the white man in this country will be gladly received by the people of Mississippi, as we are very much in need of labor."[12]*

The migration continued. In 1910, blacks comprised 56 percent of the state's population. That figure fell to 52 percent in 1920, 50

---

* Bilbo's sentiments were echoed by whites throughout the state. Even the planters and businessmen of the Delta expressed a certain ambivalence about the migration of young blacks—their future labor supply—to the North. In the 1920s, the Indianola Rotary Club published a brochure ("Sunflower County, Mississippi: Where the Richness of the Soil Makes Living Easy and the Folks There Make Life Worthwhile") to encourage Northern whites to settle in their area. "Sunflower County has nearly 8,000 negro tenants and many hundred negroes in town," it said. "Most of them are good negroes [but] many of them Chicago can have. . . . The lazy, lying, crap-shooting, loafing, thieving negro is a hurt to any community. We don't want him either." The brochure concluded: "Modesty forbids much comment on ourselves, but we are a section of the old South, of Anglo-Saxon parentage and of Southern ideals of manhood and womanhood. Come look us over, You may like us."

percent in 1930, 49 percent in 1940, 45 percent in 1950, 42 percent in 1960, and 37 percent in 1970. As one black migrant put it, "I am sick of the South."[13]

The declining percentage of blacks in Mississippi had an obvious impact upon the racial composition of Parchman Farm. And so, too, did the economic turmoil of the 1930s. By the time prohibition ended, the Great Depression had begun. In Mississippi, as elsewhere, the human misery of this era—lost jobs, bank failures, farm foreclosures—fueled a sharp increase in property crimes. On the eve of the depression in 1929, there were 1729 state prisoners in Mississippi. Fifty-two percent were serving time for murder and manslaughter, only 25 percent for burglary, robbery, and grand larceny. At the height of the depression in 1935, there were 2,639 state prisoners in Mississippi—a number so large that it would not be matched again until the mid-1970s. Fifty-eight percent were serving time for burglary, robbery, and grand larceny, only 17 percent for murder and manslaughter.[14]

Poor whites were caught in this net. For the first time since Reconstruction, significant numbers of them were being convicted for crimes of hunger, not honor, crimes of "niggers" and slaves. By the mid-1930s, nearly 30 percent of those sent to the state penitentiary in Mississippi were white. (The prisoners included Elvis Presley's father, Vernon, who served a three-year term at Parchman for "check forgery" when Elvis was a boy.) Parchman would remain a predominantly black institution—though never again to the degree that its founders had intended.

IV

"One white convict gives me more trouble than three Negroes," Superintendent Oliver Tann remarked in the 1930s. His belief was widely shared. Parchman officials had long viewed white inmates as stubborn, mutinous men. Dr. A. M. M'Callum, the prison physi-

cian, told a national audience that white convicts were "almost un-
manageable without the most rigid discipline." Parchman was a difficult place for them, he thought, because field work and gang labor
simply were not in their blood. The Negro took to Parchman naturally; the white man never would.

White convicts were said to work less and complain more than
black convicts, and to consciously reject their lot. "When I tell one
of these young [whites] to take a hoe and join the field squad, I am
often met with a haughty refusal . . . ," said Tann. "We have tried the
dark cell, a bread-and-water-diet, standing them on a barrel. Such
methods don't work. I've tried them all. When persuasion fails, I
order the rebel stripped and whipped. Then I give him a day to
think it over. The second morning . . . he is whipped again. Perhaps
the third day, the same program must be followed, but not often does
the man hold out longer than that."[15]

The only recorded "strikes" at Parchman occurred in the 1930s
and the 1960s, when white convicts "bucked the line" to protest severe whippings and long hours spent in the fields. In 1947, fifteen
white inmates engaged in mass mutilations—severing their Achilles
tendons with a knife. The apparent cause, said a local religious
group, was a system that degraded white men to the point of suicide
or open revolt. They "are forced to doff their caps even to visitors
who come to the penitentiary," noted the *Methodist Advocate*. "They
are taught to be humble and servile at all times. . . . As it is now, no
matter what a man's possibilities or aptitudes were when he went
into the prison, he comes out just a cotton chopper or cotton
picker." Although statistics about escapes at Parchman do not include
race, the most serious breakouts, involving three men or more, appear to have been led by whites. "They may be a minority here," said
one Parchman employee, "but they cause ninety percent of the problems."[16]

There probably was truth to this, though racial perceptions played
a role. White convicts were expected to resist a prison environment

geared to the discipline and punishment of Negroes. And white opinion viewed white criminals as bolder and more defiant than black criminals, though far less threatening to the social order. White outlaws and "bad men" were a vital part of Southern folklore, idolized for their bravery, their battles with peace officers, their attempts to gain freedom, and their honorable ways. Mississippi had numerous examples, and Parchman saw its share. There were bank robbers with Robin Hood reputations and mountain moonshiners who had "shot it out" with the law. There were Clarence "Hogjaw" Grammar, the South's "toughest convict," and Russell Montgomery, the rodeo cowboy who escaped Parchman on a prison horse. And there was Kinnie Wagner, the most celebrated white "bad man" of them all.

The truth about Wagner was startling enough. Born in the western hills of Virginia in 1903, he left home at fourteen to join a traveling circus based in Tennessee. A huge man, at six feet, three inches and 260 pounds, Wagner worked as a barker, roustabout, and trickshot artist known for his remarkable aim. When prohibition began, he made moonshine liquor and sold it to the "local Negroes." At age twenty-two, he was arrested in Lucedale, Mississippi, for stealing a watch. Awaiting trial for grand larceny, he escaped by overpowering the jailer and taking his horse. A local posse tracked him to an isolated shack in the woods, but Kinnie shot his way to freedom, killing a deputy sheriff in the fight.[17]

The law caught up to him in Kingsport, Tennessee. This time, Wagner escaped after a shootout that left two officers dead and another badly wounded. He surrendered a week later (making certain that his family got the reward money), went on trial for murder, and was sentenced to die in the electric chair. Transferred to an "escape-proof" state prison, Kinnie broke out and made his way to Mexico, where he spent a fruitful year robbing banks and trains. Returning to the United States, he wound his way north, killing twice more, in barroom brawls, before being captured by a female sheriff in Arkansas. "You know," he insisted, "I could never hurt a woman."

The Other Parchman

By this point, three states were competing for Kinnie Wagner— two hoping to try him for murder, the other determined to execute him. Mississippi won out because his killing spree had begun there. In 1926, a jury found Wagner guilty, and the judge sentenced him to life. "They put me in handcuffs and shackles and hauled me off to Parchman," Kinnie recalled. "Long Chain Charlie watched me like a hawk."

At Parchman, he picked cotton and planned his first escape. But things did not go as expected. Betrayed by another convict, he was shot in the arm and shoulder as he broke for freedom in a hijacked prison truck. "I stayed in the hospital for a week," Kinnie said. "They beat me every day and night trying to get me to tell who hid the guns for our escape. I wouldn't snitch on a friend if they beat me to death."

In the following years, Kinnie seemed to settle down. He rose from gunman to trusty-shooter to head trainer of the prison bloodhounds. Riding alone on horseback, surrounded by his dogs, Kinnie was the best tracker Parchman had ever known. He hunted escapees all across the Delta —in fields and swamps, in abandoned barns and cabins. One day in 1940, however, Kinnie took off himself. Recaptured three years later near his mountain birthplace in Virginia, he became a model prisoner until his next escape in 1948, when he walked out the front gate with a machine gun, successfully evading the bloodhounds he had raised. Kinnie remained at large until 1956. "I have violated no laws since I have been out on escape," he claimed after a huge posse cornered him in central Mississippi, "and I am very happy to be going back to Parchman." Seriously ill, he died in the prison hospital a short time later.

But his reputation as an outlaw hero lived on. At the height of his criminal career between 1924 and 1926, the infant American recording industry produced three popular ballads about Kinnie. In the following years, he became a favorite of rural folk singers, who played up his troubles with the law.

They drove him to the river front,
On one mild April day.
And there poor Kinnie drew his guns,
Two sheriffs he did slay.
They took poor Kinnie back to jail,
The judge to him did say:
"Your sentence shall be death, my boy."
But Kinnie got away.[18]

In legend, he became the best shot, the bravest man, the greatest lover of them all. His exploits were accepted, and embellished, by national publications such as *Newsweek,* which described him as a "gunman, a killer, a ladies' man, lover, moonshiner, brawler, bandit, and a drinker." After each escape, it was said, he would gallop through town on horseback, looking to "kiss a pretty girl." When he robbed a bank, he would share the money with the poor. And he would kill his victims by shooting a perfect circle in their chest and dotting the middle with his final slug.[19]

Folklorists who have studied Kinnie Wagner explain that he fits perfectly into the white outlaw stereotype of the rural South and West. Kinnie was noble and handsome, chivalrous toward women, and generous to those in need. He lived by his wits, using great natural skills to avoid capture and to escape repeatedly. He was a free spirit, determined to protect his independence at all costs. The legend of this five-time killer reveals a powerful ambivalence—if not outright sympathy—toward bold and desperate men who flout the law. It is a legend reserved for whites.

V

Women in Mississippi were rarely sent to the state penitentiary. They committed fewer crimes than men, and their offenses tended to be minor ones, such as prostitution and petty theft, punishable by a month or two in the local jail. At no time between 1870 and 1970 did females comprise more than 5 percent of the state prison population. Their numbers were low, and their color never changed.

When Margaret Givens arrived at the state penitentiary in 1876, she was barely fifteen years old. Margaret was among the first females to be housed there following the collapse of Reconstruction, and her stay would be long. Described in her pardon petition as a "poor, simple-minded negro girl," she had been convicted of infanticide—drowning her newborn infant in a pond. Twelve years later, the "good, reputable white citizens of Clay County" petitioned the governor to overturn her life sentence and "set her loose." They argued that Margaret had been tricked into the crime by the infant's father, a "smart, shrewd black demon" who had promised to marry her if she did away with the child. The governor's pardon arrived in 1888.[20]

Margaret Givens was typical of the few females who entered the state prison system each year. Young, poor, and black, she had been convicted of a violent offense. When Parchman opened its women's camp around 1915, it housed twenty-six inmates. All were black, and seventeen had been convicted of a homicide. Ten years later, there were forty-eight blacks (and still no whites), including thirty-six murderers. Most were in their early twenties or below.[21]

Many of them had killed a husband, a lover, or a rival in a domestic dispute. Negro women "exhibit a ferocity as bloody and as savage as that exhibited by the men," wrote a white Delta resident in 1935. "They stab with deadly effect and shoot with unerring precision. They plunge icepicks into the hearts of men and women, cut throats with razors, batter heads with axes, and shoot their victims full of holes with pistols." While students of Delta life would surely take issue with this gory description, there was wide agreement that violence by and against women was common in the black community and that authorities paid it little heed. The code of chivalrous protection did not extend to the lower caste. Whites did not see these offenses as either unusual for Negroes or threatening to the social order.[22] Some black women served their state sentences at local road camps and jails, working as domestics and prostitutes for those in charge. It was an old Delta custom, journalist Hodding Carter once complained, for a "negress" in an "air-tight murder case" to wind up as the sheriff's latest cook. "She'll be made a trusty, be given the run of the local jail and courthouse, and pick up as much in tips as she made all last year."[23]

In the 1930s, a number of folklorists visited Parchman to record the songs and work chants of the prisoners. Male blues singers like Bukka White, Dobie Red, and Alabama Stewart got most of their attention. The women were recorded as an afterthought, more for their spirituals than anything else. "If evil had left its mark on these bright young faces," wrote John Lomax, "no trace appeared as they sang about a 'Motherless Child,' or found comfort in the hope of 'Hearing My Mother Pray Again.' "[24]

More personal songs were recorded and forgotten. They included "Anybody Here Wants to Buy Some Cabbage," about a prostitute "so tired of rolling for my shoes and clothes," and "Dangerous Blues," in which convict Mattie Mae Thomas described her early battered life:

> You keep talking bout the dangerous blues,
> If I had my pistol I'd be dangerous too.
> You may be a bully, but I don't know.
> But I'll fix you so you won't gimme no trouble
> In the world I know.[25]

The most valuable material was collected by David Cohn, a Delta writer with a deep interest in local folklore. A frequent visitor to Parchman in the 1930s, Cohn asked the more literate women at Camp 13 to write down their lyrics in longhand. The women responded with original verse about their families, their crimes, their sexual fantasies, and their lives at Parchman Farm. Alma Hicks noted the diverse shades of color among the inmates, none of them white:

> So many women here
> And so many different kind.
> Some high yellows
> But I'm a chocklate brown.

Willie B. Young put her feelings in a "blues poem":

> I'm a lonely prisoner
> a long-long away from home
> I have no friends and relation
> to feel and care for me.
>
> I wrote an told my mother
> to try to get me home
> an I will never leave her
> in this mean world alone
>
> My mother sent me an answer
> she says my child you must pray
> and God will guide you
> and bring you back to mother some day
>
> I wrote an told my father
> to go to chief of police
> an see if could get the Gov
> to set this poor child free

My father sent me an answer
He say child there is not a chance
You know you must be punish
for it wrong to kill a man.[26]

The women were separated from the men's quarters by acres of cotton fields and a high barbed-wire fence. Yet sex and rape were all too common in a camp supervised by male sergeants and guarded by male trusties. A former employee recalled that the men and women of Parchman "stopped at nothing in trying to get at each other" and that sometimes "we would just turn our heads and pray for all that sowing of oats to end up in a crop failure."[27]

The women at Camp 13 sang of their isolation and loneliness in playful, longing verse:

If I were a cat fish
swimming deep down in the see
I could have all these Parchman men
fishing after me.

And:

I'm goin to the free world
to get my ham bone boiled (*repeat*)
Cause these Parchman men
done let my ham bone spoil.[28]

The women slept in a large dormitory, much like the men. They canned vegetables, ran the prison laundry, and worked dawn-to-dusk shifts in a sweat-filled sewing room, making clothes, bedding, and mattresses for the entire farm. One of their songs went:

When I go home I'm gona wear my dresses
above my knees (*repeat*)

I'm gonna sell my stuff
to who I please.

You talkin bout trouble
You don't know what trouble means (*repeat*)
What I call trouble
is a Singer Sewing Machine[29]

When cotton had to be planted and picked, the women helped in
the fields. They worked in long, tight formations, surrounded by
dogs and trusty-shooters, moving in unison to the chants.

All right Gals
Um-Um
Work ain't hard
Um-Um
Sergeant ain't mean
Um-Um
Sergeant, Sergeant
Um-Um
Dis cotton is thick
Um-Um
Can't you see
Um-Um
Its making me sick
Um-Um . . .
We got twenty years
Um-Um
Seven and five
Um-Um
Wit dis cotton sacks
Um-Um
On our side
Um-Um.[30]

Their favorite song was "Evil Superintendent." The women were reluctant to perform it for Cohn, but they did write down the words:

We've got a evil superintendent
And the worst sergeant on the farm (*repeat*)
If I make it to the bushes
The Sergeant can't do me no harm.

The sun is too hot
and seven years is too long (*repeat*)
The first chance I get
I'm gonna make a start for home.

Captain, Captain please don't drive
my man so hard (*repeat*)
He ain't nothing but a hustler
Ain't never had a job . . .

When I leave this place
I will sure have something to tell (*repeat*)
I can tell the world
Just what is meant by hell.[31]

VI

Like everything else at Parchman, the women's camp was segregated by race. The blacks lived in a long shedlike structure, the whites in a small brick building, with a high fence in between. The black population ranged from twenty-five to sixty-five women each year, the white population from zero and five. "It is a fortunate thing for Mississippi that white women seldom indulge in serious crime," a Jackson newspaper noted in 1936. "Probably half of the counties would be embarrassed if they had to confine a woman in their jails."[32]

So few white females reached Parchman that a clear profile of them is impossible. Their crimes ranged from murder and infanticide to grand larceny and aiding an escape. Some, like Lucy Philips of Meridian, were viewed as "incorrigible." "We consider her one of the most daring and cold-blooded Robbers and House-Burners, male or female, within the state," said the signers of a successful petition to deny her a pardon, "and we consider her very presence a menace to the safety of our property and probably our lives. We believe that fifteen years is a light sentence for her crime, and the Penitentiary is the safest place for her."[33]

More remarkable, however, were the white women who were spared a prison term after committing a heinous crime. In 1929, Mrs. Marion Drew, a twenty-five-year old widow, confessed to killing her husband, Marlin, in Ashland, Mississippi, near the Tennessee line. The newspapers called it "one of the queerest murder cases in the history of the state." At first, Mrs. Drew and her eight-year-old daughter blamed the death on Marlin's father, who was tried and convicted of the crime and sent to Parchman Farm. When damaging new evidence emerged, Mrs. Drew made her confession in a rambling "love poem," which described her husband as an evil man seeking forgiveness at the end:

I know I've lived a sinful life
While in this world I've been;
I'd sure live a different life
If I could live again.

The time has come, my darling
When you and I must part,
The bullet of that forty-five
Has surely plunged my heart.

But kiss our little children
And tell them I am gone.
Don't let them follow my footsteps
For I have led them wrong.[34]

The judge had never sent a white woman to Parchman. After conferring with the district attorney, he accepted a guilty plea from Mrs. Drew and then released her without bond. She would remain free, he ordered, if she behaved herself in the future. Mrs. Drew never went to trial. Her father-in-law was pardoned by the governor.

A few years later, a judge in Jones County sentenced a white woman to house arrest following her conviction for murder. He did not think that prison was a proper place for her. In a more spectacular case, Sara Ruth Dean went on trial in 1934 for killing her married lover, J. Preston Kennedy, in Greenwood, Mississippi. The trial received national attention because both parties belonged to Mississippi's social register, and both were physicians. Dr. Dean was accused of slipping poison into Kennedy's whiskey glass during a "farewell midnight tryst."

Local custom favored Dean, as the prosecutor well understood. "You must consider this case as you would a man's," he told the jury. "The fact that she is a woman is no shield for crime." The state's key witness was a black servant called "Toodlums," who had seen the couple together just before the death occurred. Dean's attorney went for the throat. "The prosecution turned its sails when they placed that negro boy on the stand to insinuate something about a white woman," he thundered. "I resent it and you resent it and the womanhood of Leflore County and the South resent it!"

It took thirteen hours for the jury to find Mrs. Dean guilty of murder. "We hated to send a woman to prison," said the foreman, "but we had no choice. It was either death or life imprisonment." Another juror agreed. "We wanted to make the punishment less severe, but we could not under the verdict we had to decide on."[35]

Ruth Dean remained at home during her appeal. When that failed, Governor Mike Conner issued a full pardon on July 9, 1935, after being bombarded with mercy requests. Though Conner claimed to have new information "not available to the courts," he never said what it was. His decision rested on politics and chivalry, Conner told friends. He just could not send a woman like Ruth Dean to Parchman, no matter what she had done.

✠

CHAPTER EIGHT

Going Home

I have often heard of mercy,
and have never known what it mean,
but if mercy mean my freedom,
Lord please have mercy on me.

—"Friendless Prisoner," by Parchman
inmate Henrietta Barnes, 1936

I

Every fifth Saturday night in Jackson, the downtown railroad station
came suddenly alive. At the stroke of twelve, a crowd of black
women clamored aboard a shabby excursion train and headed north
into the Delta on the Yellow Dog Line. The train swept past mile
after mile of perfectly flat cotton fields, reaching Parchman with the
dawn. Known as the Midnight Special, it carried the wives and
lovers of the inmates—and, hopefully, good news:

Heah comes yo' woman, a pardon in her han'
Gonna say to de boss, I want mah man,
Let the Midnight Special shine its light on me.[1]

The Parchman Era

Yet seen from inside Parchman, this light was often a mirage. Convicts yearned for luck—not justice—in their freedom songs because the standards for clemency were so capricious and corrupt. Mississippi had no parole laws in this era. It would be one of the last states to institute them, in 1944. Prisoners served fixed sentences, with time off for good behavior, unless the governor intervened. "You know the one star in the night of our sorrow is the hope of a pardon," wrote an educated white inmate in a letter home. "No matter how desperate our chances, no matter how frequent or bitter our disappointments have been in the past, we cling to this hope as to life itself."[2]

As a general rule, Parchman's population rose and fell with the fortunes of the cotton economy. Good times meant full employment and fewer property crimes. But in hard times, Parchman filled up with young men—partly, some suspected, because the big planters had no interest in shielding surplus workers from the law. "It is obvious to me," said Governor Mike Conner in 1936, "that when labor is plentiful in the Delta, the accused is permitted to go to the penitentiary."[3]

To win an early release, an inmate had to have the backing of his camp sergeant and the Parchman superintendent. Their recommendations were essential. Next, the inmate published a petition for pardon in his local newspaper, stating the reasons for his request. The petition alerted his community, which then lobbied the governor by mail. A typical pardon file contained the letters of dozens of interested parties—sheriffs, judges, attorneys, planters, and ministers—comprising the "best" white opinion of the town. Taken together, they provided a vivid, if one-sided, portrait of the convict and his world.

Few Parchman inmates were literate enough to compose a petition by themselves, so their families, or a white patron, would hire a local attorney to do the job. Over the years, the same lawyers appeared again and again in the voluminous pardon files. With few exceptions, they tended to be members of the courthouse elite, well connected to the politicians and power brokers of their intimate one-party state.

The competition for clients led some attorneys to promise far more than they could deliver. In 1928, for example, a lawyer named William Stribling took the case of Will Chaney, a Negro sentenced to five years at Parchman for "aiding and assisting one of his race in eluding arrest." For the usual fee—about twenty dollars—Stripling composed a standard petition describing Chaney as a "good" but "sickly" negro, "unable to render the State much service."

As the months passed without a decision, Chaney became concerned. In November 1928, he sent Governor Bilbo a letter from prison, asking him to "grant me a pardon so that I can be able to send you a necktie for X-mas." When Bilbo didn't respond, Chaney wrote him a second time begging "you to forgive me," and a third time pleading "to let me go home to my wife and child."

Nothing seemed to work. Attorney Stripling had lost interest in the case, leaving Chaney on his own. In 1930, the convict sent his fourth—and final—letter to Bilbo:

> I has paid W. P. Stribling all the money that I had to obtain a pardon for me. And now I haven't heard from him since. . . . He told me that you and him were close friends and you would issue the pardon for him. And I taken him at his word. Now I beg thee for you to look into the matter and do something.[4]

Will Chaney received his pardon in 1932, a few months before his sentence was due to expire.

II

In a prison system where most inmates were black and outside authorities were white, racial etiquette played a crucial role. There was a distinct ritual to the pardon process that everyone understood. In practical terms, it meant getting a number of prominent whites to vouch for the inmate's good character. The tone of these appeals was deeply paternalistic, with the writer extending his good name, and noble blessing, to a clearly "inferior" being. "Carson Alexander has lived on my place nearly all of his life," a planter assured the governor in 1911. "This darkey's reputation is far above the average, in fact he is a white man's negro." Or, "I have known Lewis Luckett ever since he was born. . . . He was a faithful slave and since the surrender has been a good and dependable citizen."[5]

The "faithful slave" ideal did not die out with slavery. When the white "friends" of Charlie Berry petitioned the governor for his release in 1897, they compared him, with obvious affection, to the "old-time uncles" who "stood so nobly by our own people during the gloom of war, when 'old master' was away on distant battlefields fighting 'neath the grandest battle flag that ever hovered over our land." And when a wealthy merchant requested a pardon for his favorite house servant in 1935, he did so, he wrote, "to show my appreciation for this humble and penitent negro's many years of loyalty and unusual service."[6]

Paternalism had its limits, however. Many whites simply wanted their workers back. A planter from Lula, Mississippi, asked for the release of Ben Jeter, "as I need him to pick cotton." And another requested clemency for John Cook, "an exceptionally good negro who is under contract to me." "I need [him] to help me out on the farm," the planter added, "and want you to parole him for ninety days, so he can complete his crop."[7]

The most revealing pardon files often belonged to the violent offenders who were facing long terms at Parchman Farm. Since black-on-black crime was the common thread in these cases, a racial explanation was essential. The most common one, by far, depicted knifings and shootings among Negroes as ordinary events in the lives of a savage, impulsive race. Time and again, a pardon would be requested—and granted—on the grounds that the murder occurred "at a negro frolic" or that "it was just a normal case where one nigger killed another."[8]

Most petitions contained a humdrum excuse for the murder: liquor was involved; the gun went off accidentally; it was a matter of self-defense. The more inventive ones suggested that the dead man had thoroughly deserved his fate. In 1909, Governor E. F. Noel pardoned a black field hand who had gunned down a rival in a domestic dispute. While the facts of the killing were somewhat muddled, the larger issue was crystal clear. The victim "had attended a negro college for a term or two and was so highly educated as to be a full-fledged, good-for-nothing negro bully." The murderer, by contrast, "was not only a hard working, honest negro, but a white man's friend from rind to core."[9]

It was a rare attorney who did not attempt to portray his client as a "good" and "humble" Negro. But such descriptions were often challenged by local whites. A typical case involved a "one-legged negro barber" named Ed Cottrell, who had requested clemency on the grounds that a murder he committed was an "unfortunate accident." Cottrell claimed to have fired a pistol at a "negro man in the heat of passion," but "the ball had missed its intended mark and [struck] a negro woman, from which wound she died shortly thereafter." Endorsed by two dozen prominent whites, the petition expressed Cottrell's "deep regret" for the incident, adding that he had "entertained no malice toward the woman, as [they] were on friendly terms."

Things looked good for him until a letter arrived from a white merchant, informing the governor about Cottrell's violent past. "This is the *second* time he has been sent to the penitentiary for murder," it began. "The first time, the enemies of law and order and justice . . . succeeded in causing the pardon power to be misapplied. So this bastard yellow negro murderer was turned out. Now the same interested parties are creating another petition ... to turn him out again."[10]

The letter provided a compelling reason for Cottrell's powerful white support. "Under the guise of a barber shop," it explained, "this negro ran one of the most notorious 'blind tigers,' or whiskey joints, in defiance of the law." And the white men who had composed and signed his petition were part of the "illicit liquor influence" that had been corrupting northern Mississippi for years.

The governor rejected Cottrell's petition, taking note of the convict's previous pardon from a life sentence. "A murderous purpose against one individual, resulting in the death of another, makes murder complete," he replied. "Under the circumstances I could not do otherwise than let the law takes its course." Ed Cottrell would remain at Parchman until a new governor took office.[11]

Perhaps no other case illustrated the perils of the "bad negro"— or the skills of the "good" attorney—better than that of Prince Berry, a Delta field hand sentenced to life in prison for a murder he committed at a "negro frolic." Berry had waited nine years, an eternity in such matters, before submitting his first petition to the *Lexington Advertiser*, his hometown newspaper. Written by W. P. Tackett, a local attorney, it stressed that Berry had been confined to the prison hospital "on account of heart and lung problems, and is now a physical wreck ... unable to perform further service to the state."[12]

This was a common strategy. Hard work was the driving force behind convict life in Mississippi, and those unable to do it were often set free. But the white people of Lexington were quite content to let Berry rot in jail. Berry had a history of violent behavior; his reputation was such that Governor Noel, who came from nearby Yazoo City, could recall this convict's sordid past. There was little chance that Noel would accept the "good Negro" argument in Berry's case, and Tackett did not push it very hard. "I have no desire to force the matter upon you," he wrote Noel in 1908, "for we both know this negro. But whatever his character may have been in the past, [his] physical condition . . . appeals to executive clemency."[13]

Noel was dubious. As a favor to Tackett, an old friend, he wrote personally to the prison doctor, inquiring about Berry's health. "In regard to this convict," came the reply, "I will say he is unable to do very hard work, but is fully able to do the work required of him— milking cows."[14]

This was not what Tackett wanted to hear. With his case in shambles, he made a final plea to Governor Noel, insisting that a pardon for Berry would not endanger the white community because his crimes had always been committed against blacks. In Tackett's chilling words, "Wouldn't it be the wisest course to grant Berry's pardon, turn him out, and take chances on his killing another negro?"[15]

The answer was no. Prince Berry would remain at Parchman. Blacks who killed other blacks were routinely pardoned, but only if white opinion did not vigorously object. It was part of a larger pattern of neglect in Jim Crow Mississippi, and it would be very slow to change. "One nigger cuts another's throat . . . and that is the last heard of it," a Hattiesburg editor explained in 1903. "Perhaps not one third of the [killers] are ever arrested. It is like dog chewing on dog and the white people are not interested in the matter. Only another dead nigger—that's all."[16]

This was hardly a revelation to Mississippi's beleaguered black community. There had long been complaints that white indifference to black crime had fueled high levels of violence among Negroes and created a cynical disregard for the law. It was a matter of record, wrote the black-owned *Delta Leader*, that the criminal justice system did not care "what a negro does as long as the white people are not involved."[17]

Ordinarily, blacks did not attempt to write the governor about their views in a particular clemency case. The gesture was not only futile, it could also be dangerous by pitting the writer against powerful white forces in his town. Still, the black community's deep interest in the pardon process can be gleaned from the letters and petitions sent by whites. In one case, J. P. Morris, a state senator, wrote the governor about a black convict named Charles Collins, who had been sentenced to the gallows for killing a "colored fiddler" at a Negro frolic near Shaluba, Mississippi. Morris described Collins as an "industrious boy, polite and popular with whites." But he freely admitted that the blacks in town wanted Collins to hang. "The colored people do not like him because they say he is wild and reckless, and especially so when at all under the influence of whiskey. He was convicted wholly on their evidence."

Morris helped get the sentence reduced to life. And the arguments he put forth would soon be used to win Collins his freedom as well:

> We are asking that you take his good character and youth into consideration, and that it was a negro frolic where . . . there was plenty of whiskey, and also the fact that the whites think well of him, that your Excellency will let him have the benefit of merciful clemency.[18]

The fears of the black community were easily forgotten.

III

In the spring of 1884, a judge from Okolona, in the Mississippi hills, asked Governor Robert Lowry to pardon a sharecropper named Squire Horton, who had been sentenced to four years in prison for "assault and battery with intent to murder one Henry Knowles." It was an ordinary case—"both negroes were drunk, a row ensued, Horton drew his pistol, Knowles had a knife"—requiring, at best, a routine plea for compassion. Squire Horton had a "wife and large family of children," the judge explained, who were "now dependent upon the charities of a cold and unfeeling world for their daily bread."

Going Home

But the judge went further. Pardoning this convict would be more than a stroke of human kindness; it would be an act of racial justice as well:

> To get drunk and shoot a negro is no very great offense if it be a white man who does the shooting. I find it a hard matter to convict a white man for *any* offense, and particularly of such offense as that. . . . If we would make friends of our colored population, let us deal kindly and gently and mercifully with them where we can. Let's have a rule which deals out to crime an equal punishment—not tortures with the horrid lash.[19]

This was a far bolder plea. There was a big difference between common compassion, with its paternalistic nod in the direction of "inferior" blacks, and equal punishment, which challenged the basic assumptions that held the caste system in place. Yet it was not uncommon for whites to argue privately that the pardon power should be used to rectify obvious injustices based on race. Squire Horton benefited from this strategy, and he was not alone. In 1915, a common thief named Ada Johnson won an early release after her trial judge urged the governor to "turn this negro a loose" on the grounds that "she would not have been convicted had she been a white woman." "You know as a matter of fact," the judge continued, "what little show the average negro gets before a jury."[20]

This strategy was also effective in pardon cases involving black assaults against whites, where the punishment was intentionally severe. The number of such cases was never very large; blacks did not normally confront whites in Mississippi, and those who did were sometimes denied the luxury of a trial. But when a Negro was sent to prison on this charge, clemency could play a vital, mitigating role.

Such was the case with Napoleon Carter, a sixty-year-old night watchman at the railroad depot in the central Mississippi town of Water Valley. One evening in 1908, Carter got into an altercation with a white conductor named Charles Anderson, who had a reputation for trouble. Though neither man was seriously hurt, Carter was charged with "assault and battery with intent to kill and murder." At his trial, a witness recalled, "the negro was not represented by counsel, and, of course, made no defense for himself." The white jury sentenced him to ten years in prison.[21]

Carter had a good reputation in Water Valley. Whites there liked him and knew he had been provoked. But his aggression was a serious matter, and a spell at Parchman would send the right message to other blacks. When Carter's white "friends" petitioned for his release in 1910, they described him publicly as a chastened man. "Napoleon is an old negro," they said, "who has been sufficiently punished for his offense." In private, however, a different message emerged. Everyone knew that race had determined the verdict. "Had Napoleon struck another negro or a white struck Mr. Anderson under the same circumstances, there would have been no conviction at all," a local merchant admitted to Governor Noel. "If you grant the pardon I am sure that it will be approved by nine-tenths of the white people who know the facts in the case."

This undoubtedly was true. Having done their obvious duty by sending this Negro to prison, the whites of Water Valley now felt compelled to bring him back home. "He has served more than twenty months for an offense where but slight injury was made upon the assaulted party," wrote another white patron, "and that with an instrument which has never been recognized as a deadly weapon—a shovel."

Carter was pardoned a few weeks later. The issue of unequal punishment, raised discreetly by the white "friends" of a "humble old negro," had proved essential in deciding his fate. But other such cases would have very different results. For every "good Negro" like Napoleon Carter, it seemed, there was a "bad Negro" like Man Cook.

Cook had also been arrested in 1908 for much the same crime: assaulting a white conductor in the town of Pascagoula, on the Mississippi Gulf Coast. According to Cook's attorney, his client had been sitting quietly in the "colored" section when the conductor, noticing a razor in Cook's pocket, rudely ordered him from the train. Cook refused, a policeman was summoned, and a "scuffle ensued." As the conductor beat him with brass knuckles, Cook grabbed the officer's pistol and fired one shot, "slightly wounding" his attacker. A white jury sentenced Cook to ten years in prison. "He was fortunate," a witness noted, "to get off with his neck."[22]

Cook's basic defense was similar to Carter's: both rested on the issue of inequality. "It is one of those . . . instances," wrote Cook's attorney, "where a negro . . . got into trouble with white men and came out best." Man Cook, he said, was the "unfortunate victim of race prejudice."

In this case, however, the lawyer stood virtually alone. Cook was no humble Negro. He had wrestled with a police officer, ignored a white man's order, and shot him in the fray. Now his pardon request added insult to injury by defending this behavior as an "act of self-preservation," a legitimate response to the "unwarranted conduct" of racist whites.

The reaction was severe. Dozens of angry letters crossed the governor's desk. "This was a notoriously bad case," wrote the district attorney who prosecuted Cook. "He is a high-tempered, vicious negro," fumed a local banker. "This is one of the worst negroes [around]," claimed the county sheriff. "When an officer has succeeded in landing one of these dangerous darkies in the penitentiary, it is discouraging, to say the least of it, to have him pardoned and again turned loose on the community to be a source of worry and danger."

Cook's petition was rejected. "I believe that the best place for negroes of his character is on the farm where he can serve the state infinitely better than as a free citizen," a white merchant had written, and the governor obviously agreed. Man Cook would remain at Parchman for the full ten years.

IV

Winning a pardon did not necessarily require a lawyer's fee. One of the simplest ways out, in fact, was to become a burden to the state. The pardon files are crammed with successful pleas from convicts who were too old or too sick to work in the fields. And some prisoners took matters into their own hands, quite literally, by drinking poison, slitting their wrists, severing Achilles tendons, or chopping off a limb, a process of self-mutilation known as "knockin' a joe."

The body could be "helpful" in other ways. Mississippi had a long history of using its convicts in medical experiments. Those who took part and survived were granted clemency for "meritorious service." The list of diseases included malaria, yellow fever, and sleeping sickness, to name a few. "Hell," said one volunteer, "this is a lot easier than picking cotton."[23]

Mississippi was the site of the most successful prison experiment of this century. It involved the "red flame" of pellagra, which struck the American South with deadly force in the early 1900s. Medical opinion at that time agreed on the symptoms: severe back pain, a sore mouth, listlessness, mental depression, and a deep red rash on the hands, feet, and face. Yet the cause of pellagra was anyone's guess. Some scientists linked it to heredity, others to poor sanitation, still others to spoiled corn or bad cotton seed. Health officials in Tennessee declared pellagra to be a transmissible disease, requiring the quarantine of its victims. As a result, pellagrans were treated like lepers in much of the South.

There was another theory. Dr. Joseph Goldberger of the Public Health Service viewed pellagra as a nutritional disease. "From what

I've seen," said Goldberger, "the big difference between folks that die of pellagra and those who never get it, is that the pellagrans are poor." And the "big difference between rich and poor," he added, "is that the poor don't get the right stuff to eat."[24]

But what about pellagra's regional base? Why did it strike so many in the South and so few in the North? The answer, said Goldberger, lay in the monotonous "3-M diet" of the Southern poor: meat (fatback), meal, and molasses. Pellagra was not a starvation disease, since its victims got plenty of calories. What they lacked was the protein that came from fresh meat, milk, and vegetables.[25]

The problem was worst in Mississippi. More than sixteen thousand cases of pellagra (resulting in fifteen hundred deaths) were reported by state officials in 1915 alone. A nutritional study done in the Delta showed about half of the residents with serious protein deficiencies. Few families owned a cow, and gardens were rare because the plantation owner demanded that cotton be planted right up to the doorstep of their shacks. Were it not for the growing of greens at odd seasons and the fish caught in local ponds and rivers, the sharecropper diet would have contained almost no protein at all.

In 1914, Dr. Goldberger ran a series of experiments in two pellagra-ridden Mississippi orphanages. Within a year, he had wiped out the disease in both places by adding milk, green vegetables and fresh meat to the normal fare of grits, lard, cornbread, salt pork, and molasses. The next step was more dangerous, however, as Goldberger well understood. Having cured pellagra by adding protein to the diets of suffering children, the doctor now hoped to induce the disease by removing protein from the diets of healthy adults.

Goldberger chose the state penal farm because pellagra had never been a problem there. Despite brutal working conditions, the prisoners were reasonably well fed. Their diet included milk and eggs and various green vegetables. After getting the governor's approval, Goldberger rounded up twelve male convicts for his experiment by promising them a full pardon for their services. All they had to do was spend the next six months in isolation, eating the same food consumed every day by the poor folk of Mississippi.

These convicts had much in common. They were strong, healthy, and white. (Goldberger insisted on this because statistics showed that adult white males were less likely to contract the disease than adult black males.) The group also included some of the most notorious convicts in Mississippi: seven of the twelve were serving life terms for murder, and two others—the Atkinson brothers—were responsible for the most spectacular bank failure in state history. Serving seven years each for embezzlement, they were now gambling with their lives.[26]

The story of Dr. Goldberger's experiment is well known. The men got progressively weaker as time went by. They lost considerable weight, despite a diet of three thousand calories a day. Some complained of joint pains; others became moody and depressed. After five months, the telltale red rashes appeared on several of the men. Goldberger was ecstatic. "This is beyond anything I anticipated," he wrote his wife from Mississippi. "The most I had hoped for, the most I had prayed for, was two cases. We have five!"[27]

The ending to this story had a secret twist. As the experiment entered its final stages, several of the prisoners begged to be let out. "We have gone through with six months of the worse torture 12 men ever were subjected to," convict Guy James wrote the governor. "Not for a single day have we been given the diet Dr. Goldberger promised us, and we never get enough to satisfy [our] hunger. . . . For God sake, come to our relief."[28]

The governor ignored him. And the convicts got no sympathy from Goldberger, whose courage and dedication were legendary among his peers. Goldberger had purposely contracted almost every illness he studied, including yellow fever, typhoid fever, dengue fever, and Stramberg's disease. To demonstrate that pellagra was not infectious, he had injected himself with the blood of its victims, eaten pieces of their scaled-off skin, and even swallowed a vial containing the feces of a woman "very sick with a true case of the red disease." Goldberger could not conceive of quitting an experiment before its completion. For the convicts under his control in this secret endeavor, there would be no turning back, no escape from the pain.[29]

All of the men recovered. They were hailed as heroes, handed their pardons, and given five dollars and a new suit of clothes. "I have been through a thousand hells," said a tearful volunteer, adding that there were moments when he would have welcomed a bullet to the head.[30]

The news of these pardons was far less popular in the convicts' hometowns. From the Delta hamlet of Itta Bena came urgent pleas to keep Guy James locked up in jail. His crime was "one of the worst we ever had," wrote the local editor, "the cold-blooded killing of an unarmed man." Furthermore, James had publicly threatened the prosecutors at his trial. "If he is turned loose," a minister warned, "the belief is that he will return to this place and kill these men. If possible, do not pardon him; if you do, make it on the condition that he leave the state."[31]

It was too late, of course. The people would never know that Guy James had been promised a pardon in advance for joining the experiment or that he had begged to drop out when the suffering became intense. What they did know—improbable as it sounded—was that twelve dangerous men had eaten their way to freedom. Guy James did not carry out his threats against the prosecutors, although he and several others in the experiment would spend a lifetime in conflict with the law.

V

Clarence E. Grammar was known as Hogjaw to fellow inmates because of his huge head and burly physique. He had served two terms at Parchman in the 1930s for larceny and criminal assault. In 1940, he was sentenced to a life term for drowning an old man after blasting him with a shotgun. Had Grammar been a Negro, he probably would have died in the state's traveling electric chair, Instead, his hard fists and mean disposition won him instant respect at Parchman, whose officials made him a trusty.

Grammar relished the role and exploited its benefits. In 1947, he earned a pardon for "meritorious service" by killing a prisoner who was trying to escape. But trouble followed him like a shadow, and his freedom did not last. Returned to prison in 1949 for another assault, Hogjaw was given a promotion. He became the keeper of Parchman's prized bloodhounds, a job that allowed him to track down criminals throughout the state.

In 1950, Grammar led a manhunt against three whites who had butchered a black family near the town of Kosciusko. Using his best bloodhounds—Nigger, Alabama, and High Rollin' Red—Grammar directed the posse to a cabin on a cotton farm where the men were hiding. As the sheriff demanded their surrender with a bullhorn, Hogjaw charged the cabin and captured the fugitives by himself, badly wounding their leader. "While [he] posed proudly, cigarette dangling from his lips, deputies rushed up to arrest the killers and photographers to record the stirring scene. Said Hogjaw, with an old con man's bland and innocent eye: 'I did it because I wanted to be something more than just a number at Parchman.' "[32]

What he really wanted was another pardon for his efforts. And he might well have received one had not the media raised a fuss. The tradition of releasing a trusty who killed or wounded an "escaping" convict was as old as Parchman itself. A glance at the prison's musty discharge book shows case after case of one convict winning his freedom at the expense of another convict's life. In 1907, for example, trusty-shooter Robert Garrison was released "for meritorious service as guard, killing Silas Todd and wounding . . . a second convict attempting to escape with Todd." And George Pat was pardoned "for shooting and killing George Thomas trying to escape, both balls entering his head."[33]

In the early 1920s, the state legislature had redefined meritorious conduct to exclude the shooting of escapees after a rash of well-publicized killings. But problems quickly arose within the ranks of the trusties, who had come to count on their marksman's skills as a ticket out of Parchman. As their morale plummeted, the escape rate soared. For prison officials, the choice was clear enough: restore the old rules or hire professional guards to replace the trusties at a cost of almost $200,000 a year.[34]

The old rules were quietly restored. In 1929, Parchman superintendent J. W. Williamson wrote Governor Bilbo:

> A [negro] in the plow gang at Camp #8 broke and ran for freedom today, and was shot from a considerable distance by negro convict guard Andrew Coleman, #1104. This shot negro made the statement before being put to sleep on the operating table, that he was running to escape and that he intended to get away. . . .
>
> I feel that it is necessary to release this guard immediately to keep up the wonderful morale that now exists all over the institution among our guards.[35]

Bilbo knew what was at stake. He released Coleman at once.

The pardon requests for trusty-shooters provided ample evidence about their pasts. Most of them were like Hogjaw Grammar: violent men with nothing to lose. An escape attempt in 1933 showed this all too well. One summer afternoon, ninety prisoners and six trusties were returning to the barracks at Camp Eight when three men broke through the guard line and ran into the brush. "Convict guard Lindsey Matthews managed to stop prisoner Abe Jones without doing him any bodily harm," the superintendent noted, "[but] prisoners John Henry Nixon and Luther McCullough would not heed the command to stop. Convict guards Gus Black and Will Rutledge opened fire. A bullet from Rutledge's rifle stopped McCullough. The wound proved fatal, McCullough dying a few minutes later. A bullet from Black's rifle struck Nixon in the foot and he was apprehended without any further injury."

The superintendent then listed the crimes and sentences of the six men involved. The escapees were serving "three years for burglary," "seven years for burglary," and "five years for burglary and larceny." By contrast, the trusties were serving "life for murder," "life for murder," and "20-years for manslaughter." A few weeks later, the superintendent requested, and received, a pardon for the three convict guards.[36]

This tradition would continue into the 1970s, when a federal court finally stepped in to abolish the trusty system. At that time, a psychological profile of the trusties showed that 40 percent of them were mentally disabled and that 71 percent had serious personality disorders. "Armed inmate trustees, selected without objective criteria, [still] perform the primary guard function at Parchman," the court noted in 1972. "They . . . have shot, maimed, and physically mistreated scores of inmates subject to their control."[37]

On one point, however, Hogjaw Grammar would have disagreed. Whatever the failings of this brutal system, the main criterion for choosing its trusties had always been very clear. "I'm one scary son-of-a-bitch," said Hogjaw.

VI

Every so often, a newspaper story would appear about a local Negro serving an interminable sentence at Parchman because no one cared enough to get him out. As time went by and these stories piled up, the press began to describe a class of "forgotten men." In the 1930s, Governor Mike Conner decided to take a look for himself. Traveling to Parchman, he offered a personal hearing to any convict who had served a sentence of at least ten years. Conner called it a "mercy court." His opponents dubbed it an "amnesty for ancient coons."[38]*

More than a hundred convicts took advantage of the governor's offer. Most had been convicted of violent crimes—murder, manslaughter, and criminal assault. They were blacks who had killed other blacks in a drunken brawl, a game of chance, or a domestic dispute.

"What are you here for?" Conner asked an elderly inmate.

"I was shootin craps, cap'n, an' killed a nigger."

"Why did you kill him?"

"I made my point, suh, and he wouldn't recognize it."[39]

One of the convicts, seventy-three-year-old Tom ("Drybone") Robinson, had been sentenced to life in 1924 for beating his "woman" to death. Robinson did not deny the crime; he simply wondered, with a perverse kind of logic, why he had to go to Parchman for committing it. At the time of the murder, Drybone had been working as an enforcer on a large Delta plantation, keeping other Negroes in line. His job included collecting debts for the owner and preventing tenant families under contract from moving away. By his own count, Robinson had killed twelve people without ever being arrested. Each time, his "boss man" had interceded with the law.

Then a problem arose. The "boss man" died, Drybone killed again, and a judge sent him to Parchman Farm. Somehow this murderer's tale of woe made a deep impression on the governor. It may

---

* Conner was struck by the black children in prison stripes, a common sight at Parchman, where one inmate out of five was under twenty years of age. Among the boys who caught Conner's eye were Homer Reed, age twelve, Jabo Dean, twelve, and his brother Pratt Reed, eleven. All three had been convicted of grand larceny for stealing some merchandise at a store in Philadelphia, Mississippi. After lecturing the boys about honesty, Conner sent them home to their "mammies."

The Parchman Era

have been Robinson's advanced age, or his striking candor, or the fact that a Negro killing other Negroes was viewed as a trifling offense. Perhaps it was all three. On May 10, 1935, Tom Robinson walked out of Parchman a free man.[40]

Mixed in among the young thieves and elderly killers were a number of cases concerning the most explosive crime in Mississippi, rape. Governor Conner studied two of them at length. One case involved a black man and a white woman, the other a black man and a black child.

Charlie Bennett had been in Parchman for thirty-one of his forty-nine years. Arrested in 1905 for the attempted rape of a white woman in Winona, Mississippi, Bennett had been lucky to escape with his life. A local judge, fearing the worst, had rushed him to nearby Greenwood only hours before a mob had stormed the Winona jail carrying torches, kerosene, and a rope. Bennett needed armed protection just to make it into court for his arraignment.

As the case unfolded, the white jury began to have doubts. Bennett's eighteen-year-old accuser, Josie Hudson, had already earned a reputation around Winona as a "woman of bad repute." There were rumors that she fraternized with black men and even enticed them to her home. According to Hudson's account of the crime, she had crawled into bed one night to find a "kinky-haired" Negro already lying there. Her screams had awakened her father, who burst into her room to see a black man diving out the rear window. The muddy footprints led directly to Charlie Bennett's shack.[41]

Several jurors were skeptical of her story. They suspected some kind of consensual relationship, though they dared not say so in public. Sex between a black man and a white woman was the ultimate taboo. It could not be described as voluntary in a Southern courtroom; it had to be rape. So the jury ruled that "*Charlie Bennett,* on the 9th day of October, A.D., 1905, did violently and carnally ravish one *Josie Hudson,* a female, against her will." It fixed his punishment "at imprisonment in the State Penitentiary for life."[42]

Going Home

Bennett languished there for years. More than a decade passed before he filed an unsuccessful petition for pardon in 1920. It noted, as many others did, that Bennett had been a good worker at Parchman, and it contained a reference from his sergeant, calling him a "pretty-good nigger." Six years later Bennett tried again. This time his petition caught the eye of Governor Henry Whitfield, who asked an old friend in Winona, Judge Vernon Rowe, for details about the twenty-year-old case ("whether it was a white or negro woman, etc."). After talking to the long-time residents, Rowe offered his confidential opinion. Charlie Bennett, he wrote, "had been having sexual intercourse with a [white] woman with her consent."[43]

On the night in question, Rowe believed, the noise of their love-making had awakened Josie's father. As he approached her room, she had rushed Bennett out a window and begun screaming for help. Fearful of her father's violent reaction, Josie claimed that an unknown Negro had tried to rape her. The simple fact, Rowe concluded, was that Charlie Bennett had been framed by a "bad woman."

But nothing came of this. Governor Whitfield died suddenly in office, leaving no record of his feelings about the Bennett case. ("I believe he would have pardoned the negro," Rowe said later.) In the following years, Bennett scrawled personal appeals to three different governors, painfully pressing his case. "I have made a model prisner for 25 years," he pleaded in 1931, "and truly with all my heart will certonly apreciote what ever yo do for me in any way to help and I kinly ask you to please pardon me as I have no one to help me now Govnor. I am depending on you and only you for help."[44]

Governor Conner learned of Bennett's plight while making a routine visit to Winona in 1933. Judge Rowe told him that an innocent black man was now serving the twenty-ninth year of a life sentence at Parchman, because "nobody ever had enough interest in him to let the real facts . . . be known." When Conner expressed a willingness to look into the case, Rowe framed a new petition for Bennett with extraordinary care. At no point did it challenge the word of Josie Hudson or the verdict at the trial. Consensual sex was never mentioned. Instead, the petition humbled the convict and reaffirmed his "guilt." "Charlie Bennett has been sufficiently punished," it said, "for the crime he committed" in 1905.

The petition was supported by Winona's "best" white citizens. It even contained the signatures of the three remaining survivors of the mob that had tried to lynch Charlie Bennett at the Winona jail. But something more was needed, and getting it would not be easy. Because a white female had been "ravished" by a Negro, there had to be some assurance that the woman's kinfolk would not view the pardon as a blot upon the family's good name. Governor Conner wanted this matter put to rest before he made his next move.

In the following weeks, Winona's sheriff tracked down members of the Hudson clan. Josie had "wandered away" from town shortly after the trial, he wrote Governor Conner. Her father had died many years ago, and a brother had been murdered. There were only two relatives left in the county. "One is a sister who lives here in town, lives in a negro quarter, and associates with negroes. The other is a half brother who is as fine a citizen as Mississippi has. . . . He does not care if Charlie is turned out and told me if you wanted to write him in regard to this negro's pardon he would be glad to write you about same."[45]

Conner sent the letter at once. And C. A. Hudson proved good to his word. "I beg to state that I have no objections, whatever, to a pardon being granted to Charlie Bennett," he replied. "I think he has been sufficiently punished, and that a pardon is proper." The last hurdle had been cleared.

On his visit to Parchman in 1935, Governor Conner gave Charlie Bennett the good news: "an indefinite suspension of sentence, pending good behavior." Bennett had been in Parchman for thirty-one years, longer than anyone else. He was given a firm handshake by the warden, who told reporters what the governor himself had been unable to admit: "I am firmly convinced that this negro should never have been convicted."[46]

VII

The same words also could have been said about John Randolph, a black field hand sentenced to life at Parchman for raping a Negro girl, "about ten or eleven years old," near the Delta town of Drew, Mississippi, in the spring of 1920. Randolph did not know his age. He was thought to be about twenty-two when the "crime" occurred. At the time, the case against him seemed airtight. The girl and her foster mother had both identified Randolph as the rapist, and Randolph himself had pleaded guilty to the charge before the trial even began.

On the surface, his life sentence seemed harsh. The Mississippi courts did not normally consider the rape of one Negro by another to be a serious crime. But the victim had been a little girl, and that fact alone made Randolph a "dangerous" Negro whose sexual appetite might lead him one day to commit the ultimate outrage: the rape of a white woman or child.[47]

In 1926, Randolph filed his first petition for pardon in the local *Drew Leader*. But unlike Charlie Bennett, who dared not criticize his white accuser, Randolph now claimed to have been the "innocent victim" of a "malicious connival" between the black girl and her mother. He provided no proof for this reversal, because he had none. Convicts were always changing their stories and charging they had been framed. As a tactic for Southern Negroes, it rarely succeeded. Contrition was far more effective. Randolph's pardon was denied.[48]

In this case, however, the convict had been framed. There was no rape; mother and daughter had made up the story. Worst of all, Judge R. B. Smith, who handled the indictment, had discovered evidence of John Randolph's innocence almost immediately after the verdict was rendered. He simply never got around to fixing the problem until he read about Governor Conner's mercy court in the local newspaper. By that time, Randolph had been in Parchman for fifteen years.

In 1935, the judge wrote Conner a remarkable letter about the workings of justice in the Delta. John Randolph's case was not really unique, he explained, because the average black defendant, being too poor to hire a lawyer, had one appointed for him by the court. And the lawyer's primary function was not to serve his client but rather to save the county the time and expense of a public trial. Naturally, a "large percentage" of the cases never reached a jury. Instead, a deal was cut between the district attorney and the defendant's lawyer in which the "defendant enters a plea of guilty, and accepts so many years, or perhaps life, in the state penitentiary." If the Negro happened to be innocent—"we are all human and make many mistakes," the judge acknowledged—then a white "friend" would take up the case and help him win a pardon. If he did not have a white friend, "Well: he is just there!"[49]

John Randolph had been one of those "many mistakes." At his mercy trial on March 27, 1935, he was asked about the alleged rape:

Randolph. I was going with a woman named Nora and this girl was working for her and I caught [Nora] giving another man my money. I told her I was going to quit her. In about three weeks I caught her again and quit her. I quit her for another woman and Nora . . . turned around and had me arrested, claimed I had raped this little girl.

Conner. Were you guilty?

Randolph. Governor, your honor, they found me guilty but I was not guilty. . . .

Conner. Did you plead guilty?

Randolph. The lawyer told me if I didn't plead guilty they would hang me.

Going Home

Conner. Did you hire a lawyer or did they appoint one?

Randolph. They appointed one.[50]

Conner asked the convict if he had ever "given up hope":

Randolph. Yes, sir. I had nobody to do nothing for me; and if none of you good white folks won't do nothing for me, I am lost.

Conner. Do you know anybody who would help you prove [your innocence]?

Randolph. Yes sir. Here he is.

Conner. You brought a witness with you?

Randolph. Yes, sir.

The witness was Judge R. B. Smith. He had come to Parchman, at long last, to take up Randolph's cause:

Conner. Tell me what you know.

Smith. This negro was brought before me in February 1920 accused of rape. . . . Nora [Washington] was the main prosecutor. . . . She testified against him. So did the little girl. Pretty damaging testimony. All I could do was to hold him and await action of the grand jury. They indicted him and gave him life.

The very next year, Smith continued, he had gone to Rome, Mississippi, to "try a negro up there for attempted rape." To his surprise, the "victim" in the case turned out to be none other than Nora Washington's little girl. "I suspected something [was wrong]," the judge recalled, "so I had a local doctor examine this child. He said she had never been entered."

Though Smith dismissed the rape case in Rome, he did nothing to help John Randolph, who languished in prison. Conner was furious. He pushed the judge hard. "Did you ever call this to the attention of the Governor?"

The Parchman Era

Smith. No, sir.

Conner. That was 13 [*sic*] years ago. . . . This is a horrible thing to think about.

In handing John Randolph his pardon, however, the governor took a more traditional line. There was nothing wrong with the way Mississippi treated its Negroes, he said, but "plenty wrong" with the way its Negroes treated each other. "If you are innocent, the law did not send you here, and the courts did not send you here," the governor intoned. "It was done by your own color who testified against you." John Randolph dared not disagree. "Yes, sir. Yes, sir," he kept repeating, his eyes frozen to the ground. This was the price of freedom, and it had to be dutifully paid.[51]

Randolph left Parchman that afternoon with forty other "forgotten men." No transportation had been provided for them and no civilian clothes. They were "clad in their prison overalls," a witness observed, "with scarcely a bundle in their possession. Some said they would hitchhike to their destinations. Others said they would call on friends."

John Randolph had no clear destination and no one to call. He was last seen walking down the two-lane blacktop in the blazing Delta sun.

✠

CHAPTER NINE

Executioner's Song

It ain't but one thing I done wrong,
I stayed in Mississippi just a day too long.

—Parchman prison song

I

On a warm October afternoon in 1940, a white ex-convict named Jimmy Thompson drove his brand new pickup truck to the state capitol grounds in Jackson, where a large crowd had gathered to meet him. The pickup, costing $4,000, had been carefully outfitted in Memphis at the public's expense. It contained a switchboard, a generator, six hundred feet of cable wire, and a big wooden chair with three straps to hold a body in place. A journalist described the vehicle as the "weirdest rolling stock that ever streaked down a highway." Jimmy Thompson called it his personal "killing machine."[1]

With the crowd around him, Thompson explained how it worked. His pitch was so compelling—he had toured the Southern carnival circuit as "Dr. Alzedi Yogi, world famous hypnotist" after serving a stretch for armed robbery at Parchman—that several of the spectators fainted when he turned on the power. As one newspaper

205

The Parchman Era

reported: "The only thing lacking at Thursday's formal and public exhibition of the state's new electric chair . . . was a victim."[2]

Thompson, age forty-four, was Mississippi's first traveling executioner, a position created in response to the public's growing opposition to the gallows. In the 1930s, a series of bungled hangings had led to calls for a change. With electrocution now viewed as a more humane and dignified substitute, state officials had hoped to centralize the process by housing a permanent electric chair at Parchman. But problems quickly arose. For one thing, executions in Mississippi had long been a local affair, occurring in the counties where the crime had been committed. For another, the residents of Sunflower County did not relish the idea of a "death house" on their home turf. "Place that thing at Parchman," warned a local politician, "and you will have riots and a wholesale breakout to descend hundreds of criminals down upon our people."[3]

As a compromise, the state legislature decided on a portable electric chair, a truly American contribution to capital punishment. Thompson's job was to drive this contraption from county to county in order to implement the death sentences handed down by the state courts. Paid one hundred dollars per execution, plus expenses, he "juiced" his first victim—"a little, sawed-off, tar-colored wife-killer named Willie Mae Bragg"—in Lucedale, Mississippi, on October 11, 1940.

The execution drew rave reviews. Local newspapers carried photographs of the event with meticulous explanations. "At the left, Bragg sits in the chair and looks on as guards strap his arms," wrote the *Jackson Clarion-Ledger*. "The picture at the right was made as the first flash of electricity surged through his body. . . . Note Bragg's hands gripping the chair and his neck bulging in death's throes." Jimmy Thompson took a less clinical approach. The victim departed "with tears in his eyes," he explained, "for the efficient care I took to give him a good clean burning."[4]

Executioner's Song

The portable electric chair would remain in use until 1955, when Mississippi brought its executions under state control and a gas chamber was constructed at Parchman. In that fifteen-year period, seventy-three people were put to death: fifty-six black males, sixteen white males, and one black woman. Most of these executions were held inside the county jail so as to avoid the public spectacles of the past, yet people often surrounded the building to listen for telltale signs of Jimmy Thompson's work. Author Florence Mars recalled the execution of a killer in her hometown of Philadelphia, Mississippi, in 1942: "A crowd gathered late at night on the courthouse square with chairs, crackers, and children, waiting for the current to be turned on and the street lights to dim."[5]

Thompson took great pride in his work. His goal was to give each victim the "prettiest death a guy can have." That meant keeping his equipment in top shape, treating the electrodes with "salt solutions," and fitting them "very tight and snug." "Condemned men seem to trust me," said Thompson, "and I never let 'em down."[6]

But some executions proved harder than others. Thompson claimed that rapists needed "more voltage" than murderers, because of their strength and sexual drive. And the "condemned men" he spoke about were not always adults. In 1947, two fourteen-year-old Negroes were given death sentences for the pistol slaying of a white lumberman in Woodville, Mississippi. When the governor refused to intervene, the boys' attorney offered Thompson some caustic advice. "I suggest that you seat them as we do our children at the dinner table," he said, "that you place books underneath them in order that their heads shall be the proper height to receive the death current; and I further urge that the books used for this purpose be the 'Age of Reason,' 'The Rise of Democracy in America,' a copy of the 'Constitution of the United States,' and an appropriately bound edition of the Holy Bible."[7]

Thompson was not amused. He electrocuted the boys an hour

apart at the Wilkinson County jail. A job was a job, after all, and this one—"a double-header," he called it—earned him two hundred dollars for a quick morning's work.[8]

II

For several hundred convicted felons, capital punishment became the fatal alternative to Parchman Farm. As expected, the process was deeply rooted in race. According to a comprehensive report of legal executions in Mississippi, blacks accounted for 87 percent of the 433 people put to death there since the Civil War, a figure slightly above the Southern average of 80 percent. The report listed the crimes for which blacks had been executed (331 males and 4 females for murder, 33 males for rape, 8 males for armed robbery), as well as the race of their victims (41 percent of the murders, 85 percent of the rapes, and all of the armed robberies were committed against whites). Not surprisingly, black-on-white crime—a marginal phenomenon in comparison to black-on-black crime—accounted for more than half of the legal executions in Mississippi.[9]

Of the sixty-one whites put to death in this period, all were convicted murderers, and all but one had killed another white (or whites). What this meant, among other things, was that every single person executed for rape and armed robbery in Mississippi was a Negro and that only one white person had ever been executed for an interracial crime. His name was Mel Cheatham.[10]

In the summer of 1889, Cheatham was tried and convicted for the murder of James Tillman, a plantation worker known to whites as a "good," "reliable" "inoffensive," "churchgoing" Negro. Cheatham had ambushed Tillman on a lonely road, killed him with a shotgun blast, and dumped his body into the Yalobusha River, near Granada, Mississippi, where it was found caught on a log. "There was no mystery to the murder," wrote a local historian. "Everyone in the little community knew who had killed [the Negro] and why." Tillman had just told a grand jury about the notorious gambling den that Cheatham ran behind his general store, and he was set to testify again. In this particular case, the black man spoke for law and order, so his death could not easily be ignored.[11]

The jury took less than an hour to decide. Cheatham went to the gallows on March 19, 1890. He walked briskly, "made a short prayer, said 'Boys, good-bye,' then firmly, 'I am ready.' Sheriff Jones cut the rope holding the trap with one clean stroke of a hatchet, and Mel J. Cheatham dropped into eternity, strangling slowly when the fall failed to break his neck."[12]

III

Scholars have long debated the relationship between lynchings and executions. Did these lethal punishments complement each other or serve as alternatives? Did their numbers rise and fall in tandem (the "reinforcement" effect), or did an increase in one mean a decrease in the other (the "substitution" effect)? Or was there no correlation at all?[13]

On the surface, Mississippi appears to provide a textbook example of the substitution effect. Between 1882 and 1930, it experienced more lynchings (463) and fewer executions (239) than any other state in the Deep South. Yet these totals are deceiving, for they are not spread evenly over time. In the first decade of the twentieth century—the turbulent era dominated by James K. Vardaman—Mississippi witnessed an absolute flood of lynchings *and* legal executions. In 1902 alone, nine blacks were murdered by local mobs, while five whites and twenty-one blacks were legally hanged—the highest combined total ever recorded by an individual state in a single year. This suggests, of course, that both lynchings and legal executions rose dramatically in times of racial stress. Lethal punishment signaled social control.[14]

Furthermore, the attempt to separate lynchings from legal execu-

The Parchman Era

tions may well be futile, for the line between them is sometimes narrow, at best. Mississippi was among the last states to abolish public executions and to bring them under state control. As a result, these events frequently resembled mob actions in which a predetermined verdict was followed by a gruesome carnival of death.

There are numerous examples. In 1934, as national attention was riveted upon the fate of nine black youths accused of raping two white women near Scottsboro, Alabama, authorities in Mississippi arrested three Negroes for "criminally assaulting" a white high school student named Mildred Collins in the town of Hernando, fifteen miles south of Memphis. The suspects, described in local press reports as "black terrorists" and "lust-craven wretches," were tracked down after a frantic manhunt involving "practically every law enforcement officer" in northern Mississippi.[15]

Determined to avoid a multiple lynching, Governor Mike Conner ordered the prisoners held in Jackson until the day of their trial. In February 1934, the "heavily shackled negroes" were taken from their cells, marched to the train station by dozens of national guardsmen, placed in a steel baggage car, and transported north to Hernando, a distance of two hundred miles. The train made several stops along the way to pick up additional troops. It was met in Hernando by a large detachment of guardsmen from Clarksdale, Greenville, and other Delta towns.

In all, more than 350 soldiers ringed the De Soto County courthouse, where the young men went on trial for their lives The scene was reminiscent of a war zone, with barbed wire, machine-gun emplacements, and soldiers in full battle gear with fixed bayonets. Yet the crowd of several thousand refused to back down. There was so much firepower on both sides that General T. J. Grayson, the commanding officer, struck a desperate bargain with the girl's father, C. W. Collins. In return for a note from Collins asking the mob to go home, Grayson would use his influence to see that the father got to kill these "niggers" *himself* by acting as the hangman at their execution.

The bargain seemed to work. The crowd slowly dispersed after hearing Collins's words. ("No matter what passions well up in the breast of all of us," his note read, "I hope and pray no attempt will be made to interfere with the natural and normal course of the courts in this case.") The only reported casualty was Sheriff W. M. Birmingham, who died of a heart attack attributed by local doctors to "mental and physical exertion."[16]

The trial itself was an afterthought. The jury took seven minutes to find the defendants guilty, and the judge sentenced them to death. The three Negroes—Isaac Howard, twenty-five; Ernest McGehee, twenty-two; and Johnnie Jones, twenty-one—offered no defense. "We was drinking, I guess that was the reason," Howard was quoted as saying. "We intended just to rob [her] but this other thing just got into our minds."[17]

But then a problem arose. Word of the private bargain at Hernando reached the state attorney general, who ruled that Mr. Collins could not be deputized as the hangman because he did not reside in De Soto County, site of the planned executions. The ruling set off a furor; it seemed to violate the code of personal vengeance and family honor that many held dear. Within days, state senator H. Clay Collins, a cousin of the assault victim, proposed a remarkable piece of legislation that gave each county sheriff the authority to appoint any Mississippi resident as an executioner. His so-called "hanging bill" passed the state senate by a vote of eighteen to fifteen.

Some residents did not exactly welcome this privilege. The bill was not only barbaric, they believed; it also embarrassed Mississippi on the national stage. Did civilized people settle private scores by hanging each other? sniffed the *Clarion-Ledger*. Of course not! Retribution was honorable *only* when exacted by representatives of the law. "There is a vast difference between a sheriff impersonally performing this grim duty, as a duty," it said, "and another citizen performing it to satisfy personal vengeance."[18]

Such criticism stalled the bill's momentum. House leaders quietly tabled the measure, fearing the dreadful publicity it would bring. "There will be no legalized butchery in Mississippi, no matter who favors it," fumed Walter Sillers, chairman of the House Judiciary Committee. "This bill is not civilized."[19]

Shortly after midnight on March 17, the condemned men were brought back to Hernando to be hanged. A reporter traveling in the huge motor convoy described them as remarkably composed. Isaac Howard chanted the words "Lawd, Lawd, Lawd, Jesus, Jesus, Jesus," over and over again. "I ai'nt 'fraid o' no mob but I don't like that rope," he whispered. "If I had a razor I'd cut my throat. I don' wanna walk out of dem gallus."[20]

As a security measure, the new sheriff, Roscoe Lauderdale, had moved up the execution from 11:00 A.M. to daybreak without informing the town. Howard, McGehee, and Jones were allowed a last meal of ham and eggs and a visit with a minister. "It remained for Rev. Roberts, a Negro Methodist preacher, to elicit from the condemned blacks the admission that the death penalty in their case is one of justice," wrote a white reporter on the scene. With that, he added, "spiritual hymns were sung by the negroes with an effectiveness peculiar to their race."[21]

Word of the early executions circulated quickly through the town. At dawn, as the prisoners were led in shackles to the prison yard, a crowd of several hundred already surrounded the gallows. Sheriff Lauderdale acted as the hangman, with C. W. Collins standing at his side. "The spectacle went on for over an hour," a witness noted, and the father "smiled through it all."[22]

One by one, the condemned blacks confessed to their sins and warned others away from temptation. "Don't do what I've done," McGehee told the crowd. "Let alone them things that don't concern you." And one by one, they broke into song as the black hood was placed over their heads. Isaac Howard went first, singing "I'm ready to Go." He was "midway through the second stanza when Sheriff Lauderdale pulled the lever."

Things did not go smoothly. The trap stuck, and Howard remained standing. He dropped on the second try, but the rope proved too short, leaving him barely conscious for fifteen minutes until his heart stopped beating. It took even longer for Ernest McGehee to die. ("Aw, hell," someone yelled, "knock him on the head with a hammer.") Sweating deputies lengthened the rope and smeared it with grease. When Johnnie Jones mounted the platform, all was finally in order. The snap of his broken neck could be heard a block away.

The three corpses were packed in rough wood coffins, tossed into a pick-up, and driven to the Negro cemetery. Dozens of whites followed the truck in a noisy procession of honking automobiles. As the dirt was being shoveled, the crowd serenaded a small group of mourners. Their song was "Bye, Bye, Blackbird."[23]

IV

Public executions made powerful theater. They had their own cast of characters—the judge, the sheriff, the minister, the grieving families, the condemned—and a common set of scenes. First came the long procession through the dense, howling crowd, sometimes five thousand strong. There followed the climb to the gallows, the admission of guilt (or protest of innocence), the final prayer, the placement of the hood, the slam of the trap, the deafening roar. Public executions were akin to festivals in rural Mississippi, with merchants hawking their goods under colorful awnings and political candidates debating one another from the scaffold itself. Food and drink were everywhere, as a New York journalist discovered while attending an execution near Starkville in 1915. "The people are to be congratulated on their healthy appetites," he mused. "Doubtless public killings are becoming commonplace when a mob can witness one and not miss a mouthful of its lunch."[24]

Public hangings are part of Mississippi folklore, a mosaic of fact and legend and faded memories. In 1901, a white man named Clyde Harveston rode to the gallows in an ox-drawn cart, seated upon a box that was to be his coffin. When offered a last chance to speak, he shouted: "My hands are free of human blood and God will give you a sign that I am telling the truth!" At that very instant, water poured down from a cloudless sky. They hanged Clyde Harveston in the rain.[25]

Others were more fortunate. In 1894, the town of Columbia, Mississippi, prepared to hang Will Purvis, leader of a white vigilante group that terrorized "successful Negroes" in the area. Purvis had been convicted of killing a local planter who objected to the whipping of one of his black servants by another white man. Purvis admitted to the whipping but not to the murder. On the scaffold, he made a final plea: "You are taking the life of an innocent man."

Seconds later, Purvis dropped through the trap. But the rope failed to hold him, and he crashed hard to the dirt floor below. As Purvis arose, dazed and bleeding, a preacher rushed to his aid. "All who want to see this boy hanged a second time," he yelled, "hold up your hands."

The crowd was silent. Not a hand went up. "All who are opposed to hanging Will Purvis a second time," cried the preacher, "hold up your hands." First a few, then dozens, then hundreds responded. Hands shot up, someone recalled, "as if magically raised by a universal lever."

The local sheriff intervened. The law required that Purvis be "hanged by the neck until dead," he declared, and the law must be obeyed. But the heavily armed crowd would have none of this, and he sheriff backed off. Purvis was returned to his jail cell, where he remained for several years until pardoned by the governor. In 1917, another man, on his deathbed, confessed to the killing. Will Purvis was voted $5,000 by the Mississippi legislature as compensation for the time he had "wrongly spent" behind bars.[26]

In most cases, these executions had strong public support. They were outlets for community vengeance, community warnings, community rage. And they remained alive as physical reminders of subordination and racial caste.

For condemned blacks in Mississippi there were no happy endings, no last-minute reprieves. In place of a Will Purvis one finds men like George Walton, a "one-legged darkey" sentenced to death for shooting another Negro in an argument over a woman. Walton was hanged in front of thousands of spectators, white and black, after confessing on the scaffold and reciting a prayer. According to press accounts, it took three tries to kill him. Amazingly, Walton mouthed his confession before each failed attempt. At one point, after dangling for almost two minutes, he whispered, "For God's sake, take me down and hang me again!" The final try took fifteen minutes, with Walton "kicking in the air and suffering untold agony." His head almost fell from his body, which was "placed in a coffin and buried immediately near the spot."[27]

In 1902, two men were hanged in Oxford, Mississippi, for the brutal murder of a white girl. They surely would have been lynched had not the sheriff promised to hold the trial, the sentencing, and the execution without a moment's delay. The dusty streets were clogged with ice cream and lemonade vendors, an observer noted, and a "striking feature of the crowd was the large number of women, young and old, who accompanied their fathers, husbands, and brothers . . . for the express purpose of seeing two young men die an ignoble death on the gallows."

Though double hangings were not uncommon in Mississippi, this one had a novel twist. For the first time in the state's history, men of different races were executed side by side for the same offense. And their behavior, according to local newspaper accounts, conformed to the racial stereotypes of the time. Orlando Lester, "a fine specimen of negro, coal black in color, with very smooth skin," was portrayed as a calm, untroubled savage, who, having cheerfully admitted his guilt, was quite prepared to die. Lester said a few parting words to the people, blaming whiskey for his crimes. The crowd responded with cries of "Kill that nigger three or four times" and "Hang him up by the heels." A huge roar was heard as he plunged through the trap.

The white prisoner, William Mathis, looked "nervous" and "grim." He said little and appeared to be "ashamed" of what he had done. At the last moment, Mathis glanced at his suffering young wife, a model of Southern womanhood in her white sunbonnet and faded blue dress. "Her complexion is clear and beautiful," the newspaper reported, "and her white teeth show clearly behind perfectly formed lips of sensual redness. With the advantages of culture and fashion, she could have been a reigning beauty." When the trap door opened for William Mathis, the crowd was more subdued. Though few would mourn his violent passing, there seemed to be genuine sympathy for the shame he had brought upon his family and for their visible presence at his death.[28]

Executions were meant for men. Only four women were ever put to death in Mississippi, and their similarities were clear.* All were black; all were executed with a male Negro accomplice; all were convicted of gruesome killings; and all but one of their victims were white. In 1922, Pattie Perdue and Leon Viverett were hanged for the slaying of Alton Page, a white man whose body had been hacked to pieces, burned in a stove, and buried in a Negro cemetery. A lynching was barely avoided. In 1937, Mary Holmes and Selmon ("Dad") Brooks went to the gallows for killing a prominent white planter in a

---

* Very few women have been legally executed in the United States. Most states have not executed a single female since 1924 (when accurate statistics on capital punishment generally begin). That includes such leaders in the field as Texas, which executed more than 350 males in this period, and Florida, which executed more than 200. Georgia executed one woman out of more than 400, and North Carolina two out of more than 300.

burglary attempt. Seven years later, Mildred James was electrocuted for the murder of an "aged [white] spinster" in Vicksburg. "She gave only one quick, slight start as the current hit her the first time," a newspaper reported, "and relaxed as the body slumped down into the chair."[29]

Ann Knight was the only one of these women to be executed for killing a fellow black. She and Will Grey, her male "consort," had shotgunned Knight's husband John in order to "get him out of the way." But John Knight bore a "good reputation" with local whites, who wanted justice done. As always, the local press described this double execution in graphic detail. "Will's neck was clearly broken," wrote the *Greene County Herald*, "there being some blood exuded from his mouth afterwards and bones separated from his head. It was not so clear as to Ann's neck being broken, she having a fat neck, but as her death was quicker than the man's it was thought that . . . the weight of her body [caused] a vertebra [to] slip."[30]

V

In *Deep South,* a brilliant and long-forgotten study of "Negro life" in Natchez in the 1930s, authors Allison Davis, Burleigh Gardner, and Mary Gardner tell the story of two black convicts awaiting execution in the county jail. Nathan had murdered his wife; Roy had killed his wife and her father. (Although the authors protected their sources, it is not difficult to match Nathan with Obediah McKnight and Roy with Phil Williams. Both men were executed in Natchez in December 1934.)[31] Naturally, the authorities expected both men to confess their crimes, express their sorrow, and seek the Lord's forgiveness. These were essential parts of the "execution ceremony," the authors explained, because they upheld the "supreme powers" of God and racial caste, while absolving the white community of "any guilt or injustice" that might accompany the taking of Negro lives.[32]

Nathan did what was expected of him. He welcomed black ministers into his cell and "got religion." He was "ready to go." On the night before Nathan's execution, a white deputy said: "I guess all the preachers around here have been with him today. I have talked with him a lot, and he has told me about the crime several times; he says the Devil got in his path, and he lost his temper and killed his wife. He admits he did it all right."

But Roy was different; he would not budge. He was a "hard sinner" and a "bad negro" because he refused to confess, or apologize, or reach out to the Lord. "He has never gotten religion . . . ," a deputy complained. "I asked him the other day if he was ready for the long journey, told him it would be a mighty long trip and he ought to pray and make his peace before it started. . . . We had a preacher . . . work on him . . . but he said he 'couldn't do no good, the Devil had sealed Roy's mouth so he couldn't pray.' "[33]

The authorities kept pressing Roy, to no avail. He rejected the pleadings of the judge who sentenced him, the ministers, white and black, who visited him, and a popular Catholic priest. By refusing to pray or to repent, Roy had sabotaged a ritual of tremendous importance in the Deep South. On December 7, 1934, the *Natchez Democrat* described his execution in measured terms. "Outwardly calm and making no statement," it began, "Phil Williams (Roy), negro, was yesterday hanged in the county jail." Williams "declined to see any minister," the report went on, noting that he had brazenly requested "cigars and chicken and dumplings" for his final meal.[34]

The black community handled these deaths in very different ways. Both men were killers, and their punishment did not seem out of line, but Roy was cast as a hero for resisting white authority, while Nathan was seen as a coward for accepting his subordinate caste role. "Dis' guy Nathan, he war chicken-hearted lak," said a man who visited the body at a local funeral home. "Dey tell me he couldn't get enough religion." A fellow standing alongside him agreed. "Nathan wazn' nervy lak the firs' one. The fis' didn't change at all, but a man at the jail tol' me that this felluh was jus' about dead when they went to get him this morning. They say he jus' folded right up an' they had to lif him up."[35]

Stories of Roy's brave defiance—some false, most exaggerated—seemed to pop up everywhere. "Dey couldn' mek him talk about no religion or nuthin' lak dat," said one admirer. "[He] went up on dem galluhs with jes' what he had in himself, you see what I mean. Not whut preachin' an' a lot of singin' and prayin' an stuff had put in him." A favorite story had Roy calmly telling Nathan that they would meet again in a different place. ("He say dat on his way to die!") Another had Roy "bustin' down" the door to hell and "breakin' off de Devil's horns."[36]

To many blacks in Natchez, Roy had become a living example, an authentic version, of the mythical black outlaw known as Stagolee. In the songs of Delta bluesmen, Stagolee was no Kinnie Wagner—no champion of the common people with noble instincts and a heart of gold. Stagolee was a "ba-ad nigger," a "mean son-of-a-bitch," who frightened everyone and lived by his own set of rules:

> Now Stackerlee, he was a bad man,
> He wanted the whole world to know,
> He toted a .32-20
> And a smokeless .44.

Stagolee killed when he was angry, or irritable, or for no reason at all:

> Say, boys,
> What do you think of that?
> Stackolee killed his best friend
> Bout a five-dollar Statson hat.
> Oh bad man. Stackolee.

Sheriffs feared him:

> The high sheriff said, "Go bring me
> dat bad man Staggerlee here."
> The deputy pulled off his pistols and
> he laid them on the shelf.
> And said, "If you want dat bad man
> you got to go 'rest him by yo'self."

And judges too:

> Stackolee was on the gallows,
> He got mad and cussed.
> The judge said, "Maybe we better hang him
> Fo he kills one of us."
> Oh that bad Stackolee.

But he was not easy to kill:

> De hangman put de mask on,
> tied his han's behin' his back,
> Spring de trap on Stagolee,
> but his neck refused to crack.

And he made hell itself a more dangerous place:

> When de devil wife see Stack comin'
> she got up in a quirl,—
> "Here come dat bad nigger
> an' he's jus' from de udder worl'."

> All de devil' little chillun
> went scamblin' up de wall,
> Say, "Catch him pappa,
> befo' he kill us all." . . .

Stagolee took up de pitchfork
an he laid it on de shelf—
"Stand back, Tom Devil,
I'm gonna rule Hell by myself."[37]

Like Stagolee, Roy killed for the sheer pleasure of it, showing no hint of remorse. Like Stagolee, he defied white rules and rituals, staying fearless to the end. And like Stagolee, he allowed a powerless community to live vicariously through his feats. A local Negro said it well: "Roy wasn't much good at livin,' but he knew how to die."

VI

For all of Roy's defiance, his victims had been black. What most frightened the white community were the rare instances in which a Negro killed "outside" his own race, showing no fear, not hint of deference, no remorse. The crime and execution of Alonzo Robinson, alias James Coyner, was that very nightmare come true.

On a winter's night in 1934, a young white farm couple from Cleveland, Mississippi, deep in the Delta, were found murdered in their home. Aurelius Turner had been shot through the head, his pregnant wife bludgeoned with a hammer. Her body had been "horribly mutilated," said the *Bolivar Commercial,* with "large pieces of flesh cut out and taken away by the fiend who committed the murder." A few weeks later, Alonzo Robinson was arrested at the Cleveland post office after mailing a slew of obscene letters to local white women. A search of his quarters turned up a box containing Mrs. Turner's body parts. He then confessed to the murders.[38]

White authorities could take some small comfort in Robinson's background. Born in the Delta, he had moved to Indiana and Ohio as a young man. He was well educated and well spoken—in short, a foreigner, an "uppity nigger" contaminated by Northern racial experiences and ideas. To prevent a lynching, the governor brought the suspect to Jackson to await his trial. It came quickly. Inside the courtroom, Robinson looked bored and sleepy as the state militia patrolled the streets. When asked if he had regrets, he said, "No, no more than if I had spilled a glass of milk. What's done is done. What's bothering me now is that this jailhouse is cold."[39]

Robinson's crime and demeanor were a shocking departure from traditional ways. The local newspapers barely mentioned the case once it was solved. The trial itself was quick and rigidly formal. According to one account, blacks showed far more interest in the proceedings than whites, who wished only to have it go away. It was as if both races understood that a sick, cold-blooded Negro had brutalized an innocent white family in much the same manner that sick, cold-blooded whites had been brutalizing innocent Negroes for years.[40]

Robinson was hanged at four o'clock one morning to "minimize outside interference." He declined a minister, made no final statement, and showed "not the slightest trace of nervousness" as the rope was placed around his neck. Asked if he had made his peace and was "ready to go," Robinson uttered his last words. "One time," he said, "is as good as another."[41]

✠

CHAPTER TEN

A Farm with Slaves

While confinement, even at hard labor and without compensation, is not necessarily cruel and unusual punishment, it may be so when conditions and practices become so bad as to be shocking to conscience of reasonably civilized people.

—Federal District Judge William C. Keady, 1972

I

The evolving method of execution—from the gallows to the electric chair to the gas chamber in 1954—marked a major reform in Mississippi, where events moved glacially in matters of punishment and race. At Parchman, nothing seemed to change; the years turned to decades in an environment almost frozen in time. In 1925, Superintendent Jim "Big Boss" Williamson expressed a lonely complaint in his biennial report to the legislature: "If Mississippi is to take rank with many of the more progressive states in caring for her prisoners, she must get away from the idea that Parchman is alone a profit making machine . . . and realize her obligation to society and to those who are making this profit for the State." Exactly thirty-two years and six superintendents later, another Parchman official expressed the identical sentiment in *his* biennial report: "We realize that our farming is excellent and is very necessary, but our young men whom we are responsible for rehabilitating, need something more than a plow or hoe. Which is more valuable, a bale of cotton or a citizen returned to society?"[1]

The answer was obvious. Blacks came to Parchman as field workers and left the same way. That was their lot in life. Anything more was anathema in a culture where white supremacy and unskilled Negro labor went hand in hand. In Mississippi, rehabilitation was a dangerous word.

For most of its existence, Parchman remained a stable and profitable operation, dependent on the rhythms of nature and the fortunes of King Cotton. During the Great Depression, the prison ran its first deficit when farm prices collapsed.* This was the worst time to be a prisoner at Parchman, a time of severe overcrowding and neglect, with inmates forced to sleep on the floors of the primitive cages. A sense of their deprivation was provided by a local newspaper headline in 1934: "State Convicts Will Get Shoes."[2]

But the coming of World War II brought a wild demand for cotton, and the Delta plantations boomed. In the 1940s, Parchman generated profits of almost a million dollars a year. The good times lasted into the 1950s, when an increase in foreign competition and the use of synthetic fibers depressed cotton prices once again. Still, the autumn harvest at Parchman was an extraordinary sight, as inmates picked the fields clean, battered trucks delivered raw cotton to Front

---

* Like so many of the large Delta plantations, Parchman took part in the New Deal's federal farm programs designed to raise agricultural prices by cutting back on production. "This year, complying with the Government Cotton Acreage Reduction Program," wrote Parchman's superintendent in 1933, "the penitentiary abandoned 4,150 acres of its cotton crop. The Government will pay the State for 2,000 bales of cotton destroyed on the land rented by them through this program." Parchman received more than $75,000 from the federal government in 1933, a figure surpassed only by the $115,000 allotted to its huge Delta neighbor, the 38,000 Delta and Pine Land Company.

A Farm with Slaves

Camp, "the gins hummed, buyers gathered around the administration building, and stuffed box cars swayed as they lumbered toward the processing plants of Memphis, New Orleans, and the Mississippi Delta."[3]

Parchman's inmate population remained steady in these years, at around fifty women and two thousand men. As a labor-intensive plantation, it depended far less on the tractors and cotton-picking machines that revolutionized Southern agriculture—and spurred the black migration North—after World War II. Well into the 1960s, Parchman hand-picked much of its cotton on the grounds that "the product is cleaner, the crop is picked more completely, and a tired cotton-picking inmate is less likely to promote mischief than one who stands around watching a machine do his job."[4]

Prison officials defended their philosophy by noting that, profits aside, the convicts were fed more, disciplined better, and driven no harder than field workers at other plantations in the state. "I lived on a farm until I was 21 years of age," claimed the prison chaplain, "and I know that the work day at Parchman is no longer and the work no more difficult than it was for me while I lived on a farm. A good, honest day's work is all that is expected or required of any prisoner." When a criminology professor at Ole Miss claimed that convicts were being mistreated at Parchman, Governor Hugh White told him to shut up or face dismissal, adding that prisons were "not like the Y.M.C.A." And when Hodding Carter's *Delta Democrat-Times* railed against "rampant brutality" at the farm, Superintendent Marvin Wiggins banned Carter's entire staff from the premises, claiming they were too "disreputable" to enter the gates.

In response, Carter suggested that a group of editors judge his newspaper, while a group of penologists judge Parchman. "Whoever gets the low score should take ten from 'Black Annie . . . ,' " he quipped. "We feel ourselves getting sorry for Marvin's backside already. But on second thought, since we don't believe in the lash like

Marvin does, we suggest as a substitute if he loses, he be required to read a book on present–day penal methods."[5]

II

Carter's view had little public support in Mississippi. Most whites thought of Parchman as a model prison, and the press carried endless stories of its profitable ways: "Parchman Is A Self-Supporting Institution," "Penitentiary Crops in Excellent Shape," "Prison System Puts Money in State Coffers and Makes Inmates Healthy." "Mississippians," gushed a reporter from the *Memphis Commercial-Appeal,* "you have a wonderful penal institution down at Parchman."[6]

Mississippi's most celebrated authors took a more measured approach. William Faulkner lived in Oxford, only eighty miles east of the farm. "Everyone around here knows about Parchman," said an Oxford resident, and "everyone knows someone who has served time there." That list included E. J. Banks, who escaped four times from Parchman while serving a life term for murder, and A. J. Tabor, who refused a pardon from Governor Bilbo in 1932 after spending seventeen years at the prison. "You can't beat this place for comfort," Tabor declared, "and I'll be right here when the Lord calls me."[7]

Many of Faulkner's characters spent long stretches at Parchman, mostly for murder. In Faulkner's view, the prison represented both a throwback to slave times and an escape from the pain and responsibilities of the modern world. The inmates toiled in isolation, reasonably well fed and cared for, "doing the only work they knew how to do." In Faulkner's *Old Man,* the "tall convict" remembers "the barracks at night with screens against the bugs in summer and good stoves in winter and someone to supply the fuel and the food too. . . ." In *The Mansion,* Mink Snopes, a convicted killer, toils "in the rich black cotton land" of Parchman, memorizing the rules that will keep him alive: "To do whatever they tell me to do. Not to talk back to anybody. Not to get into any fights. That's all I got to do for jest twenty-five or maybe even jest twenty years."[8]

A character in Shelby Foote's 1950 novel, *Follow Me Down*, describes Parchman in much the same way. "They have no cells . . . no walls, no barbed wire. . . . It's a . . . plantation like back in slavery days—eighteen thousand acres, mostly cotton. . . . You go out in the morning, eat in the field, and come back at sundown. . . . It ain't bad. Stay in line, you'll be all right. Otherwise the sergeant's got a strap—Black Annie."[9]

These portraits partly resembled the ones provided by the convicts themselves. But the long-time inmates remembered a parallel environment in which dawn-to-dusk labor was rewarded with assorted pleasures from outside. In daylight, the smart convict did his work, deferred to authority, and "stayed in line." At night, the cages hummed with the sounds of music, gambling, and sex. "The camps was wide open," a convict recalled. "You could get everything you ever wanted. There was always cash being smuggled in. The trusties ran the drugs, there was ladies on weekends, and dice rollin' all the time." Some camps had their own still tended by an expert moonshiner. Dozens of inmates used opium, a Delta favorite; others sniffed paint thinner and lighter fluid. "I never saw but one or two sergeants who tried to put a stop to this," said an inmate with almost forty years of prison under his belt. "Most of them were part of the action or just looked the other way."[10]

III

The flush times of World War II ushered in some minor reforms. In the 1940s, the superintendent began a system of incentives for "well-behaved" convicts that included a ten-day Christmas furlough and weekly visitations with family members at the farm. The furlough program was a great success. More than a quarter of the inmates went home for Christmas, and the return rate was close to a hundred percent. "Our murderers and manslaughterers are our best releases," said one Parchman official. "Most of the time you find those are a one-time deal. The burglars, arsonists, and armed robbers are the worst, because they're repeaters."[11]

In 1944, the Mississippi legislature created a parole board after years of bitter debate. Parole had the potential to change the day-to-day operations at Parchman because, as one penologist put it, the reform threatened the "superintendent's ability to control the size and makeup of the convict population . . . and compromised the most vital component of the [farm's] internal incentive system." As things turned out, the parole board rubber-stamped most of the superintendent's recommendations, leaving old Parchman largely in place.[12]

Small programs in basic education and vocational training were also begun. A tiny budget permitted white convicts to attend classes after their work day was over. Black convicts were excluded. Instead, the prison allowed a "negro preacher" named Marion Enochs, serving a life-term for murder, to educate these convicts on his own. "Enoch has a deep understanding of the psychological makeup of fellow members of his race," a reporter noted. His idea was to teach basic mathematics "through the medium of negro spirituals" such as "Swing Low, Sweet Chariot" and "Hear Dem Bells." Even better, the classes could be held right in the fields. "Negroes in prison stripes chanting the multiplication tables in the rhythm of their beloved spirituals heralds a new policy trend . . . ," the reporter added. " 'Five times five is twenty-five, five times six is thirty, five times seven is thirty-five, and five times eight is forty,' they sing-song as they tend to their [cotton] under the sole guard of 'trusties.' "[13]

In 1954, Parchman added a Maximum Security Unit (MSU), a low-slung brick-and concrete bunker in the middle of a former cotton field, surrounded by four guard towers, two razor-wire fences, and a series of electric gates. The MSU housed the state's new gas chamber, a solitary confinement wing, and a series of individual cells—a first at Parchman—for the isolation and punishment of disruptive convicts. It was the place, a long-time inmate recalled, "where they just beat the living crap out of you. It was death row in one wing, crazy people in another wing, and folks sent to be kicked and stomped in the rest. Everything went at MSU. It got the meanest sergeants and the worst trusties on the farm. We called it 'Little Alcatraz.' Nobody left there without bumps and busted bones."[14]

Between 1954 and 1964, when a nineteen-year national moratorium on capital punishment went into effect, Mississippi executed thirty-one prisoners in the gas chamber at Parchman. That number included twenty-three blacks, nine of whom were sentenced for the rape of white women. Racial tensions were rising; a new cycle of violence had begun.

IV

The reason seemed clear enough. In 1954, the Supreme Court's ruling in *Brown v. Board of Education* set off an explosion of white anger across the South. "Mississippi cannot and will not abide by such a decision," stormed the *Jackson Daily News*. James O. Eastland, the state's senior U.S. senator, went a step further. "On May 17, the Constitution was destroyed," said Eastland, whose huge cotton plantation sat a few miles from Parchman Farm. "You are not required to obey any court which passes out such a ruling. In fact, you are obligated to defy it."[15]

Eastland made these remarks in a speech to the Citizens' Council, an organization formed by Robert "Tut" Patterson, a Sunflower County plantation manager, to fight the *Brown* decision and uphold white supremacy "through all legal means." Comprising mainly white businessmen—some dubbed it "the middle-class Ku Klux Klan"—the Citizens' Council spread quickly across the South. In Mississippi, its members used their economic clout to punish local blacks who joined the NAACP, or spoke up for integration, or tried to register to vote. Blacks were laid off, their credit lines cancelled and their mortgages called in. "If the NAACP thinks we have the slightest idea of surrendering our Southland to a mulatto race," said a Citizens' Council leader in Jackson, "the NAACP had better think again."[16]

In the summer of 1954, a black, fourteen-year-old Chicago boy named Emmett "Bobo" Till, visiting relatives in the Delta, was murdered for allegedly flirting with a white woman at a country store. Local police arrested the woman's husband and his half-brother after Till's beaten, decomposed body was fished from the Tallahatchie River with a heavy fan around its neck. Neither the killing nor the murder site generated much surprise. "That river's loaded with niggers," a local resident explained. The two suspects were tried before a jury restricted to white males over the age of twenty-one. They were acquitted after a deliberation lasting one hour and seven minutes. "If we hadn't stopped to drink pop," a juror noted, "it wouldn't have taken that long."[17]

The Till case received enormous national publicity, due, in large part, to the victim's age and Northern background. But other racial murders in Mississippi were barely noticed, if at all. In the Delta town of Sumner, where the Till case had been tried, another jury acquitted a white cotton-gin manager who had shot and killed a Negro filling-station attendant for giving him the "wrong amount" of gas. It hardly mattered that the evidence was overwhelming or that the case, unlike Emmett Till's, had no sexual overtones. "There's open season on the Negroes now," said a local white man. "They've got no protection, and any peckerwood who wants to can go shoot himself one, and we'll free him."[18]

In the wake of *Brown* the Mississippi legislature passed a series of bills tightening segregation in public facilities, banning "controversial" speakers from college campuses, and organizing a State Sovereignty Commission to uphold "traditional values" through education, propaganda, and, it turned out, the monitoring of civil rights groups like the Student Nonviolent Coordinating Committee, the Congress of Racial Equality, and the NAACP. On its list of required reading was *Black Monday,* a tirade against the *Brown* decision by Judge Tom Brady, a future member of the Mississippi Supreme Court, which portrayed blacks as subhuman creatures whose "social, economic, and religious preferences . . . remain close to the caterpillar and the cockroach."

As the struggle for civil rights unfolded, state officials turned up the heat. No threat to segregation went unchallenged. In 1958, a thirty-seven-year-old black teacher named Clennon King attempted to register for summer courses at the all-white University of Mississippi in Oxford. King was arrested by highway patrolmen and rushed to the county courthouse, where a "lunacy warrant" was issued on the grounds that "any nigger who tried to enter Ole Miss *must* be crazy." After spending two weeks in a mental hospital, King was declared "competent" in return for his promise to leave the state. "I'm disillusioned," he said as he boarded a plane for Georgia. "I don't feel free in Mississippi."[19]

A more tragic incident occurred the following year, when Clyde Kennard sought to break the color line at Mississippi Southern College. Described by Myrlie Evers as a "brilliant, soft-spoken young Negro," Kennard had served as an army paratrooper in Germany and Korea before enrolling at the University of Chicago in 1953. After completing his junior year, Kennard returned to the family farm near Hattiesburg when his stepfather fell ill. Determined to finish his education, he applied to Mississippi Southern, fifteen miles away.

Kennard, an NAACP member, refused the organization's offer of legal support. In a letter to his local newspaper, he emphasized his desire for a slow-paced integration that both races could accept. "I admit that we have . . . lower economic and moral standards than many of our white neighbors," he wrote. "However, we must realize that this condition is not the cause . . . but the effect of segregation and discrimination. . . . Teach men to do a job and then give them the job to do, and high morality will follow as the day follows the night."[20]

State officials had no intention of admitting Kennard to MSC. Their plan was to avoid a national incident by convincing him to voluntarily withdraw his application. When Kennard persisted, the response was severe, Mississippi had a law on the books stating that no one convicted of a felony could attend a state college. Within weeks, Kennard was arrested for stealing $25 worth of chicken feed from a local warehouse. Despite clear evidence of a frame-up, an all-white jury took ten minutes to find Kennard guilty, and the judge sentenced him to the maximum term of seven years at Parchman Farm.

Kennard did common labor at the prison, working the "long line" in the fields. At night, he wrote letters home for illiterate convicts and taught a number of them to read and write. In 1962, suffering from severe stomach pains, Kennard was moved to a Jackson hospital, where surgeons removed a cancerous growth from his colon. He returned to Parchman eleven days later, despite a medical report that recommended immediate parole "because of the extremely poor prognosis in this rather young patient." Sent back to the fields, Kennard lost forty pounds and could barely walk. Yet Parchman officials cancelled his medical checkups, claiming he did not need additional care.

Thurgood Marshall, the NAACP's leading attorney, took Kennard's conviction to the U.S. Supreme Court in an unsuccessful attempt to get it overturned. Meanwhile, local activists mobilized a campaign that caught the attention of national figures like comedian Dick Gregory and Martin Luther King, Jr. At an NAACP banquet in Jackson, field secretary Medger Evers broke down while describing Kennard's Parchman ordeal. "Medger had always looked on crying as a weakness in men," recalled Myrlie Evers. But "tears streamed down his face as he spoke, and he just gave way. He stood there in front of hundreds of people and cried as though his heart would break. A woman called out, 'That's all right son. We all feel the same way,' and Medger, nodding, began once more. This time he finished what he had to say, and by the time it was over, hundreds of us had cleansed our hearts with tears."

Kennard was released from Parchman in the spring of 1963. Mississippi's new governor, Ross Barnett, did not have a visible soft spot for blacks. He pardoned Kennard to minimize the state's role in news stories concerning the prisoner's desperate plight. Kennard's supporters rushed him to a hospital in Chicago, where he died on July 4, 1963—"a victim more of Mississippi justice," wrote Myrlie Evers, "than the cancer that caused his death."[21]

The Kennard case introduced a new element into the civil rights struggle: Parchman Farm. In the 1960s, Mississippi officials used the Delta prison to house—and break down—those who challenged its racist customs and segregation laws. On the eve of the Freedom Rides, the *Jackson Daily News* boasted of Parchman's Southern "charm":

ATTENTION: RESTLESS RACE-MIXERS
Whose Hobby is Creating Trouble

Get away from the blackboard jungle. Rid yourself of fear of rapists, muggers, dopeheads, and switchblade artists during the hot, long summer.

FULFILL THE DREAM OF A LIFETIME
HAVE A "VACATION" ON A REAL PLANTATION
Here's All You Do

Buy yourself a Southbound ticket via rail, bus or air.

Check in and sign the guest register at the Jackson City Jail. Pay a nominal fine of $200. Then spend the next 4 months at our 21,000-acre Parchman Plantation in the heart of the Mississippi

Delta. Meals furnished. Enjoy the wonders of chopping cotton, warm sunshine, plowing mules and tractors, feeding the chickens, slopping the pigs, scrubbing floors, cooking and washing dishes, laundering clothes.

Sun lotion, bunion plasters, as well as medical service free. Experience the "abundant" life under total socialism. Parchman prison fully air-cooled by Mother Nature.

(We cash U.S. Government Welfare Checks.)[22]

Parchman was already well known to civil rights workers in Mississippi and beyond. "We had all heard of [it], of course," said CORE's James Farmer, "the most fabled state prison in the South." Farmer got to see Parchman for himself in the spring of 1961, when he was arrested at the Jackson bus depot with other Freedom Riders after ignoring Police Captain Ray's now-famous query: "Are y'all gonna move on out of this heah station?" Fined $200 for "breach of the peace," the Freedom Riders chose prison instead.[23]

Forty-five male demonstrators were packed into army trucks at midnight and driven north through the Delta on Highway 61. The drivers swerved their vehicles on the flat, deserted blacktop in order to jolt and sicken their human cargo. The trucks reached Parchman at dawn. Surrounded by trusties with shotguns, the protestors were marched to the administration building, where Superintendent Fred Jones, a cigar-chewing planter from Sunflower County, was waiting with his sergeants. "We have some bad niggers here," Jones told them. "Niggers on death row that'll beat you up and cut you as soon as look at you." As the superintendent barked instructions, a commotion arose in the rear. Two white Freedom Riders who refused to leave the truck were being dragged, feet first, along the stone-and-gravel drive. "Ain't no newspapermen out here, what you actin' like that for?" a sergeant asked. "We refuse to cooperate because we have been unjustly imprisoned," the man replied.[24]

The group was taken inside and told to undress. When the two resisters went limp, trusties shocked them with cattle prods before tossing them into a cell. The others were sent to the shower room, where a crowd of white men had gathered to watch.

"Holy Christ, look a' that lil' nigger there! He got one like a hoss."

"But look a' that one. He ain't hardly got nuthin'. And that one there—ya cain't hardly see it."[25]

Governor Barnett left explicit instructions to keep the Freedom Riders safe. Break their spirit, he suggested, but not their bones. With the news media and the FBI watching his every move, Barnett ordered the demonstrators placed in the maximum security unit for their own protection. (Other inmates had threatened to "kick their asses.") A few days later, a well-dressed visitor appeared in the cell block—a middle-aged white man with a potbelly and a sun-reddened face. "Are they treating you all right?" he drawled. It was Governor Barnett.

As the weeks passed, hundreds of new Freedom Riders entered Parchman's gate. Life was hard and monotonous for them, but the danger had passed. The protestors lived two to a cell in stifling eight-by-ten compartments, segregated by sex and race. They left only to shower twice a week. There was a no fresh air or exercise time, no cigarettes or reading material except the Bible and a racist tract about the inferiority of blacks. The food was bug-ridden and drenched in salt. The women wore striped prison dresses, the men ill-fitting underwear. When someone complained, a young Bible student cut him off. "What's this hang-up about clothes?" he said. "Gandhi wrapped a rag around his balls and brought the whole British Empire to its knees."[26]

To ease the boredom, the Freedom Riders did calisthenics and sang freedom songs. Their loud, energetic voices grated on the guards, who warned them to pipe down. When the prisoners refused, their bedding was taken away. One of the memorable scenes from Parchman involved a tall, reed-thin Howard University student named Stokely Carmichael being dragged along the cell-block floor on his mattress, singing "I'm Gonna Tell God How You Treat Me."

Without their ultimate weapon, brute force, the guards did what they could. "You boys don't stop that singin', " Deputy Tyson told them, "and y'all gon' be singin' in the rain." The Freedom Riders mocked him in verse:

Ole big man Deputy Tyson said,
I don' wanna cause you pain,
But if you don't stop that singin' now
You'll be singin' in the rain!

Minutes later, Tyson and the trusties blasted the prisoners with a fire hose, flooding their cells. Then powerful exhaust fans were turned on to create a chilling draft. But the singing continued, louder than before. Tyson seemed thoroughly deflated, like a fighter unable to throw his best punch. In his mind, Farmer could hear the confused deputy pleading with Barnett: "But, Guv'nor, how we gon' stop their singin' if we cain't go up 'side their heads."[27]

The Freedom Riders were released after serving thirty-nine days. They became national heroes, bold survivors of the toughest prison in America's most repressive state. Though their treatment had been far better than the public imagined, the demonstrators viewed Parchman as vital training for the road that lay ahead. "We had learned to sleep on steel, to eat slop, to sing when we must and to make a game of periodic floods . . . ," a veteran recalled. "The younger ones had left a little of their youth in the prison cells. They had aged, matured. The older were surely younger now, more enthralled with freedom, imbued with its quest."[28]

A Farm with Slaves

V

The walls of segregation did not tumble quickly or peacefully in Mississippi. Freedom had its price. In Oxford, an angry mob tried—and failed—to block the admission of James Meredith, a black army veteran, to Ole Miss. Two people died and hundreds were injured, including twenty-eight federal marshals hit by gunfire. In the Delta town of Winona, not far from Parchman, police officers forced Negro prisoners to assist them in the savage beatings of local activists, including Fannie Lou Hamer. In Jackson, Medger Evers was gunned down in the carport of his home. Near Philadelphia, Mississippi, the bodies of three missing civil rights workers were discovered in an earthen grave, murdered by members of the revitalized Ku Klux Klan, aided by local police.[29]

Some of the worst trouble occurred in Natchez, a place of intense poverty and elegant antebellum mansions where, its boosters claimed, "The Old South Still Lives." Led by Charles Evers, brother of the slain civil rights leader, black demonstrators packed the tense downtown streets in defiance of a court order against marching and picketing to protest the segregation of public facilities. Hundreds were arrested, denied bail, and bused to Parchman Farm.[30]

This time, the treatment was rough. These prisoners were local people, with no friends in Washington or the national press. Lacking both the moral fervor and celebrity status of the Freedom Riders, they faced a far more dangerous fate. When their buses arrived at Parchman, the demonstrators were stripped naked, beaten, marched to the maximum security unit, and packed eight to a cell. "The first night we were quiet as lambs," said one, "but after we were made to feel freezing we shouted that we wanted our clothes. . . . My jaw was so cold I couldn't eat hard food."[31]

Jammed together with no soap or towels or toilet paper, the demonstrators were force-fed laxatives by the guards. The single latrine in each cell quickly backed up onto the floor. The stench and sickness were overpowering. "They ordered me to take medicine, which made me run to the toilet," a middle-aged black woman recalled. "They tore my blouse off. We nearly froze to death. We only had one meal on Sunday. It was terrible. I never thought people could be so mean."[32]

Their suffering was not in vain. It focused attention on Parchman as a civil rights problem and made it part of the larger black struggle. Among the hundreds of activists who traveled to Mississippi in the 1960s were several dozen attorneys representing the NAACP Legal Defense Fund and the Lawyers' Committee for Civil Rights Under the Law. They had come, for the most part, to protect the Northern students and ministers who faced beatings, police harassment, and jail, but their roles naturally expanded to include the broader aspects of Negro life in Mississippi, from school integration to welfare rights, from health services to prison reform. Known as the Farish Street lawyers (their office address in the black commercial district of Jackson), they faced a legal system that fiercely resisted social change.[33]

Following the Parchman incident, the Lawyers' Committee filed two civil damage suits in federal district court. The first one involved a fourteen-year-old black youth, serving ninety days for shoplifting, who had been shot in the face by a trusty at the Leflore County prison farm, causing total blindness and permanent brain damage. The second one concerned the mistreatment of the Natchez demonstrators at Parchman Farm.

By avoiding the state courts and their all-white juries, the Lawyers' Committee got positive results. In *Roberts v. Williams,* the federal court awarded $185,000 in damages to the wounded boy's family, ruling that Leflore County had been grossly negligent in the training of its prison trusties. And in *Anderson v. Nosser,* it held the Parchman superintendent liable for punishment so cruel as to violate the Eighth Amendment to the U.S. Constitution. "We deal with human beings," the court reminded state authorities, "not dumb driven cattle."[34]

For the Farish Street lawyers, these victories underscored two basic points. First, the mistreatment described in *Anderson v. Nosser* was no aberration; inmates routinely faced these conditions at Parchman, and no one seemed to care. Second, the long-term solution to penal problems in Mississippi would have to come from the outside. The federal courts would have to lead the way.

VI

In *Delta Time,* Tony Dunbar's nostalgic journey down the back roads of modern-day Mississippi, a middle-age black man recalls the changes he has seen since the "big troubles" of the 1960s. "But now, it's bad to say, but this is the bottom line," claims Sunflower County native Tiny Brown. "Everything that was done for black people in the state of Mississippi that was worthwhile was done through a federal court order."[35]

This surely is an exaggeration. The role of the executive branch, of civil rights groups, of courageous outsiders and local people have all received widespread attention and credit, yet the thrust of Tiny Brown's recollection is largely correct. When black people needed justice and protection in Mississippi in the 1960s, there were few places to turn. The local courts were virtually useless. The entire state contained three black attorneys. Even the federal district judge for southern Mississippi, Harold Cox, was a hard-core racist who referred to blacks in his courtroom as "niggers" and "chimpanzees."

That left Greenville's William C. Keady, the federal district judge for northern Mississippi. The son of an Irish saloon keeper, Keady had to overcome tremendous obstacles in his early life, including the death of both parents and a birth defect that left him with one arm. A brilliant student, he won a full scholarship to the Washington University (of St. Louis) Law School, a far more progressive environment than Ole Miss, the usual training ground for Delta attorneys. Returning to Greenville in 1937, Keady joined the prestigious law firm of William Alexander Percy, the planter-poet-attorney best known for his aristocratic pretensions and moderate racial views. With Percy's help, he won a seat in the state legislature, where he chaired the Senate Judiciary Committee and took an interest in prison affairs.[36]

Keady quit the political arena in 1945. "I decided it wasn't for me," he recalled. "I could see the fate of a man [in] public office without his own wealth." Keady thrived in private practice, earning the nickname "Cash" for his ability to win large settlements for his clients. His friends included Ross Barnett and Senator John Stennis, who recommended him for the federal bench in 1968.[37]

Keady considered himself a traditionalist in matters of politics and race. "Like most people my age, I grew up in a segregated society, and I was happy with it," he said. The difference between Keady and Barnett, however, was the former's willingness to accept racial integration as an inevitable, and ultimately beneficial, force in Southern life. During the James Meredith crisis at Ole Miss, Keady tried to keep Barnett from leading the segregationist mob. "His phone was off the hook or something," Keady recalled. "I wanted to tell Ross that the finest name in the South was Robert E. Lee and even he knew when to surrender."[38]

On the federal bench, Keady faced a dilemma of his own. "I am not a crusader, it was never my intention to strike dramatic reforms but to advocate gradualism," he insisted. Yet the issues that came before his court—voting rights, school desegregation, racial and sexual bias in jury selection—left Keady little choice. He became a guardian of civil rights through his simple determination to uphold the law. As a local attorney put it: "He was someone the minorities in this state could turn to and know that the Constitution was alive and well."[39]

A large, imposing man, respected by lawyers for his intelligence and even-handed demeanor, Keady got far less media attention than neighboring federal judges like Frank Johnson, a liberal activist, or the reactionary Harold Cox. It was not until 1972 that reporters flocked to Keady's Greenville courtroom in force. The reason was a federal lawsuit filed by four Mississippi convicts alleging "massive violations" of their constitutional rights. The case, *Gates v. Collier,* would profoundly affect the treatment of prisoners throughout the United States.

VII

Gates v. Collier was the brainchild of a thirty-one-year-old attorney named Roy Haber, who quit his New York City divorce practice to join the civil rights struggle in the South. Based at the Lawyers' Committee's Farish Street office, Haber became interested in prisoners' rights while working on *Anderson v. Nosser.* Coworkers described him as a fearless loner, with a scraggly beard and the first "Afro" haircut ever seen in Mississippi. State officials view him as a dangerous troublemaker: a northern Jew intent on stirring up the races. Roy Haber, said one newspaper, "has probably made more high-placed enemies in Mississippi than any of the other 'outside agitators' who have espoused civil libertarian causes here during the last ten years."[40]

In 1970, Haber began taking statements from Parchman inmates about conditions at the farm. Getting them to talk was not easy. The convicts feared retribution from prison officials, who made their feelings all too clear. After his first meeting with Haber, inmate Matthew Winter, a convicted murderer, was told by his sergeant "that he was on the bad list [and] would never be paroled if he continued to 'fool around with those fucking civil rights people.' " After seeing Haber again, Winter was sent to the maximum security unit, beaten by trustees, handcuffed to bars and left that way for entire nights.[41]

Intimidation was routine. Convicts who came to see Haber were often brought to the interview room in chains. Armed trusties manned the door and the hallways outside. "I remember one time I had to go to the bathroom," said a legal assistant on Haber's tiny staff. "Walking down this narrow corridor, I brushed into a young white trusty leaning on the wall. I kept moving, not looking back, until I heard this loud click, an incredibly scary sound. The guy had cocked his Winchester, and I thought, 'Jesus, he's gunna shoot me in the back.' I tried not to panic, but my legs almost gave way. I figured this bastard could kill me for free because he was already serving life. After that, no more bathroom breaks. I grinned and held it in."[42]

Haber was a rock. His courage and determination convinced hundreds of prisoners to come forward with stories of unspeakable brutality and neglect. The group included Nazareth Gates, a black career criminal serving ten years for manslaughter, whose name would head the class action suit filed by Haber in 1971. Gates viewed Haber as an indispensable asset—a pipeline to both the media and the courts. "Several of the guys here at Camp Two would like an appointment with you," he wrote the lawyer in 1971. "If you will help us to help these men [and others], I am thanking you very much."[43]

Within weeks, Haber had all the information he needed. His most damning document was a list of murders, rapes, beatings, and tortures at Parchman between 1969 and 1971, running to more than fifty single-spaced pages. The allegations included:

Bogard, William	Was compelled to stand (days) and sit (nights) for three entire days, without interruption, on a coke crate.
Collins, Matthew	Murdered by J. C. Dunnican (trusty) on order of Ollis Hitt.
Goodwin, Frank	"Jumped on" and had an ear ripped off by inmate Danny Williamson.
Hayes, Jessie	Shot by trusty John Horn for refusal to engage in homosexual acts. . . .

Humes, George	Handcuffed to bars, on tiptoes for 2 days without food, water, or bathroom facilities.
Marino, Hilliard	Hair cut and pulled out while forced to kneel nude on concrete floor. . . . Assaulted with others in MSU with . . . brass knuckles . . . causing blindness, constant pain.
Nathan, Walter	Handcuffed and hung from tree.
Tackett, Bob	That another inmate named Cantrell kicked out one of his eyes which was lost; that he was beaten by a trusty.
Waldie, Donald	Required to maintain a mid-suspended position which one assumes during course of doing push-ups, and at that time was guarded by J. D. Gilmer, who shot above or below him if he moved.
Wells, William	Shot fatally by Sgt. West.
Williams, Jessie	Shot fatally by Walter Griffin, a trusty, on orders of Obar (driver).[44]

Haber's intervention brought tensions at Parchman to a boil. Fights erupted between inmates supporting the proposed lawsuit and those loyal to their sergeants and trusties. At Camp 5, white convicts slit their wrists to protest the beatings of three men sympathetic to Haber's cause. At Camp 8, black inmates rioted after a sergeant burned some of their mail. A hundred men at Camp 11 "bucked the line" to protest long workdays and homosexual assaults. In retaliation, Haber charged, the strikers "are being forced to sleep in, on, or near sewerage ditches after spending fourteen hours in the fields."

Amid this chaos, the body of a young Parchman inmate named Danny Bennett was sent home for burial. The name was familiar to many people, for Bennett, who was white, had been a high school football star before an injury ended his promising career. The prison doctor listed heat stroke as the cause of death, but the local under-taker found burns and bruises covering the body, leading to an autopsy that turned up broken ribs, a crushed thorax, and massive hemorrhages in both lungs. Danny Bennett had been beaten to death.

Haber jumped on the case. If this could happen to a white man serving "light time" for burglary, he charged, then no one was safe. The state legislature, traditionally sympathetic to Parchman, formed a committee to investigate Bennett's death. Witness after witness said much the same thing: Bennett had fallen face down in the cotton rows while working the "long line" on a 100-degree afternoon. Un-able to rise, he was shocked with cattle prods, beaten with ax handles, and tossed on to the back of an open truck, where he remained—unconscious in the broiling sun—until he died.

The committee report minced no words. Concluding that Ben-nett had been murdered, it blamed a security system in which hard-pressed sergeants chose the most intimidating convicts to be their trusties. The report described Bennett's sergeant as mentally unstable. (A newsman close to the case called him a "barely functional mon-key.") About the trusty who led the beating, the report said:*

J. D. Gilmer was sentenced to Parchman in 1950 to serve a life term for murder and was paroled in 1960. In February 1962 . . . he was recom-mitted to the Penitentiary to serve another life term for the crime of rape. This is the character of the criminal, the trusty, who had direct and ex-clusive supervision of the work detail to which Danny Bennett was as-signed on the day of his death.[45]

---

* J. D. Gilmer was tried and convicted for the murder of Danny Bennett. Returned to Parch-man, he was reappointed as a trusty "dog-boy" by the superintendent in an apparent effort to separate him from the inmate population. As a safety move, it failed miserably. At his new job, Gilmer either fell or was pushed into a vat of tick dip. Badly burned, he died a short time later.

The report struck an ominous note. If the legislature did not move quickly to clean up Parchman, it said, the federal courts would surely step in. The warning was prophetic; it simply came too late.

VIII

On February 8, 1971, Haber filed suit in federal court on behalf of inmates Nazareth Gates, Willie Holmes, Matthew Winter, and Hal Zachery. The plaintiffs charged that "deplorable conditions and practices" at Parchman deprived them of rights guaranteed by the First, Eighth, Thirteenth, and Fourteenth amendments to the U.S. Constitution. In a bold stroke, Judge Keady determined that the case qualified as a class action under federal guidelines, covering all inmates at the prison. And he added a subclass of black convicts, who faced additional hardships based solely on their race.

Keady visited Parchman on four occasions, once taking his minister along. Wandering through the cages, talking privately to the inmates, he discovered an institution in shambles, marked by violence and neglect. The camps were laced with open ditches, holding raw sewage and medical waste. Rats scurried along the floors. Electrical wiring was frayed and exposed; broken windowpanes were stuffed with rags to keep out the cold. At one camp, Keady found "three wash basins for 80 men which consist of oil drums cut in half." At all camps, he saw filthy bathrooms, rotting mattresses, polluted water supplies, and kitchens overrun with insects, rodents, and the stench of decay.

The convicts told him stories that supported Haber's claims. Parchman was a dangerous, deadly place. Shootings and beatings were common; murders went unreported; the maximum security unit was a torture chamber. Trusties brutalized inmates, who, in turn, brutalized each other. "One part of me had always suspected such things," the judge recalled. "The rest of me was angry and ashamed."

In August 1971, the U.S. Justice Department filed a pathbreaking brief in support of the convicts. Never before had the federal government intervened in a prison reform case on the state level. Mississippi officials did not respond. Determined to avoid an embarrassing public trial, Governor William Waller told Judge Keady: "We are, in effect, your Honor, admitting that the constitutional provisions have been violated." His confession left Parchman's future almost completely in Keady's hands.[46]

On October 20, 1972, the judge released his "Findings of Fact and Conclusions of Law." There were few surprises in the twenty-one-page opinion, apart from the passion of the words. "We all expected Keady to find for the plaintiffs," a newsman recalled. "What struck many of us was the tone he used. This case reached deep down into his soul."[47]

Keady condemned Parchman as both an offender of the Constitution and an affront to "modern standards of decency." Its policy of segregating inmates by race "is in violation of the Equal Protection Clause of the Fourteenth Amendment," he wrote. And its failure to provide adequate housing, medical care, and physical protection "is in violation of the Eighth Amendment's prohibition against cruel and unusual punishment."

Keady described the living quarters at Parchman as "unfit for human habitation" and the medical facilities as primitive and unsafe. He noted that the failure to classify prisoners by personality and criminal background had encouraged "physical assaults, abuses, indignities, and cruelties." In daylight, he wrote, the inmates were guarded by poorly trained trusties; in darkness, they were left to themselves. According to Parchman's own statistics, trusties had shot thirty men in the previous two years and had beaten dozens more. Rapes and stabbings were nightly affairs. "When the lights go out," the superintendent admitted, "there is no way that anyone can guard the safety of an inmate in the Parchman situation."

Keady also focused on conditions at the maximum security unit, which contained the gas chamber, death row, and the so-called black hole, a windowless compartment six by six feet, without a sink, a bed, a light, or a toilet. Before entering solitary confinement, the convict had his head shaved with heavy-duty clippers. He was given minimal food and water, denied soap and toilet paper, and kept there without clothing for up to seventy-two hours. "The record is replete with innumerable instances of physical brutality and abuse in disciplining inmates who are sent to MSU," Keady declared "They include . . . handcuffing inmates to the fence and to cells for long periods of time, shooting at and around inmates [in the yard] and using a cattle prod to keep [them] standing or moving."

Keady followed these findings with a sweeping order for "immediate and long-range relief." Starting at once, Parchman officials were to eliminate "all racially discriminatory practices" at the prison, "increase the protection of inmates from the assaults of fellow inmates," and prohibit the use of corporal punishment "of such severity as to offend present-day concepts of decency and human dignity." To accomplish these goals, the court demanded an "orderly desegregation" of inmate facilities, an end to the trusty system, and the hiring of professional guards. Getting rid of the trusty-shooters was priority number one. "Defendants shall exert every effort to obtain competent civilian personnel," the order said, "making special appeals to the black community for qualified persons."

Turning to "long-range relief," Keady posed some vital questions about Parchman's future. Did state officials intend to keep the prison as a penal farm, without serious vocational training or rehabilitation programs for the inmates? Did the long history of operating Parchman at a profit really save the state money in the long run? Did a system based on intimidation and fear provide the best methods for disciplining inmates in the modern age? Keady insisted on a set of "comprehensive plans" for eliminating the "unconstitutional conditions" described in the injunction, including such things as the construction of better housing and a modern hospital, facilities for sewage treatment and clean drinking water, and a system for isolating hardened criminals from nonviolent inmates and first offenders.

"The court reserves the power to issue further and supplemental orders in aid of the provisions of this injunction," Keady concluded. To speed the process and ensure its success, he directed the state to pay more than $50,000 in attorneys' fees to Roy Haber and his team, a figure that would rise dramatically in the coming years. Whatever the future held for this prison, the old days were gone. No longer would Parchman match the apt description that Haber and Nazareth Gates had used when the case began: "a farm with slaves."

✠

Epilogue

I

Reform came slowly to Parchman. Prison officials did all they could to derail the *Gates* decision, forcing endless compliance orders from the federal district court. In one instance, they "desegregated" Parchman by placing a single black inmate in an all-white camp and a single white inmate in an all-black camp. In another, they encouraged "goon squads" to roam the cages, beating "radical" inmates. "There was a lot of obstinancy," Judge Keady recalled. "There were some dark days because of the ineptitude [of officials] running the penitentiary."[1]

Yet Keady prevailed. Mixing threats with patience, he helped give Mississippi a "constitutional prison," staffed by true penologists and civilian guards. Along the way, he closed the worst camps, ordered an inmate classification system, established a prison law library, upheld the right of Black Muslims to meet and worship, and required at least fifty square feet of living space for each new convict. In 1976, Mississippi created a Department of Corrections to oversee Parchman and other facilities. "It is safe to say that no other state has come such a long way with its prisons," said one authority, "although perhaps no other state had such a long way to go."[2]

These reforms had inevitable consequences—some unintended,

249

many quite severe. A step forward in one area often caused a step backward in another. The end of racial segregation, for example, led to a surge of gang activity in the cages, as whites and blacks squared off to protect themselves, boost their status, and gain territorial control. Integrating a prison was not like integrating a high school or a restaurant, a Parchman official complained: "In most cases we are dealing with the scum of the earth. . . . Power is the game. It is won in two ways: by physical force and by appeals to the worst prejudices. . . . That builds black and white gangs that stalk each other, do horrible shit to each other, and hold together with constant reminders of the blood that flows."[3]

The average convict was safer from violence after the *Gates* decision than before. The number of homicides dropped as civilian guards took the place of gun-toting trusties. Yet in an odd way, the federal court had shifted the balance of terror from the keepers to the inmates—from Black Annie and trusty-shooters to homemade weapons and prison gangs. In 1990 alone, the Parchman emergency room treated 1,169 inmate-on-inmate and 1,136 inmate-on-staff assaults. "I've sat and watched a young man cry," wrote a Mississippi prison activist, "begging me to get the officials to keep him in the Maximum Security Unit after he had been brutally raped by men in an open dormitory unit. I sent condolences to his family a few months later when another prisoner stabbed him to death in a rage because he was sitting on somebody's bed."[4]

Inmate violence has been a problem in all prisons, of course, including the Parchman of old. Yet many believed that Keady aggravated the problem by encouraging an end to forced labor in the fields. Following *Gates,* the great bulk of Parchman's prime land—more than 13,000 acres—was leased to local growers. The prison no longer fed and clothed its inmates with home-grown crops. The once-profitable, self-sufficient plantation disappeared.

Nothing fully took its place. Prison support jobs, such as maintenance and cooking, did not provide inmates with nearly enough work. Well-intentioned efforts at adult education and vocational training were poorly funded, and attempts to create small prison industries ran into strong opposition from competing private firms. The result was too many convicts with too little to do. "You stay in these cages all day, you build up a lot of hostility," said one inmate, "and it's got to get out somehow."[5]

II

When Judge Keady made his first ruling in 1972, Parchman seemed to offer unique possibilities for change. Unlike other prisons, it did not have much invested in a paid workforce or a physical plant. The prison had few sturdy buildings, few cell blocks, few guards. "Mississippi had a clean slate to write on," noted one observer, and a federal court to push things along.[6]

In 1973, a group of national prison experts drew up a master plan for the state. It called for "decentralized reform": the growth of regional facilities and community programs, which threatened to make Parchman obsolete. Their plan, however, faced strong opposition from the start. Most localities did not want a prison in their midst. And the people of Mississippi still conceived of Parchman as the perfect place for convicts, especially blacks. "I don't want prison facilities lost and scattered all over the state," said one political leader. "If you're sent to prison, you should feel you're going away somewhere. And when you come out, you should feel you're going back towards society."[7]

The plan faced other obstacles as well. In the 1970s, the belief that prisons should embrace rehabilitation was seriously challenged by studies concluding, as one author put it, that "nothing works." Counseling, job training, education—all seemed futile in getting inmates to change their criminal ways. At the same time, Mississippi began to toughen its sentencing policies in response to public outcries about drugs and violence in a slowly urbanizing culture. Along with other states, it passed laws providing mandatory sentences,

tougher penalties for repeat offenders, and tighter controls on proba-
tion and parole.[8]

These changes put tremendous pressure on the prison system.
There was no room for the growing number of convicts, with their
required fifty square feet each. Caught in the crossfire between a
fearful public and a determined federal court, the Mississippi legislature opened the coffers of America's poorest state, allocating huge
sums for the construction of new facilities at Parchman. Between
1904 and 1970, the prison had housed between 1,800 and 2,500 inmates—the ideal number for a plantation of that size. Between 1970
and 1995, that figure more than tripled, to 6,500 with thousands
more expected down the line. Parchman's budget rose to almost $60
million a year. As Mississippi's only major state prison, it became one
of the largest penal institutions in the United States.

III

Parchman remains a distant, isolated place, known through legend
and folklore, far removed from public view. Along the side of the
Delta's flat, two-lane Route 49, a small sign appears telling motorists
that they have entered prison land and warning them not to pick up
hitch-hikers. Several miles later, one sees a brick-and-glass guard
booth and a single "security gate" with large letters reading: "Mississippi State Penitentiary." The gate stands alone, attached to nothing.
Down the road a few yards is a weathered billboard from an earlier
time. "WELCOME TO PARCHMAN MS, it says. "Coke is it!"

Parchman today is a mixture of the present and the past. The convict population remains about 70 percent black, stable since the 1930s,
while the rate of recidivism—a depressing 49 percent—is slightly
higher than before. Parchman is now an all-male prison; convict
women were moved to a separate facility near Jackson in the 1980s.
The all-white prison staff is a thing of the past. Today the majority of
guards, and a large percentage of administrators, are black. They come

from all over the Delta, and few would ever think of living on the prison grounds. Parchman is a job to them, not a way of life.

To become a guard, an applicant must pass a written test and be a high school graduate, at least twenty-one years old. These are tough restrictions in the Delta, where the high school drop-out rate exceeds forty percent. Those who qualify are given a quick month's training in the basics of corrections and prison life. Almost half the guards at Parchman are black women, mainly single, heading households on their own. "They are the ones who graduate high school in the Delta," said a black official. "They are the ones who can pass the written exam and will work an eight-hour shift for less than $20,000 a year." He added: "It's a shameful procedure—not just here, but all over. Corrections is not a discipline to most of them. The work is hard and stressful, and they do their best. But can you think of another job where someone with this salary, this level of education, and this sort of training has so much power over the lives of others?"

From Highway 49, the prison seems little more than a maze of gravel roads and dusty fields. Yet further inside, the new Parchman appears. There is a sweeping administration building with thick carpets and bustling computer rooms. There is a modern hospital, a handsome Spiritual Life Center, a fully equipped gymnasium, and a sizeable law library, perhaps the most popular spot of all. Some of the ancient cages are still in use. Drab but clean, they are filled with minimum security inmates, often the elderly, who tend the camp grounds. The old maximum security unit—Little Alcatraz—now houses parole violators as well as the gas chamber and an adjoining room for lethal injections. Mississippi changed its method of execution after a series of mishaps involving the chemical gas mixture led to the slow torture of two condemned men.*

---

* In 1983, convict Jimmy Lee Gray, convicted of raping and killing a child, died an agonizing death in the gas chamber, his mouth foaming, his eyes rolling, his head slamming into an iron pipe by the chair. The following execution had problems as well. To prevent further trouble,

Epilogue

Parchman has a new maximum security unit, a "state-of-the-art" facility where more than a thousand inmates spend twenty-three hours a day in their individual cells, with a bunk, a sink, and a seatless toilet, leaving once each morning to shower alone, and once each afternoon for a short stay in an exercise yard surrounded by razor-wire. All meals are eaten in their cells; radio and television are banned. Some of these convicts are too dangerous to be housed anywhere else. Others have been moved there temporarily for violating prison rules. Most are serving long (often fixed) sentences for serious crimes, with few privileges or incentives, and faint hope of parole.

The majority of Parchman convicts live between these two extremes. They are the medium security inmates, housed in crowded barracks with barred doors and pillbox windows, sharing their space with seventy or more men. They can leave for meals, medical problems, special classes, legal visits, or work details. But much of their day is spent in the "cage," sleeping, watching television, killing time. It is here that most of the trouble occurs. "You don't sit on another man's bunk unless he says okay," an inmate explained. "Don't even walk up the aisle of his bed. You're liable to get stabbed or get your brains knocked out. You live in your own world. . . . It's a cautious way of life. You learn a lot about survival."[10]

A Parchman official agreed. "These are not submissive inmates," he said. "Those days are long gone. A lot of the people we get have no roots. They have no discipline. They are very angry. They resent us more than they fear us, and they need more help than a prison can provide."[11]

Mississippi is not standing still. It has opened a number of branch facilities and community work centers across the state for minimum

---

the executioner tested two rabbits and a turtle in the chamber before his next job. "The bunnies went *poom*," he recalled, "but that turtle was one tough sumbitch. He held his breath or something. We took him back, and he just swam off into the sunset. You cannot gas a turtle." Mississippi went to the lethal injection shortly thereafter.

security inmates, and it is experimenting with privatization, the currently popular idea of allowing private companies to operate prisons as a business venture. At Parchman itself, the prison industries program has been revitalized, and large-scale farming—in hogs, poultry, and vegetables, not in cotton—is being resumed in the hope of cutting costs and putting convicts back to work. Parchman's most heralded new program is Regimented Inmate Discipline (RID), a six-month boot-camp operation for nonviolent offenders staffed by drill instructors, job counselors, and teachers. "It's small and showy and we don't know its long-run results," said a prison official, "but it's a lot better than Alabama with its chain-gangs breaking rocks."[12]

A group of old-timers at Parchman spoke recently about the changes they had seen. These men, three black, two white, are veterans of Black Annie, hand-picked cotton, and dawn-to-dusk labor in the fields. They can recall the beatings and shootings by the trusties, and the raw sewage that ran through their camps. One of them was a plaintiff in the *Gates* case, and all are grateful for the good it did. Yet these men also insisted that the new Parchman can learn something from the old. What is missing today, said Horace Carter, a prisoner for almost fifty years, is "the feeling that work counted for something," that the farm had a rhythm, "awful bad as it was in most camps, that kept us tired and kept us together and made me feel better inside."

"I'm not looking to go backwards," he said. "I know the troubles at old Parchman better than any man alive. I'm seventy-three years old. But I look around today and see a place that makes me sad."[13]

✠

Notes

Prologue

1. William Faulkner, *The Mansion* (New York, 1955), pp. 43–44, 47–48; William Ferris, *Blues from the Delta* (New York, 1978), pp. 32–33; Robert Palmer, *Deep Blues* (New York, 1981), pp. 79–82; Sheldon Harris, *Blues Who's Who* (New York, 1979), pp. 552–553.
2. J. Watts to Governor Charles Lynch, November 29, 1833, RG 27, vol. 18, Mississippi Department of Archives and History.
3. *Columbus Democrat,* November 25, 1837.
4. John H. Moore, *The Emergence of the Cotton Kingdom in the Old Southwest; Mississippi, 1770–1860* (Baton Rouge, La., 1988), pp. 116–155; William B. Taylor, *Brokered Justice: Race, Politics, and Mississippi Prisons, 1798–1992* (Columbus, Ohio, 1993), p. 10.
5. D. Clayton James, *Antebellum Natchez* (Baton Rouge, La., 1968), pp. 254–273; William Hogan and Edwin Davis (eds.), *William Johnson's Natchez: The Ante-Bellum Diary of a Free Negro* (Baton Rouge, La., 1993).
6. *Semi-Weekly Mississippian,* July 21, 28, August 15, 18, 22, 1854.
7. Dwyn Mounger, "Lynching in Mississippi, 1830–1930" (master's thesis, Mississippi State University, 1961), pp. 23–24; *Mississippi Free Trader,* May 16, 1839.
8. *Niles Register,* August 8, 1835, p. 401.
9. Mounger, "Lynching," p. 32.

10. John Wunder, "American Law and Order Comes to Mississippi Territory: The Making of Sargent's Code, 1798–1800," *Journal of Mississippi History* 38 (May 1976): 131–155; *Mississippi Free Trader,* July 24, 1838.

11. E. Bruce Thompson, "Reforms in the Penal Code of Mississippi, 1820–1850," *Journal of Mississippi History* 7 (1945): 53–54.

12. *Ibid.,* pp. 57–58.

13. *Ibid.,* pp. 56–57.

14. Edward Ayers, *Vengeance and Justice: Crime and Punishment in the 19th-Century American South* (New York, 1984), p. 61; Michael Wayne, *The Reshaping of Plantation Society: The Natchez District, 1860–1880* (Baton Rouge, La., 1983), p. 16.

15. Lyda Shivers, "A History of the Mississippi Penitentiary" (master's thesis, University of Mississippi, 1930), pp. 12–25. On the Auburn system, see Blake McKelvey, *American Prisons* (Chicago, 1936), pp. 8–10; Larry Sullivan, *The Prison Reform Movement* (Boston, 1990), pp. 9–16.

Chapter 1: Emancipation

1. William L. Nugent to his wife, August 19, 1861, in John K. Bettersworth, *Mississippi in the Confederacy: As They Saw It* (Baton Rouge, 1961), p. 63.

2. Ibid., March 13, 1864, in Bettersworth, *Mississippi,* p. 213.

3. See William C. Harris, *Presidential Reconstruction in Mississippi* (Baton Rouge, 1967), pp. 18–36; Frank E. Smith, *The Yazoo River* (New York, 1954), pp. 169–186; Hodding Carter, *Lower Mississippi* (New York, 1942), pp. 289–291.

4. James W. Garner, *Reconstruction in Mississippi* (New York, 1901), pp. 119–130; Vernon L. Wharton, *The Negro in Mississippi* (Chapel Hill, 1947), pp. 216–218; Edward L. Ayers, *Vengeance and Justice* (New York, 1984), pp. 199–200; James T. Trotter, "Last Charge to the Court of Desoto County, Miss., 1866," 930, Southern Historical Collection, Chapel Hill, North Carolina.

5. Smith, *Yazoo River,* pp. 169–170.

6. John T. Trowbridge, *The Desolate South* (reprinted, New York, 1956), pp. 159–160; *The Reminiscences of Carl Schurz,* vol. 3: *1863–1869* (New York, 1908), pp. 198–199.

7. Wharton, *Negro in Mississippi,* pp. 232–233; Leon Litwack, *Been in the Storm So Long* (New York, 1979), pp. 262–263.

8. Trowbridge, *Desolate South,* pp. 189–190.

9. James L. Roark, *Masters Without Slaves* (New York, 1977), pp. 111–155; Michael Wayne, *The Reshaping of Plantation Society* (Baton Rouge, 1983), pp. 31–71; Wharton, *Negro in Mississippi,* pp. 216–217. In his recent study of antebellum Mississippi, John Hebron Moore noted that white farmers "to a man expected to become planters before they died. They were, in fact, one of the most optimistic agricultural working classes that the world has ever known. . . . Because so many of them actually realized this goal of becoming planters, the remainder saw themselves as having a stake in the slave-worked plantation system." See Moore, *The Emergence of the Cotton Kingdom in the Old Southwest: Mississippi, 1770–1860* (Baton Rouge, 1988), p. 145.

10. Whitelaw Reid, *After the War* (Cincinnati, 1886), pp. 417–418. See also William C. Sallis, "The Color Line in Mississippi Politics, 1865–1915" (Ph.D. diss., University of Kentucky, 1967), chaps. 1, 2, for an excellent discussion of Northern attitudes toward the Magnolia State.

11. Quoted in Wharton, *Negro in Mississippi,* p. 28.

12. Autobiography of Charlie Davenport, in George P. Rawick (ed.), *The American Slave: A Composite Autobiography* (Westport, Conn., 1977), Supplement, ser. 1, vol. 7, *Mississippi Narratives,* pt. 2, p. 566.

13. Autobiography of Ebeneezer Brown, in Rawick, vol. 6, pt. 1, pp. 251–252.

14. Autobiography of George Coleman, in Rawick, vol. 7, pt. 2, p. 426.

15. Eric Foner, *Reconstruction: America's Unfinished Revolution* (New York, 1988), pp. 79–84; William Cohen, *At Freedom's Edge: Black*

Mobility and the Southern White Quest for Racial Control, 1861–1915 (Baton Rouge, pp. 23–43; Wharton, *Negro in Mississippi,* pp. 106–124; Roark, *Masters without Slaves,* p. 200.

16. Autobiographies of Angie Floyd, vol. 7, pt. 2, p. 737; July Ann Halfen, vol. 8, pt. 3, p. 898; and Vinnie Busby, vol. 6, pt. 1, p. 310; all in Rawick, *Mississippi Narratives.*

17. Dan Carter, *When the War Was Over* (Baton Rouge, 1985), p. 157. Carter notes that the sample may not accurately represent the entire slave population because, in his words, "most of those interviewed during the 1930s were under twenty years of age at the time of emancipation and thus were likely to be more mobile than the general black population." He adds, however, that the "extraordinarily high percentage of individuals who moved tends to reinforce the earlier stereotypes of a black population in turmoil." See also autobiographies of Simon Durr, vol. 7, pt. 2, p. 656, and Angie Floyd, vol. 7, pt. 2, p. 738, in Rawick, *Mississippi Narratives.*

18. Wharton, *Negro in Mississippi,* p. 18; Sallis, "Color Line in Mississippi Politics," pp. 1–15; Reid, *After the War,* pp. 417–418; Vincent Harding, *There Is a River: The Struggle for Freedom in Black America* (New York, 1981), p. 311.

19. Sallis, "Color Line in Mississippi Politics," p. 6.

20. Ibid., pp. 6, 11; Wharton, *Negro in Mississippi,* p. 80.

21. Claude Nolen, *The Negro's Image in the South* (Lexington, Ky., 1967), pp. 3–28; Joel Williamson, *The Crucible of Race* (New York, 1984), pp. 11–43; Wayne, *Reshaping of Plantation Society,* pp. 32–71; Roark, *Masters without Slaves,* p. 139.

22. Wharton, *Negro in Mississippi,* p. 49; Walter Fleming, "Deportation and Colonization: An Attempted Solution of the Race Problem," *Studies in Southern History and Politics* (1925): 30.

23. Sallis, "Color Line in Mississippi Politics," p. 13; Wharton, *Negro in Mississippi,* pp. 53–57.

24. Harris, *Presidential Reconstruction in Mississippi,* pp. 104–120; Foner, *Reconstruction,* p. 191.

25. *Mississippi House Journal* (1865), Appendix, pp. 44–46.

26. Daniel A. Novak, *The Wheel of Servitude* (Lexington, Ky., 1978), pp.

1–8; Harris, *Presidential Reconstruction in Mississippi,* pp. 121–153; Wharton, *Negro in Mississippi,* pp. 80–96.

27. Wharton, *Negro in Mississippi,* pp. 91–105; Harris. *Presidential Reconstruction in Mississippi,* p. 141.

28. Foner, *Reconstruction,* pp. 276–280; David Sansing, "Congressional Reconstruction," in Richard A. McLemore, *A History of Mississippi* (Jackson, Miss., 1973), pp. 571–589; Wharton, *Negro in Mississippi,* pp. 157–164; Sallis, "Color Line in Mississippi Politics," pp. 57–98.

29. Charles Nordhoff, *The Cotton States in the Spring and Summer of 1875* (New York, 1876), p. 301.

30. "Fights in the Legislature of 1870," in Mississippi Department of Archives and History, Subject File: Dueling, Jackson, Miss.

31. Dwyn Mounger, "Lynching in Mississippi, 1830–1930" (master's thesis, Mississippi State University, 1961), p. 51; William H. Russell, *My Diary, North and South* (New York, 1863), pp. 154–160; Wharton, *Negro in Mississippi,* pp. 216–217.

32. William Harris, *Day of the Carpetbagger,* (Baton Rouge, 1979), p. 379; Carter, *When the War Was Over,* p. 21.

33. Sallis, "Color Line in Mississippi Politics," p. 62; Litwack, *Been in the Storm So Long,* p. 283.

34. *Congressional Globe,* 39th Cong., 1st sess., pt. 1, pp. 94–95; Sallis, "Color Line in Mississippi Politics," p. 63: Mounger, "Lynching in Mississippi," p. 68.

35. Wharton, *Negro in Mississippi,* pp. 216–233.

36. Sallis, "Color Line in Mississippi Politics," pp. 155–159.

37. Ibid. Also see Mounger, "Lynching in Mississippi," pp. 50–75; Foner, *Reconstruction,* pp. 425–431. "Anonymous Autobiography," in Rawick, *Mississippi Narratives,* vol. 6, pt. 1, p. 2.

38. Thomas B. Carroll, *Historical Sketches of Oktibbeha County* (1931), pp. 131–149.

39. Sallis, "Color Line in Mississippi Politics," pp. 167–170; John K. Bettersworth, "The Reawakening of Society and Cultural Life, 1865–1890," in McLemore, *History of Mississippi,* pp. 622–624; Litwack, *Been in the Storm So Long,* p. 486.

40. Wharton, *Negro in Mississippi,* p. 245. Some historians believe that

Wharton missed a larger truth: that the demise of black *and* white public schools in this isolated, impoverished region was due less to sporadic violence than to pervasive indifference and neglect. At least one historian claims that Klan violence against the public schools was not nearly as severe as Wharton alleged. See Harris, *Day of the Carpetbagger,* pp. 327–330.

41. Carter, *When the War Was Over,* p. 195.
42. For information on the Meridian riot, see ibid., pp. 188–190; Foner, *Reconstruction,* p. 428; Harris, *Day of the Carpetbagger,* pp. 396–398; Sallis, "Color Line in Mississippi Politics," pp. 160–165; William H. Hardy, "Recollections of Reconstruction in East and Southeast Mississippi," *Publications of the Mississippi Historical Society* 7 (1903): 204–206.
43. Dunbar Rowland, *History of Mississippi, Heart of the South* (Jackson, Miss., 1925), 2:172; William Gillette, *Retreat from Reconstruction, 1869–1879* (Baton Rouge, 1979), pp. 170–172.
44. Mounger, "Lynching in Mississippi," pp. 50–75; Stephen Whitfield, *A Death in the Delta* (New York, 1988), pp. 1–14; Neil McMillen, *Dark Journey: Black Mississippians in the Age of Jim Crow* (Urbana, Ill., 1989), pp. 228–233.

Chapter 2: The Mississippi Plan

1. Michael Wayne, *The Reshaping of Plantation Society* (Baton Rouge, 1983), p. 145.
2. Claude Nolan, *The Negro's Image in the South* (Lexington, Ky., 1967), pp. 14–16.
3. Ibid.; Wayne, *Plantation Society,* pp. 144–145; William C. Harris, *The Day of the Carpetbagger* (Baton Rouge, 1979), pp. 27–28.
4. Eugene Genovese, *Roll, Jordan, Roll* (New York, 1972), pp. 599–609; Nolan, *Negro's Image,* pp. 14–15.
5. William Sallis, "The Color Line in Mississippi Politics, 1865–1915" (Ph.D. diss., University of Kentucky, 1967), p. 6; Dwyn Mounger, "Lynching in Mississippi" (Master's thesis, Mississippi State University, 1961), pp. 50–75; Vernon L. Wharton, *The Negro in Mississippi*

(Chapel Hill, 1947), p. 237; Edward L. Ayers, *Vengeance and Justice* (New York, 1984), p. 176.

6. Stephen Cresswell, *Mormons, Cowboys, Moonshiners and Klansmen: Federal Law Enforcement in the South and West, 1870–1893* (Tuscaloosa, Ala., 1991), pp. 60–61.

7. Ayers, *Vengeance and Justice*, p. 176; Alrutheus A. Taylor, *The Negro in the Reconstruction of Virginia* (Washington, D.C., 1926), p. 46.

8. Autobiography of Squire Irvin, in George P. Rawick (ed.), *The American Slave: A Composite Autobiography* (Westport, Conn., 1977), Supplement, Series 1, vol. 8, "Mississippi Narratives," pt. 3, p. 1082; Wharton, *Negro in Mississippi*, pp. 234–236.

9. Autobiography of Gabe Butler, in Rawick, *American Slave*, vol. 6, p. 317.

10. Lyda Shivers, "A History of the Mississippi Penitentiary" (master's thesis, University of Mississippi, 1930), pp. 26–45; Ayers, *Vengeance and Justice*, p. 187.

11. Beulah Price, "The Mississippi-Louisiana Career of Colonel Edmund Richardson," *Journal of Mississippi History* 50, no. 2 (May 1978): 184–186; "Edmund Richardson," in *Goodspeed's Biographical and Historical Memoirs of Mississippi* (Jackson, Miss., 1891), 2:666–669.

12. *Annual Report of the Superintendent of the Mississippi State Penitentiary* (Jackson, Miss., December 15, 1871); Malcolm Moos, *State Penal Administration in Alabama* (Tuscaloosa, Ala., 1942), p. 6.

13. Edythe McCraw, "World's Greatest Cotton-Grower," *Mississippi News and Views* (September 1967): 11–13; "The Late Colonel Edmund Richardson," *Planter's Journal* (February 1886): 1–2; *Pontotoc* (Miss.) *Democrat*, August 2, 1888; *Goodspeed's Memoirs*, p. 669; "Sketch of Life of Colonel Edmund Richardson," 630-Z, Southern Historical Collection, Chapel Hill, N.C.

14. Ruby Cooley, "A History of the Mississippi Penal Farm System" (master's thesis, University of Southern Mississippi, 1981), pp. 3–35. Criticism of the convict lease among black legislators would occasionally surface. In 1875, for example, six of them published a statement claiming that the convicts leased out to Delta plantations had become "slaves of the state, controlled by masters whose only inter-

est is to expose them to bad, unhealthy labor, and to get as much service out of them as they can, regardless of their lives or their bodily or moral welfare." "It is demoralizing to the poor men," they added, "and grossly inhuman." See *Mississippi House Journal* (1875), p. 305.

15. Sallis, "Color Line," p. 236; Eric Foner, *Reconstruction* (New York, 1988), p. 561.

16. James W. Garner, *Reconstruction in Mississippi* (New York, 1901), pp. 331–337; Harris, *Day of the Carpetbagger,* pp. 646–649; Foner, *Reconstruction,* p. 58; George C. Rable, *But There Was No Peace* (Athens, Ga., 1984), pp. 158–159.

17. Otis Singletary, *Negro Militia and Reconstruction* (Austin, 1957), pp. 86–99; William Gillette, *Retreat from Reconstruction,* p. 153.

18. William Harris, *Day of the Carpetbagger* (Baton Rouge, 1979), pp. 660–661; Jackson *Daily Clarion,* September 6, 1875; Charles S. Brough, "The Clinton Riot," *Publications of the Mississippi Historical Society* 6 (1902): 53–63; Edgar Wilson, "The Bloody Clinton Riot," *Jackson Daily News,* October 5, 1928.

19. Sallis, "Color Line," pp. 215–216; Wharton, *Negro in Mississippi,* p. 184.

20. Gillette, *Retreat from Reconstruction,* p. 163; Frank E. Smith, *The Yazoo River* (New York, 1954), pp. 163–168; Sallis, "Color Line," p. 236.

21. Gillette, *Retreat from Reconstruction,* p. 163; Foner, *Reconstruction,* p. 562.

22. Wharton, *Negro in Mississippi,* pp. 237–238; J. H. Jones, "Penitentiary Reform in Mississippi," *Publications of the Mississippi State Historical Society* 6 (1902): 116.

23. Wharton, *Negro in Mississippi,* p. 137; Neil McMillen, *Dark Journey* (New Haven, 1989), p. 221; John Dollard, *Caste and Class in a Southern Town* (New Haven, 1937), p. 376.

24. *Mississippi Laws,* 1876, c. 110, sec. 1, 3, pp. 194–195; Rause Echols Pardon File, Governor's Papers, RG 27, vol. 142; Lewis Luckett Pardon File, vol. 144; Robert Hamber Pardon File, vol. 166: all at

Mississippi Department of Archives and History (MDAH), Jackson, Miss.

Although some whites were convicted under the Pig Law, very few were sent to prison. And those who wound up there usually won a quick pardon from the governor. One such convict was M. L. Parker, a small farmer sent to "the Walls" for stealing a hog in the early 1880s. From the letters in his pardon file, one gathers that Parker was a difficult man, which may explain why he found himself in prison. "I have known Mr. Parker for 30 years," one of his neighbors wrote to Governor Lowry in 1885. "I have lived within six miles of him, was in the same company with him during the Confederate war, and so far as I know he is all right—though I have heard some hard talk about him." Parker got his pardon. See M. L. Parker Pardon File, RG 27, vol. 145, MDAH.

25. Walter Blake Pardon File, RG 27, no. 214, MDAH; Julius Hoy Pardon File, RG 27, no. 13, MDAH.

26. "Account Book, Hearn and Jones," 1884, David Hearn Family Papers, Box 1, MDAH.

27. "Jones S. Hamilton," Subject File, MDAH; Rowland Dunbar, "Jones Stewart Hamilton," *Mississippi Contemporary Biography* 3 (1907): 311–313; *Hinds County Gazette,* January 30, 1878.

28. "Jones S. Hamilton," Subject File.

29. See especially Jones, "Penitentiary Reform," pp. 111–125; E. C. Wines, *The State of the Prisons and of the Child-Saving Institutions in the Civilized World* (1880), pp. 109–114; Dr. A. M'Callum, prison doctor, Parchman, "Mississippi and Her Convicts," *Proceedings of the Annual Congress of the American Prison Association* (1910), pp. 120–124.

30. "Report of the House Investigating Committee," *House Journal,* Mississippi (1888), Appendix, pp. 3–4; *Raymond* (Miss.) *Gazette,* May 8, 1884; Shivers, "Mississippi Penitentiary," p. 48.

31. Charles Scott to Warden M. L. Jenkins, May 4, 1896; J. H. O'Donnell to Jenkins, March 4, 1896; both in RG 49, no. 3, file 1896, MDAH.

32. The records of the numerous leasing plantations can be found in

RG 49, subgroup 1, vols. 4, 5, 6, MDAH; see also, Randle Ivy to Board of Control, May 4, 1896, no. 3, File, 1896, MDAH.

33. "Governor's Pardon Book, John M. Stone," Governor's Records, RG 27, vol. 218; also Penitentiary Doctor to Governor Lowry, May 9, 1888, RG 27, vol. 150; H. L. Sutherland to Warden Jenkins, June 17, 1896, RG 49, no. 3, file, 1896: all in MDAH.

34. R. D. Farish to Board of Control, May 23, 1896, RG 27, no. 228; E. J. Turner to Sec., State Board of Health, Oct. 12, 1896, RG 49, no. 3, file, 1896.

35. George Washington Cable, *The Silent South* (New York, 1885), pp. 168–171.

36. Frank Johnston, "Treatment of Juvenile Offenders in Mississippi," *Journal of Criminal Law and Criminology* 1 (1910–1911): 946–947.

37. The repeated defeat of the reformatory bill dramatically altered the strategy of local prison reformers on this particular issue. A 1911 pamphlet, *Mississippi's Boy Convicts,* circulated by the Juvenile Reformatory Association, said: "We have Agricultural High Schools without negroes; we have a State Normal School without negroes; we have elections without them; surely we can have a Juvenile Reformatory without them if it is deemed necessary." But this new race strategy was doomed to failure. Because the all-white juries rarely sent white juveniles to prison in Mississippi, the problem was hardly an urgent one. And state officials feared that the construction of a white facility would stir up demands for a black facility under the U.S. Supreme Court's "separate but equal" doctrine in *Plessy* v. *Ferguson* (1896).

38. Robert Mennel, *Thorns and Thistles* (Hanover, N.H., 1973), p. 76; "Mary Gay Pardon Petition," April 7, 1882, RG 24, vol. 139, MDAH, Judge Upton Young of Vicksburg wrote the governor: "We deem her worthy, by reason of her tender years, of your executive clemency." But there is no evidence to show that she received a pardon. For Will Evans, see "Original Description Book of the Mississippi Penitentiary," 1904, p. 61, both in MDAH.

39. Jones, "Penitentiary Reform," p. 114; Cooley, "Convict Penal Farm," pp. 17–18.

40. Jones, "Penitentiary Reform," p. 120.
41. *Marion* (Miss.) *Beacon,* July 16, 1887.
42. *New Mississippian,* February 21, March 20, 1888; R. H. Henry, *Editors I Have Known since the Civil War* (Jackson, Miss., 1922), pp. 134–135; "Jones S. Hamilton," Subject File; Harris, *Carpetbaggers,* p. 599. *Pascagoula* (Miss.) *Star,* April 10, June 7, 1875.
43. *Carthaginian* (Carthage, Miss.), May 12, 1888; Henry, *Editors I Have Known,* pp. 135–137.
44. *Carthaginian,* May 12, 1888.
45. *Natchez Democrat,* January 17, 1889; Albert Kirwin, *Revolt of the Rednecks* (Lexington, Ky., 1951), p. 169; Jones, "Penitentiary Reform," p. 112.
46. "Rewards—Penitentiary Convicts," RG 27, vol. 219, MDAH.
47. James P. Coleman, "The Mississippi Constitution of 1890," in Richard A. McLemore, *A History of Mississippi* (Jackson, Miss., 1973), 2:12; C. Vann Woodward, *Origins of the New South,* (Baton Rouge, 1951), pp. 321–349; Kirwin, *Revolt of the Rednecks,* pp. 58–84.
48. Woodward, *Origins,* p. 328; William Alexander Percy, *Lanterns on the Levee* (New York, 1941), p. 20.
49. Until 1890, the apportionment of the state legislature had been figured on the basis of total population, black as well as white. This gave a tremendous advantage to the more densely populated Delta counties, where blacks (recruited to the great plantations as field workers) outnumbered whites by as many as eight to one. Even after the "Revolution of 1875," as fewer and fewer blacks voted, the political power of the Delta did not decline because the huge Negro population was still counted in the apportionment of legislative seats. Quite naturally, the poorer white counties of Mississippi began to challenge this apparent inequity. Why should the Delta keep so much political power when the vast majority of its residents were black?

    The white counties saw the disenfranchisement of the Negro as the first step in curbing the political power of the Delta planters. At the 1890 constitutional convention, their delegates pressed two major demands: the removal of blacks from the political process and a reapportionment of the state legislature based on white population alone. Not surprisingly, the Delta delegates accepted the first demand but opposed the second one. To their thinking, blacks were perfectly expendable as voters so long as their bodies were counted in determining the number of legislative seats given to the Delta counties. In the end, a compromise was reached: Virtually all blacks in Mississippi were disenfranchised through a series of restrictive devices such as the poll tax and the literacy test. As for reapportionment, the Delta counties kept their full complement of legislators, while the white counties were given some additional seats.

In 1898, the Supreme Court upheld the constitutionality of the convention's disenfranchisement procedures in the case of *Williams* v. *Mississippi*. Other Southern states, realizing that the federal government would not try to defend the political rights of blacks, quickly followed suit. Once again, Mississippi had led the way in "solving" a crucial part of the so-called Negro problem.

50. *Constitution of the State of Mississippi,* 1890, Art. 10 ("The Penitentiary and Prisons"), sec. 223, 224, 225.
51. Jones, "Penitentiary Reform," pp. 117–118.

Chapter 3: American Siberia

1. J. C. Powell, *The American Siberia, Or Fourteen Years' Experience in a Southern Convict Camp* (New York, 1891), pp. 7, 12–14; Edward C. Williamson, *Florida Politics in the Gilded Age,* (Gainesville, Fla., 1976), pp. 43–45.
2. Edward Ayers, *Vengeance and Justice* (New York, 1984), p. 196. Christopher Adamson, "Punishment after Slavery: Southern Penal Systems, 1865–1890," *Social Problems* 30, no. 5 (June 1983): 555–569; Matthew Mancini, "Race, Economics, and the Abandonment of Convict Leasing," *Journal of Negro History* 63, no. 4 (Fall 1978): 339–352.
3. Quoted in Jesse Crowe, "The Origin and Development of Ten-

nessee's Prison Problem, 1831–1871," *Tennessee Historical Quarterly* 15, no. 2 (June 1956): 124.

4. Rebecca H. Moulder, "Convicts as Capital: Thomas O'Connor and the Leases of the Tennessee Penitentiary System, 1871–1883," *East Tennessee Historical Society Publications,* no. 48 (1976): 58–59; Justin Fuller, "History of the Tennessee Coal, Iron, and Railroad Company, 1852–1907" (Ph.D. diss., University of North Carolina, 1966), p. 292.

5. Moulder, "Convicts as Capital," p. 67; Clyde Ball, "The Public Career of Colonel A. S. Colyar," *Tennessee Historical Quarterly* 12 (March–December 1953): 118.

6. Frenise A. Logan, *The Negro in North Carolina, 1876–1894* (Chapel Hill, 1964), pp. 191–193.

7. Quoted in Edward Ayers, *The Promise of the New South* (New York, 1992), p. 10.

8. Quoted in Logan, *Negro in North Carolina,* p. 192.

9. See Blake McKelvey, "A Half Century of Southern Penal Exploitation," *Social Forces* 13, no. 1 (October 1934): 117; Jesse Steiner and Roy Brown, *The North Carolina Chain Gang* (Chapel Hill, 1927), pp. 55–57; and Frank Tannenbaum, *Darker Phases of the South,* (New York, 1924), pp. 85–86; Mary Ellen Curtain, "Legacies of Struggle: Black Prisoners in the Making of Postbellum Alabama, 1865–1895" (Ph.D. diss., Duke University, 1992), pp. 102–104.

10. Logan, *Negro in North Carolina,* p. 194; Hilda Jane Zimmerman, "Penal Systems and Penal Reforms in the South Since the Civil War" (Ph.D. diss., University of North Carolina, 1947), p. 129, 162–64; Donald R. Walker, *Penology for Profit: A History of the Texas Prison System, 1867–1912,* (College Station, Tex., 1988), pp. 57–61; Albert D. Oliphant, *Evolution of the Penal System of South Carolina from 1866 to 1916,* (Columbia, S.C., 1916), pp. 5–9; George B. Tindall, *South Carolina Negroes, 1877–1900,* (Columbia, S.C., 1952), pp. 267–271.

11. Ayers, *Promise of the New South,* p. 22.

12. William R. Johnson, *A Short History of the Sugar Industry in Texas,* (1961), pp. 58–60; John S. Spratt, *The Road to Spindletop: Economic*

Change in Texas, 1815–1901 (1970), pp. 229–231; Walker, *Penology for Profit,* p. 158.

13. Walker, *Penology for Profit,* p. 38; Charles S. Potts, "The Convict Lease System of Texas," *Annals of the American Academy of Political and Social Science* (1903): 426–437; George Washington Cable, *The Silent South,* (New York, 1885), pp. 156–164.

14. See testimony of H. L. Trammel, J. N. South, J. H. Weems, A. K. Addison, and W. M. Brooks, in *A Record of Evidence and Statements before the Penitentiary Investigating Committee Appointed by the Thirty-third Legislature of Texas* (1913).

15. Potts, "Convict Lease System in Texas," pp. 426–437; Tom Finty, Jr., "The Texas Prison Investigation," *Survey,* December 18, 1909, pp. 387–391.

16. Walker, *Penology for Profit,* p. 131.

17. Ibid., pp. 17–161.

18. Ibid., p. 169; Potts, "Convict Lease of Texas," p. 431.

19. Cable, *Silent South,* p. 32; Ray Stannard Baker, *Following the Color Line* (New York, 1908), p. 49; Ayers, *Vengeance and Justice,* p. 178.

20. John Dittmer, *Black Georgia in the Progressive Era, 1900–1920* (Urbana, Ill., 1977), pp. 83–84; Cable, *Silent South,* pp. 151–157; Hugh C. Bailey, *Liberalism in the New South: Southern Social Reformers and the Progressive Movement* (Coral Gables, Fla., 1969), pp. 153–160.

21. Rebecca Felton, "The Convict System of Georgia," *Forum* (January 1887): 484–490; Mancini, "Abandonment of Convict Leasing," pp. 341–342; A. J. McKelway, "The Convict Lease System of Georgia," *Outlook,* September 12, 1908, pp. 67–72.

22. C. Vann Woodward, *Tom Watson: Agrarian Rebel* (New York, 1938), pp. 48–61; E. Merton Coulter, *Georgia: A Short History,* (Chapel Hill, 1960), pp. 414–416; Derrell Roberts, "Joseph E. Brown and the Convict Lease System," *Georgia Historical Quarterly* 44, no. 4 (December 1960): 399–410; and Roberts, "Joseph E. Brown and His Georgia Mines," *Georgia Historical Quarterly* 52, no. 3 (September 1968): 285–291.

23. Woodward, *Tom Watson,* p. 51.

24. Lester Stephens, "A Former Slave and the Georgia Convict Lease System," *Negro History Bulletin* 39, no. 1 (January 1976): 505–507.

25. E. Merton Coulter, *James Monroe Smith: Georgia Planter* (Athens, Ga., 1961), pp. 13–33.

26. Ibid., p. 34; Charles Koch, "All the Land That's Next to Mine," *Farm Quarterly* 13, no. 3 (Autumn 1958): 62.

27. Coulter, *James Monroe Smith,* pp. 39–45.

28. Koch, "All the Land That's Next to Mine," pp. 104–105.

29. Dittmer, *Black Georgia,* p. 79.

30. Coulter, *James Monroe Smith,* pp. 48–51.

31. Ibid., p. 67.

32. Ibid., p. 79. Mancini, "Abandonment of Convict Leasing," pp. 348–349; A. Elizabeth Taylor, "The Abolition of the Convict Lease System in Georgia," *Georgia Historical Quarterly,* 26 no. 3–4 (September–December 1942): 273–287.

33. George W. Donaghey, "Why I Could Not Pardon the Contract System," *Annals of the American Academy of Political and Social Science* (1913): 22–30; "A Governor, 360 Convicts and the Lease System," *Survey,* December 28, 1912, p. 383.

34. Jane Zimmerman, "The Convict Lease System in Arkansas and the Fight for Abolition," *Arkansas Historical Quarterly* 18, no. 3 (Autumn 1949): 171–188; Garland Bayliss, "The Arkansas State Penitentiary under Democratic Control, 1874–1896," *Arkansas Historical Quarterly* 34, no. 3 (Autumn 1975): 195–213. Fletcher M. Green, "Some Aspects of the Convict Lease System," in Green (ed.), *Essays in Southern History* (Chapel Hill, 1949), p. 120.

35. Ray Arsenault, *The Wild Ass of the Ozarks* (Philadelphia, 1984), pp. 144–145.

36. Donaghey, "Why I Could Not Pardon the Contract System," pp. 22–30; "Smashing the Lease System in Arkansas," *Survey,* April 12, 1913, p. 54.

37. Donaghey, "Why I Could Not Pardon the Contract System," pp. 22–30.

38. "A Governor, 360 Convicts, and the Lease System," p. 384; Zimmerman, "Convict Lease System in Arkansas," pp. 184–188.

39. Jerrell H. Shofner, "Forced Labor in the Florida Forests, 1880–1950," *Journal of Forest History* (January 1981): 17; Robert N. Lauriault, "From Can't to Can't: The North Florida Turpentine Camp, 1900–1950," *Florida Historical Quarterly* 67, no. 3 (January 1989): 310–328.

40. Richard Barry, "Slavery in the South Today," *Cosmopolitan Magazine* (March 1907): 488.

41. Powell, *American Siberia,* p. 5.

42. Ibid., pp. 15–16.

43. Ibid., p. 332.

44. Ibid., pp. 36, 60, 62–63.

45. Ibid., p. 22; Barry, "Slavery in the South Today," p. 487.

46. Powell, *American Siberia,* pp. 104–106. For the training of fox hounds, the dogs of choice in tracking down runaways, see M. N. Goodnow, "Turpentine: Impressions of the Convict Camps of Florida," *Survey,* May 1, 1915, pp. 103–108.

47. N. Gordon Carper, "Martin Tabert: Martyr of an Era," *Florida Historical Quarterly* 52, no. 2 (October 1973): 117–123.

48. Ibid., pp. 116–117.

49. Quoted in "A Victim of Convict 'Slavery,' " *Literary Digest,* April 21, 1923, p. 42.

50. Quoted in Carper, "Martin Tabert," p. 127.

51. Ibid., pp. 128–129.

52. Jerrell H. Shofner, "Postscript to the Martin Tabert Case: Peonage As Usual in the Florida Turpentine Camps," *Florida Historical Quarterly* 60, no. 2 (October 1981): 161–173.

53. Wayne Flint, Poor But Proud: Alabama's Poor Whites (Tuscaloosa, Ala., 1989), p. 114.

54. Robert D. Ward and William W. Rogers, *Convicts, Coal, and the Banner Mine Tragedy* (Tuscaloosa, Ala., 1987), pp. 26–50; Ethel Armes, *The Story of Coal and Iron in Alabama* (New York, 1910), 420–460; Justin Fuller, "Henry F. DeBardeleben, Industrialist of the New South," *Alabama Review* 39, no. 1 (January 1986): 3–18; Fuller, "History of the Tennessee Coal, Iron, and Railroad Company," pp. 282–312.

55. Cable, *Silent South,* pp. 27–28.

56. Carl V. Harris, *Political Power in Birmingham, 1871–1921* (Knoxville, Tenn., 1977), pp. 121–124; Ward and Rogers, *Banner Mine Tragedy,* p. 4; E. Stagg Whitin, *Penal Servitude* (New York, 1912), p. 1.

57. Ward and Rogers, *Banner Mine Tragedy,* p. 54.

58. Curtin, "Legacies of Struggle," pp. 170–196.

59. Quoted in ibid., p. 192.

60. Flynt, *Poor But Proud,* p. 137; Ward and Rogers, *Banner Mine Tragedy,* pp. 55–56.

61. Zimmerman, "Penal Systems in the South," pp. 277–278; Cable, *Silent South,* p. 166; Malcolm C. Moos, *State Penal Administration in Alabama* (Tuscaloosa, Ala., 1942), p. 18.

62. Curtin, "Legacies of Struggle," pp. 102–104.

63. Zimmerman, "Penal Systems in the South," p. 160; Moos, *State Penal Administration,* p. 16.

64. See Harris, *Political Power in Birmingham,* pp. 202–207; Moos, *State Penal Administration,* pp. 1–15.

65. W. D. Lee, "The Lease System of Alabama," *Proceedings of the Annual Congress of the National Prison Association of the United States* (1890), pp. 110–116; Allen Going, *Bourbon Democracy in Alabama, 1874–1890* (Tuscaloosa, Ala., 1951), p. 178.

66. Quoted in Clarissa Olds Keeler, *The Crime of Crimes; or, The Convict System Unmasked* (Washington, D.C., 1907), p. 9.

67. See "A Cash-Nexus for Crime," *The Survey,* January 6, 1912, p. 1546; Alex Lichtenstein, "Twice the Work of Free Labor? Labor, Punishment, and the Task System in Georgia's Convict Mines," in Gary Fink and Merl Reed (eds.), *Race, Class, and Social Community in Southern Labor History* (Tuscaloosa, Ala., 1994), pp. 146–165.

68. Quoted in Ward and Rogers, *Banner Mine Tragedy,* p. 120.

69. Quoted in Harris, *Political Power in Birmingham,* p. 203.

70. In its *Annual Report* for 1890, TCI claimed that its convict miners were "well-treated, in good health, and cheerful and contented." But the report turned truthful when it added: "They do their work well and regularly, and in case of strikes they can furnish us enough

coal to keep at least three of the Ensley Furnaces running and possibly all four of them."

71. The fullest account of the Tennessee convict war can be found in Karen Shapiro, "The Tennessee Coal Miners' Revolts of 1891–1892: Industrialization, Politics and Convict Labor in the Late Nineteenth-Century South" (Ph.D. diss., Yale University, 1991). The best published accounts include Archie Green, *Only a Miner* (Urbana, Ill., 1972), pp. 155–191; Pete Daniel, "The Tennessee Convict War," *Tennessee Historical Quarterly* 34, no. 3 (Fall 1975): 273–292; "Miners' Insurrections. Convict Labor, *Southern Exposure* 3–4 (Winter 1974): 144–158.

72. William A. Percy, *Lanterns on the Levee: Recollection of a Planter's Son* (New York, 1941), p. 23.

73. Quoted in Ward and Rogers, *Banner Mine Tragedy,* p. 30.

74. "Remarks of Mr. Henley of Alabama, and P. D. Sims, Chairman of the Board of Prisons, Tennessee," *Proceedings of the Annual Congress of the National Prison Association of the United States* (1890), pp. 119–121.

75. See Fuller, "History of Tennessee Coal, Iron, and Railroad Company," pp. 308–312.

76. Lawrence D. Rice, *The Negro in Texas, 1874–1900* (Baton Rouge, 1971), p. 249; Dr. S. H. Blitch, "The Negro Criminal," address to the Prison Physicians' Association, in *Proceedings of the Annual Congress of the National Prison Association of the United States* (1905), pp. 273–278. Robert D. Ward and William W. Rogers, "Racial Inferiority, Convict Labor, and Modern Medicine: A Note on the Coalburg Affair," *Alabama Historical Quarterly* 44, no. 3–4 (1982): pp. 203–210.

77. Quoted in Fuller, "History of Tennessee Coal, Iron, and Railroad Company," pp. 285–286.

Chapter 4: The White Chief

1. Frank Smith, *The Yazoo River* (New York, 1954), pp. 267–280; William Holmes, *The White Chief: James Kimble Vardaman* (Baton

Rouge, 1970), pp. 3–21. The newspaper quotations are found in Eugene White, "Anti-Racial Agitation in Politics: James Kimble Vardaman in the Mississippi Gubernatorial Campaign of 1903," *Journal of Mississippi History* 7 (January 1945): 101–103.

2. Holmes, *White Chief,* p. 6.

3. Ibid., p. 25; George Osborn, "A Country Editor Finds Himself: James K. Vardaman Champions Reform," *Journal of Mississippi History* 8 (April 1946): 81–93.

4. William A. Percy, *Lanterns on the Levee: Recollections of a Planter's Son* (New York, 1941), pp. 3–24; David L. Cohn, *Where I Was Born and Raised* (South Bend, 1967), pp. 15–21; V. O. Key, Jr., *Southern Politics in State and Nation* (New York, 1949), pp. 230–246; Hodding Carter, *The Lower Mississippi* (New York, 1942), pp. 392–393.

5. Chester Morgan, *Redneck Liberal* (Baton Rouge, 1985), pp. 12–14; William Cooper and Thomas Terrill, *The American South* (New York, 1991), pp. 568–571; William M. Strickland, "James Kimble Vardaman: Manipulation through Myths in Mississippi," in Cal Logue and Howard Dorgan, *The Oratory of Southern Demagogues* (Baton Rouge, 1981), pp. 67–82; Nannie McLemore, "The Progressive Era," in Richard McLemore, *A History of Mississippi* (Jackson, Miss., 1973), 2:29–68; Hortense Powdermaker, *After Freedom: A Cultural Study in the Deep South* (New York, 1939), pp. 20–24.

6. Strickland, "James Kimble Vardaman," p. 79; Wilbur Cash, *The Mind of the South* (New York, 1941), pp. 54–55.

7. Holmes, *White Chief,* pp. 81–115; Joel Williamson, *The Crucible of Race* (New York, 1984), pp. 378–381; Claira Lopez, "James K. Vardaman and the Negro: The Foundation of Mississippi's Racial Policy," *Southern Quarterly* 3 (January 1965): 155–178; Albert Kirwin, *Revolt of the Rednecks* (Lexington, Ky., 1951), p. 146.

8. *Greenwood Commonwealth,* November 28, 1902.

9. The best accounts of the Minnie Cox incident can be found in Willard Gatewood, "Theodore Roosevelt and the Indianola Affair," *Journal of Negro History* 13 (January 1968): 48–69, and Marie Hemphill, *Fevers, Floods and Faith: A History of Sunflower County, Mississippi, 1844–1976* (Indianola, Miss., 1980), pp. 736–745. The

quotation about popping one's head up is found in John Dollard, *Caste and Class in a Southern Town* (New Haven, 1937), p. 300.

10. Gatewood, "Indianola Affair," p. 58.

11. Ibid., pp. 60–61; Neil McMillen, *Dark Journey* (Urbana, Ill., 1989), p. 62.

12. Percy, *Lanterns on the Levee,* p. 143; Smith, *Yazoo River,* p. 277; Kirwin, *Revolt of the Rednecks,* pp. 180–181. In his brilliant account of Southern politics, V. O. Key described Vardaman in this way: "His contribution to statesmanship was advocacy of repeal of the Fifteenth Amendment, an utterly hopeless proposal and for that reason an ideal campaign issue. It would last forever. The rednecks—and some Delta planters—did not know that they were being humbugged and they loved it." See Key, *Southern Politics in State and Nation,* p. 232.

13. McMillen, *Dark Journey,* pp. 72–83; Strickland, "James Kimble Vardaman," p. 73; Lopez, "Vardaman and the Negro," p. 166.

14. Judge Gilbert Stephenson, "Education and Crime among Negroes," *South Atlantic Quarterly* 16 (January 1917): 14–20; Stuart Noble, *Forty Years of the Public Schools in Mississippi* (New York, 1918), pp. 122–125.

15. Holmes, *White Chief,* p. 37; Ray Stannard Baker, *Following the Color Line* (New York, 1908), p. 69.

16. W. Fitzhugh Brundage, *Lynching in the New South* (Urbana, Ill., 1993), pp. 49–85; White, "Anti-Racial Agitation," p. 99.

17. Strickland, "James Kimble Vardaman," pp. 73–74.

18. White, "Anti-Racial Agitation," pp. 97–99; Percy, *Lanterns on the Levee,* pp. 143–145; James W. Garner, "A Mississippian on Vardaman," *Outlook,* September 12, 1903, p. 139; Kirwan, *Revolt of the Rednecks,* pp. 153–154.

19. White, "Anti-Racial Agitation," p. 105; Kirwin, *Revolt of the Rednecks,* p. 146.

20. Governor James K. Vardaman, "To the Officers of the Counties, Cities, Towns, and Villages of Mississippi," copy on file at Mississippi Department of Archives and History (MDAH), Jackson, Miss.

21. Edward Ayers, *The Promise of the New South* (New York, 1992), pp. 133–134; George Fredrickson, *The Black Image in the White Mind* (New York, 1971), pp. 256–282; Williamson, *Crucible of Race,* pp. 109–139.

22. Philip A. Bruce, *The Plantation Negro as a Freeman: Observations on His Character, Condition, and Prospects in Virginia* (New York, 1889), pp. 129–130.

23. Charles Otken, *The Ills of the South* (New York, 1894), pp. 210, 218–235.

24. Dunbar Rowland, "A Mississippi View of Race Relations in the South" (delivered to the Alumni Association of the University of Mississippi, June 3, 1902), copy at MDAH. Frissel is quoted in D. H. Ramsey, "Negro Criminality," *Lectures and Addresses on the Negro in the South,* Phelps-Stokes Fellowship Series, University of Virginia, October 1915, p. 104.

25. Robert B. Bean, "The Negro Brain," *Century Magazine* (September 1906): 778–784; W. M. Bevis, "Psychological Traits of the Southern Negro," *American Journal of Psychiatry* (July 1921): 70–74.

26. Winfield H. Collins, *The Truth about Lynching and the Negro in the South* (New York, 1918), pp. 72–93.

27. R. W. Shufeldt, *The Negro: A Menace to American Civilization* (Boston, 1907), pp. 124, 128, 134.

28. Charles McCord, *The American Negro as a Dependent, Defective, and Delinquent* (Nashville, 1914), p. 189.

29. Ibid., pp. 217–221, 282, 293.

30. Walter Wilcox, "Negro Criminality," in Alfred Holt Stone, (ed.), *Studies in the American Race Problem* (New York, 1908); Frederick Hoffman, *Race Traits and Tendencies of the American Negro* (New York, 1896), pp. 310–329.

31. George Herbert Clarke, "Georgia and the Chain-Gang," *Outlook,* January 13, 1906, pp. 77–78.

32. Ida Joyce Jackson, "Do Negroes Constitute a Race of Criminals?" *Colored American Magazine* 12, no. 4 (April 1907): 252–255.

33. W. S. Scarborough, "The Negro Criminal Class—How Best

Reached," *Voice of the Negro* 2 (November 1905): 803; John H. Grant, "Some of the Evils Which Are Producing Desperadoes and Murderers among the Negroes, and the Remedies," *Voice of the Negro* 2 (August 1905): 545–547.

34. Scarborough, "The Negro Criminal Class." See also John T. C. Newsom, "Degeneration and Crime," *Voice of the Negro* 3 (November 1906): 495–497.

35. Monroe Work, "Negro Criminality in the South," *Annals of the American Academy of Political and Social Science* 49 (September 1913): 78.

36. W. E. B. Du Bois, "The Negro and Crime," *Independent,* May 18, 1899, p. 135.

37. W. E. B. Du Bois (ed.), *Ninth Atlanta Conference on Negro Crime* (1904), pp. 55–56, 65.

38. William F. Holmes, "Whitecapping: Agrarian Violence in Mississippi, 1902–1906," *Journal of Southern History* 25 (May 1969): 165–185; McMillen, *Dark Journey,* pp. 120–121.

39. James E. Cutler, *Lynch-Law* (New York, 1905), pp. 182–183; Terry Finnegan, "Lynching and Political Power in Mississippi, 1880–1900" (unpublished paper in author's possession); Dwyn Mounger, "Lynching in Mississippi, 1830–1930" (master's thesis, Mississippi State University, 1961), pp. 90–93; McMillen, *Dark Journey,* p. 234.

40. Arthur F. Raper, *The Tragedy of Lynching* (Chapel Hill, 1933), pp. 85–93; Mississippi Bar Association, *Mississippi and the Mob* (Jackson, Miss., 1925), pp. 11–22; Brundage, *Lynching in the New South,* p. 61; Strickland, "James Kimble Vardaman," p. 74. According to an unpublished, recently updated study by Jan Hillegas (in author's possession), more than 150 separate lynchings were reported by Mississippi newspapers in the state between 1900 and 1909. The victims included three black women and six white men, three of whom were Italian immigrants suspected of "cattle-stealing." The rest were black males accused, overwhelmingly, of crimes against whites, with murder or attempted murder being the largest category and rape or attempted rape a distant second. Among the other "crimes" were "lawlessness," "writing an insulting note," "being a bad black," and "jumping a labor contract."

41. *Jackson Clarion-Ledger,* October 2, 1902.

42. James C. Cobb, *The Most Southern Place on Earth: The Mississippi Delta and the Roots of Regional Identity* (New York, 1992), p. 114; *Vicksburg Evening Post,* February 13, 1904.

43. McMillen, *Dark Journey,* p. 234; Florence Mars, *Witness in Philadelphia* (Baton Rouge, 1977), pp. 157–161; *Neshoba Democrat,* July 10, 1902; Dollard, *Caste and Class in a Southern Town,* p. 329.

44. Carter, *The Lower Mississippi,* p. 392; Cohn, *Where I Was Born and Raised,* p. 74.

45. Florence Mars, *Witness in Philadelphia* (Baton Rouge, 1977), pp. 161–162; Chalmers Archer, Jr., *Growing Up Black in Rural Mississippi* (New York, 1992), pp. 124–142.

46. Brundage, *Lynching in the New South,* p. 37.

47. James Howell Street, *Look Away! A Dixie Notebook* (New York, 1936), pp. 11–38.

48. McMillen, *Dark Journey,* pp. 206–207.

49. Jan Hillegas, "Executions by Race and Crime in Mississippi" (unpublished paper in author's possession); *Brandon News,* July 22, 29, 1909.

50. Mounger, "Lynching in Mississippi," pp. 90–99; Vernon Wharton, *The Negro in Mississippi: 1865–1890* (Chapel Hill, 1947), pp. 224–226: *Jackson Clarion-Ledger,* October 2, 1902.

51. *Jackson Clarion-Ledger,* October 9, 1902.

Chapter 5: The Birth and Birthplace

1. William K. Holmes, *The White Chief* (Baton Rouge, 1970), pp. 150–167; William B. Taylor, *Brokered Justice* (Columbus, 1993), pp. 70–76; Paul Foreman and Julien Tatum, "The Short History of Mississippi's State Penal Systems," *Mississippi Law Journal* (April 1938): 267–269.

2. Holmes, *White Chief,* pp. 31–32.

3. *Senate Journal, Mississippi* (1908), p. 25.

4. Helen Dick Davis (ed.), *Trials of the Earth: The Autobiography of Mary Hamilton* (Jackson, Miss., 1992), pp. x, 82–89.

5. For physical descriptions of the Delta, see James C. Cobb, *The Most Southern Place on Earth* (New York, 1992), pp. 3–6; David L. Cohn, *Where I Was Born and Raised* (South Bend, 1967), pp. 12–56; Mary Hemphill, *Fevers, Floods and Faith* (Indianola, Miss., 1980), pp. 3–12; William Alexander Percy, *Lanterns on the Levee* (New York, 1941), pp. 3–5.

6. Robert L. Brandfon, *Cotton Kingdom of the New South* (Cambridge, Mass., 1967), pp. 65–90.

7. Alfred Holt Stone, "The Negro in the Yazoo-Mississippi Delta," in Stone (ed.), *Studies in the American Race Problem* (New York, 1908), p. 87.

8. Hodding Carter, *The Lower Mississippi* (New York, 1942), pp. 300–306; Cohn, *Where I Was Born and Raised,* pp. 29–30. For a closer look at the disease and its impact, see Margaret Humphreys, *Yellow Fever and the South* (New Brunswick, N.J., 1992).

9. Frank E. Smith, *The Yazoo River* (New York, 1954), pp. 243–253; Laura D. S. Harrell, "Medical Services in Mississippi," in Richard A. McLemore, *A History of Mississippi,* 2 (Jackson, Miss., 1973), pp. 516–520, 536–547.

10. Alan Lomax, *The Land Where the Blues Began* (New York, 1993), pp. 214, 217.

11. Ibid., pp. 217–218.

12. Davis, *Trials of the Earth,* pp. 98–99.

13. Hortense Powdermaker, *After Freedom* (New York, 1939), p. 75.

14. Carter, *The Lower Mississippi,* p. 392; Lomax, *Land Where the Blues Began,* p. 187.

15. Cobb, *Most Southern Place on Earth,* pp. 98–99; Percy, *Lanterns on the Levee,* p. 21.

16. John Dollard, *Caste and Class in a Southern Town* (New Haven, 1937), pp. 61–96; Cohn, *Where I Was Born and Raised,* pp. 120–141; Powdermaker, *After Freedom,* pp. 75–110; Rupert Vance, *Human Factors in Cotton Culture* (Chapel Hill, 1929), p. 266.

17. Charles S. Johnson, *Growing Up in the Black Belt* (Washington, D.C. 1941), p. 8.

18. Cohn, *Where I Was Born and Raised,* p. 133.
19. Allison Davis, Burleigh Gardner, and Mary Gardner, *Deep South* (Chicago, 1941), pp. 270–271; Betty Carter, "Mules in the Delta," Mississippi Department of Archives and History (MDAH), Jackson, Miss., *Mules and Mississippi,* (Jackson, Miss.), 1980, p. 34.
20. Lomax, *Land Where the Blues Began,* p. 96.
21. Florence Carson, "Oasis: A Mississippi Plantation 50 Years Ago," Breckenridge Family Papers, M-1311, *Southern Historical Collection,* Chapel Hill, N.C.
22. Percy, *Lanterns on the Levee,* pp. 280–282.
23. Powdermaker, *After Freedom,* pp. 86–87; Smith, *Yazoo River,* p. 182.
24. Dollard, *Caste and Class,* p. 406.
25. Powdermaker, *After Freedom,* p. 87; Dollard, *Caste and Class,* pp. 115–119; Cohn, *Where I Was Born and Raised,* pp. 138–139.
26. Davis, *Deep South,* pp. 372–373.
27. Pete Daniel, *The Shadow of Slavery* (Urbana, Ill., 1972), p. 22; Neil McMillen, *Dark Journey* (Urbana, Ill., 1989), p. 147; Ray Stannard Baker, *Following the Color Line* (New York, 1908), p. 97.
28. Governor Earl Brewer to Tom Rice, April 20, 1915, in Governor's Papers, RG 27, file 36, MDAH.
29. Tom Rice to Governor Brewer, April 21, 1915, *Governor's Papers,* no. 36, MDAH.
30. Governor Brewer to Selwyn Jones, April 20, 1915, *Governor's Papers,* no. 36, MDAH.
31. L. J. Barksdale to Governor Brewer, April 22, 1915; Brewer to Barksdale, April 23, 1915, *Governor's Papers,* no. 36, MDAH. Barksdale was the overseer at Jones's plantation.
32. Park's quotation is in his introduction to Bertram W. Doyle, *The Etiquette of Race Relations in the South* (Chicago, 1937), p. xx.
33. Johnson, *Growing Up in the Black Belt,* p. 305.
34. Ibid., pp. 4–6, 276–280.
35. Powdermaker, *After Freedom,* pp. 48–49.
36. Ibid., pp. 43–55; Dollard, *Caste and Class,* pp. 343–344.
37. Johnson, *Growing Up in the Black Belt,* pp. 274–327.

38. S. F. Davis, *Mississippi Negro Lore* (Indianola, Miss.), 1914, pp. 21–22.

39. Cohn, *Where I Was Born and Raised,* p. 80.

40. F. Rowe to Governor A. J. McLaurin, February 9, 1897, Jane Jackson Pardon File, RG 27, vol. 130, MDAH.

41. Percy, *Lanterns on the Levee,* p. 301.

42. Davis, *Mississippi Negro Lore,* p. 22.

43. "V. E. Catledge—Sheriff," file #7, *Quinn Papers,* Eugene Barker History Center, Austin, Tex. Quinn, who wrote the piece about Catledge, managed the Delta and Pine Land operation, the biggest plantation in Mississippi.

44. Percy, *Lanterns on the Levee,* p. 325.

45. Lomax, *Land Where the Blues Began,* p. 210.

46. Davis, *Deep South,* p. 499.

47. "Why So Much Blood Is Spilled in Dixie," *Literary Digest,* June 18, 1932, pp. 18–19; Mississippi State Board of Health, *Homicide Record for 1933;* Mississippi State Board of Health, *Violent Deaths—1937;* H. C. Brearley, "The Negro and Homicide," *Social Forces* (December 1930): 248–251.

48. *Jackson Clarion-Ledger,* May 19, 1904.

49. Samuel Charters, *The Bluesmakers* (New York, 1991), pp. 100–113; Robert Palmer, *Deep Blues* (New York, 1981), pp. 79–82; William Ferris, *Blues from the Delta* (New York, 1978), pp. 101–103.

50. Palmer, *Deep Blues,* p. 56.

51. *Delta Leader,* May 11, August 24, 1940.

52. See *Clarksdale Press-Register,* October 20–November 20, 1928.

53. Dollard, *Caste and Class in a Southern Town,* p. 267.

54. Powdermaker, *After Freedom,* pp. 173–174.

55. Ibid.

56. Davis, *Deep South,* p. 527.

57. *Delta Democrat-Times,* January 18, 1941.

Chapter 6: Parchman Farm

1. David Cohn, *Where I Was Born and Raised* (South Bend, 1967), p. 110.

2. Ibid., p. 103.

3. Quoted in Paul Oliver, *Blues Fell This Morning* (New York, 1960), p. 200.

4. *Biennial Report of the Board of Trustees of the Mississippi State Penitentiary* (1917), pp. 174–180.

5. Alan Lomax, *The Land Where the Blues Began* (New York, 1993), p. 256.

6. Mississippi State Penitentiary, *Description Book One,* p. 160, 1913; *Description Book G,* p. 401, 1909, MDAH.

7. For a good description of the early Parchman Farm, see Marvin Lee Hutson, "Mississippi's State Penal System" (master's thesis, University of Mississippi, 1939), pp. 7–15; "Mississippi Prison System, Parchman, Mississippi," in Paul Garrett and Austin MacCormick (eds.), *Handbook of American Prisons* (New York, 1929), pp. 523–529.

   Juveniles comprised about 20 percent of the Parchman inmate population. Virtually all the juveniles were black. See Frank Johnston, "Treatment of Juvenile Offenders in Mississippi," *Journal of Criminal Law and Criminology* 1 (1910–1911): 946–947; Mississippi Juvenile Reformatory Association, "Mississippi's Boy Convicts" (1911), pp. 2–7. See also Thomas Haines, "A Feeble-Minded Homicide in Mississippi," *Journal of Criminal Law and Criminology* 12 (1921): 76–83.

8. William L. McWhorter, "Inmate Society: Legs, Half-Pants and Gunmen: A Study of Inmate Guards at the Mississippi State Penitentiary" (1981), pp. 11–26. A copy of this valuable unpublished study is in the author's possession.

9. *New York Post,* January 9, 1957.

10. McWhorter, "Inmate Society," pp. 11–26; Hutson, "Mississippi's State Penal System," pp. 18–26. For the role played by the overseer on a slave plantation, see William Scarborough, *The Overseer: Plantation Management in the Old South* (Baton Rouge, 1966), pp. 3–19.

11. McWhorter, "Inmate Society," p. 41; interviews with convict James Louis, #31731.

12. McWhorter, "Inmate Society," p. 40–46.

13. Eugene Genovese, *Roll, Jordan, Roll* (New York, 1972), p. 378. See

also William Van Deburg, *The Slave Drivers: Black Agricultural Labor Supervisors in the Antebellum South* (Westport, Conn., 1979), pp. 3–30.

14. McWhorter, "Inmate Society," p. 24.

15. For Wimberly, see *Biennial Report of the Board of Trustees of the Mississippi State Penitentiary* (1919–1921), p. 7; for Hartfield, see *Jackson-Clarion-Ledger,* May 15, 1936; for Perryman, see *Clarion-Ledger,* December 17, 1947.

16. James Howell Street, *Look Away! A Dixie Notebook* (New York, 1936), pp. 75–76.

17. *Jackson Daily News,* January 1, 1929; "Shame to Mississippi," *Nation,* January 16, 1929, p. 62; A. Wigfall Green, *The Man Bilbo* (Baton Rouge, 1963), pp. 79–80; Dwyn Mounger, "Lynching in Mississippi, 1830–1930" (master's thesis, Mississippi State University, 1961), pp. 111–112.

18. Interview with convict Horace Carter, #23624.

19. *Mississippi State Penitentiary Investigation* (1914), vol. 4, pp. 196–197, RG 49, vol. 37, Mississippi Department of Archives and History (MDAH), Jackson, Miss.

20. Interview with James Louis.

21. "Pen Board President Demands Charges of Brutality Be Probed," Subject File: Penitentiary, 1840–1938, MDAH.

22. Interview with convict Robert Phillips, #40791.

23. J. F. Thames, "Remarks on Prison Conditions in Mississippi," *Proceedings of the Annual Convention of the American Prison Association* (1925), p. 87.

24. William Ferris, *Blues from the Delta* (New York, 1978), pp. 31–32; Lomax, *Land Where the Blues Began,* p. 260.

25. John A. Lomax and Ruby T. Lomax, "Field Notes, Southern Recording Trip, March 31–June 14, 1939, Parchman, Miss." AFS 2589–2728, 3551–3557, Music Division, Library of Congress (LC); Lomax, *Where the Blues Began,* p. 262. David Cohn, who visited Parchman frequently, collected a long list of Parchman nicknames. See "Parchman Folder," 76-13-4, David Cohn Collection, University of Mississippi Archives, Oxford, Miss.

26. Lomax and Lomax, "Field Notes, Parchman Camp #1"; Alan Lomax, "Negro Prison Songs from the Mississippi State Penitentiary," Tradition Record Notes, Music Division, LC.

27. Alan Lomax (ed.), *Afro-American Spirituals, Work Songs, and Ballads,* Archive of Folk Song, p. 23, LC.

28. Lomax, *Land Where the Blues Began,* p. 263.

29. Ferris, *Blues from the Delta,* p. 33.

30. Lawrence W. Levine, *Black Culture and Black Consciousness* (New York, 1977), pp. 212–215; Lomax, *Land Where the Blues Began,* p. 263.

31. McWhorter, "Inmate Society," pp. 10–26.

32. Hastings Hart, "Prison Planning," January 18, 1929, Russell Sage Foundation Collection, Box 38, Folder 315, Rockefeller Archives, North Tarrytown, N.Y. I am indebted to Paul Lucko for bringing this to my attention.

33. Thames, "Remarks," 1925, pp. 86–88.

34. Alan Lomax, quoted in *Jackson Clarion-Ledger,* May 22, 1987.

35. See Genovese, *Roll, Jordan, Roll,* pp. 63–67.

36. Lawrence Friedman, *Crime and Punishment in American History* (New York, 1993), p. 85. Slave Narratives of Barney Alford, vol. 6, pt. 1, p. 32; Nathan Best, vol. 8, pt. 3, p. 130; and Lewis Jefferson, vol. 8, pt. 3, p. 1137; in George Rawick (ed.), *The American Slave: A Composite Autobiography* (Westport, Conn.), ser. 1, vol. 6, *Mississippi Narratives,* Supplement, Part 1.

37. "The Whipping Post as an Instrument of Crime Control," *Journal of Criminal Law and Criminology* 35 (1944–1945): 398.

38. Lomax, *Land Where the Blues Began,* p. 257.

39. Former superintendent Oliver Tann, quoted in *Memphis-Commercial-Appeal,* July 29, 1953.

40. Craddock Goins, "Blood Harvest in Mississippi," *True Detective* 54 (1947): 40–43; *Mississippi State Penitentiary Investigation* (1914), p. 214.

41. "Pen Board President Demands Charges"; *Mississippi State Penitentiary Investigation* (1914), pp. 21–22, 86.

42. *Jackson Daily News,* January 28, 1952; *Proceedings of the Annual Congress of the American Prison Association* (1910), pp. 123–124.

43. *Jackson Clarion-Ledger,* July 20, 1935. For the minority view on whipping, see State Senator W. B. Alexander, "The Lash," 1951, copy on file at MDAH.

44. John A. Lomax, *Adventures of a Ballad Hunter* (New York, 1947), pp. 125, 160.

45. *Biennial Report of the Board of Trustees of the Mississippi State Penitentiary* (1931), p. 23; "Spiritual Emphasis Prevails at Parchman," *Baptist Record,* September 4, 1958; *Jackson Clarion-Ledger,* August 18, 1946.

46. William B. Taylor, *Brokered Justice* (Columbus, Ohio, 1993), p. 95.

47. *Jackson Clarion-Ledger,* September 19, 1977; "In Mississippi Conjugal Visiting Is Almost Considered a Right," *Corrections Magazine* (June 1979): 18–20; Columbus Hopper, *Sex in Prison* (Baton Rouge, 1969), p. 56.

48. Hopper, *Sex in Prison,* p. 93.

49. Ibid., pp. 79–80; Taylor, *Brokered Justice,* p. 95.

50. Hopper, *Sex in Prison,* p. 95.

51. "Superintendent's Report," in *Biennial Report of the Board of Trustees of the Mississippi State Penitentiary* (1917), pp. 15–16.

52. *Mississippi Senate Journal* (1912), pp. 348–349.

Chapter 7: The Other Parchman

1. *Jackson Clarion-Ledger,* August 9, 13, 1895; Dabney Marshall Subject File, Mississippi Department of Archives and History (MDAH), Jackson, Miss.

2. Ibid., August 9, 1985.

3. Ibid., August 15, 1895.

4. Dabney Marshall to Alice Shannon, September 10, 1895, Crutcher-Shannon Papers, box 8, MDAH.

5. J. F. H. Claiborne, *Mississippi as a Province, Territory, and State* (Jackson, Miss., 1880), p. 482; Edward Ayers, *Vengeance and Justice* (New York, 1984), pp. 9–33.

6. The description of Oakley Prison Farm and the convicts is found in a nine-page letter from Dabney Marshall to Alice Shannon, May 7, 1896, Crutcher-Shannon Papers, box 8, MDAH.

Notes

7. Ibid. See also Marvin L. Hutson, "Mississippi's State Penal System" (master's thesis, University of Mississippi, 1939), pp. 5–13.

8. *Biennial Report of the Board of Trustees of the Mississippi State Penitentiary* (1917), pp. 174–80; Marshall to Shannon, May, 7, 1896.

9. *Biennial Report of the Board of Trustees of the Mississippi State Penitentiary* (1925), pp. 14, 50.

10. Jessie Rials Pardon File, RG 27, no. 720, 1932, MDAH.

11. Carole Marks, *Farewell—We're Good and Gone: The Great Black Migration* (Bloomington, Ind., 1989). For a superb description of black migration from the Delta, see Nicholas Lemann, *The Promised Land: The Great Migration and How It Changed America* (New York, 1991).

12. Neil McMillen, "The Migration and Black Protest in Jim Crow Mississippi," pp. 83–99, and Carole Marks, "The Social and Economic Life of Southern Blacks during the Migration," pp. 47–48: both in Alfredteen Harrison (ed.), *Black Exodus: The Great Migration from the American South* (Jackson, Miss., 1991).

13. Population statistics can be found in John N. Burris, "Urbanization in Mississippi 1890–1970," in Richard A. McLemore, *A History of Mississippi* (Jackson, Miss., 1973), p. 369.

14. *Biennial Report of the Board of Trustees of the Mississippi State Penitentiary* (1931), p. 164, (1935), pp. 167–170.

15. For behavior of white convicts, see *Jackson Clarion-Ledger,* May 6, 1936; A. R. Beasley, "More Information about Mississippi Prison Conditions," *Mississippi Baptist Record,* September 24, 1947; John A. Lomax, *Adventures of a Ballad Hunter* (New York, 1947), pp. 136–137.

16. *Memphis Commercial-Appeal,* June 22, 1947.

17. The Kinnie Wagner Subject File, MDAH, contains a twelve-part series about Wagner's life by the *Jackson Clarion-Ledger.* Frederick W. Turner has a revealing chapter about the Kinnie Wagner legend in "Badmen, Black and White: The Continuity of American Folk Tradition" (Ph.D. diss., University of Pennsylvania, 1965), pp. 205–226.

18. See Richard Sweterlitsch, "Ballads and a Mississippi Badman," *Mississippi Folklore Register* 12 (Spring 1978): 50; Arthur P. Hudson, *Folk*

Songs of Mississippi and Their Backgrounds (Chapel Hill, 1936), pp. 243–245.

19. "Bad Day for Bad Kennie," *Newsweek,* February 13, 1956; James Howell Street, "The Story of Kinnie Wagoner [*sic*]," *Look Away: A Dixie Notebook* (New York, 1936), pp. 61–66.

20. Margaret Givens Pardon File, RG 27, vol. 150, 1888, MDAH.

21. *Biennial Report of the Board of Trustees of the Mississippi State Penitentiary* (1917), pp. 184–185.

22. David Cohn, *Where I Was Born and Raised* (South Bend, 1967), p. 108; Hortense Powdermaker, *After Freedom: A Cultural Study of the Deep South* (New York, 1939), pp. 156–174; John Dollard, *Caste and Class in a Southern Town* (New Haven, 1937), pp. 269–275.

23. *Greenville* (Miss.) *Delta Democrat-Times,* January 18, 1941.

24. Lomax, *Ballad of a Ballad Hunter,* p. 138.

25. Mississippi Department of Archives and History, Women's Heritage Series, *Jailhouse Blues* (recording).

26. Willie B. Young, "Lonely Prisoner," in Parchman File, Folder 76-13-4, David Cohn Collection, University of Mississippi Archives, Oxford, Miss.

27. Hutson, "Mississippi's State Penal System," pp. 13–14; Remarks by J. T. Thames," *Proceedings of the Annual Congress of the American Prison Association* (1925), p. 102; William B. Taylor, *Brokered Justice* (Columbus, Ohio, 1993), p. 102.

28. Bertha Mae Carson, "Catfish Song" and Henrietta Barnes, "Home Bone Boiled," both in Cohn Collection.

29. Henrietta Barnes, "Singer Sewing Machine," in Cohn Collection.

30. Bertha Riley, Cora Jones, Lillie Mae, and M. B. Barnes, "Parchman Song," in Cohn Collection.

31. Henrietta Barnes, "Evil Superintendent," in Cohn Collection.

32. *Jackson Clarion-Ledger,* April 10, 1936.

33. Lucy Philips Pardon File, RG 27, no. 214, Series E, vol. 130, MDAH.

34. *Jackson Daily News,* November 22, 1929.

35. *Greenville* (Miss.) *Commonwealth,* March 3, 1934.

Chapter 8: Going Home

1. Frank E. Smith, *The Yazoo River* (New York, 1954), pp. 205–215.

2. Dabney Marshall to Alice Shannon, May 7, 1896, Shannon-Crutcher Papers, Box 8, Mississippi Department of Archives and History (MDAH), Jackson, Miss.

3. Neil R. McMillen, *Dark Journey: Black Mississippians in the Age of Jim Crow* (Urbana, Ill., 1989), p. 216. *Biennial Report of the Board of Trustees of the Mississippi Penitentiary* (July 1, 1929–June 30, 1931; July 1, 1931–June 30, 1933; July 1, 1933–June 30, 1935); *Jackson Clarion-Ledger,* January 1, 20, 1932.

4. "Petition for Pardon: Will Chaney," 1928; Will Chaney to Governor Theo Bilbo, October 27, November 8, 1928; December 1, 1929; Chaney to Bilbo, January 22, 1930: all in Will Chaney Pardon File, RG 27, no. 579, file 125, MDAH.

5. G. G. Dement to Governor E. H. Noel, April 11, 1911, Carson Alexander Pardon File, no. 333, Charles Green to Governor T. G. Bilbo, August 23, 1930, and R. C. Russell to Governor T. G. Bilbo, August 19, 1930, Alf Hudson Pardon File, no. 133; O. A. Luckett, Jr., to Governor Lowry, December 3, 1884, Lewis Luckett Pardon File, vol. 144. All pardon files can be found in RG 27, Governor's Papers, MDAH.

6. Thomas Dickson to Governor Anselm McLaurin, December 7, 1897, Charley Berry Pardon File, no. 205; Jesse Hearin to Governor M. S. Conner, April 1, 1935, Alfred Sena Pardon File, no. 721: both MDAH.

7. M. A. Perryman to Governor Earl Brewer, October 9, 1915, Ben Jeter Pardon File, no. 390; Jesse Coleman to Governor T. G. Bilbo, March 12, 1929, George Cockerham Pardon File, no. 577; James Boyles to Governor T. G. Bilbo, May 7, 1928, John Cook Pardon File, no. 579: all MDAH.

8. See, for example, Toxey Hall to Governor M. S. Conner, February 25, 1933, Les Ratliff Pardon File, no. 720, vol. 143, MDAH.

9. N. S. Stewart to Governor E. F. Noel, July 2, 1909, Jonas Bates Pardon File, no. 333, MDAH.

10. "Petition for Pardon: Ed Cottrell," Ed Cottrell Pardon File, no. 333, file 11, MDAH.

11. Jason McCaskill to Governor E. F. Noel, January 3, 1910; Noel to W. P. Stribling, August 1, 1910: both in Cottrell Pardon File, no. 333, MDAH.

12. "Petition for Pardon: Prince Berry," Prince Berry Pardon File, no. 333, file 4, MDAH.

13. R. W. Mitchell (sgt.) to W. P. Tackett, April 14, 1907; W. P. Tackett to Governor E. F. Noel, December 7, 1908: both in Prince Berry Pardon File, no. 333 (file 4), MDAH.

14. L. B. Neal, M.D., to Noel, October 6, 1908, MDAH.

15. Tackett to Noel, December 30, 1908, MDAH.

16. McMillen, *Dark Journey,* p. 204.

17. *Delta Leader,* January 18, 1941.

18. J. P. Morris to Governor Robert Lowry, March 4, 1888, Charles Collins Pardon File, vol. 150, MDAH.

19. W. G. Orr to Governor Robert Lowry, June 18, 1884, Squire Horton Pardon File, RG 27, vol. 143, MDAH.

20. J. M. Arnold to Governor Earl Brewer, July 21, 1914, Ada Johnson Pardon File, RG 27, no. 390, MDAH.

21. E. Harris to Governor E. F. Noel, November 10, 1910; N. L. Addington to Noel, January 9, 1911; W. A. Nolen to Noel, November 29, 1910; "Members of Firm of Wagner and Co. Cotton Buyers to Noel, May 4, December 22, 1910: all in Napoleon Carter Pardon File, RG 27, no. 33, file 5, MDAH.

22. "Petition for Pardon: Man Cook, 1908; W. M. Denny to Gov. E. F. Noel, May 27, 1908; B. P. Harrison to Noel, May 4, 1908; Walter McCann to Noel, May 9, 1908; W. Chapman to Noel, May 6, 1908; A. H. Smith to Noel, May 4, 1908: all in Man Cook Pardon File, RG 27, no. 333, file 10, MDAH.

23. *Mississippi Baptist Record,* September 24, 1947; *Jackson Clarion-Ledger,* October 3, 1933.

24. Elizabeth W. Etheridge, *The Butterfly Caste: A Social History of Pellagra* (Westport, Conn., 1972), pp. vii, 3–39; Paul De Kruif, *Hunger Fighters* (New York, 1928), p. 340.

25. Etheridge, *Butterfly Caste,* pp. 65–96.

26. See "Pellagra Experiment in the Mississippi Penitentiary," Mississippi Department of Health, Pellagra File, RG 51, no. 359, MDHA; *Jackson Clarion-Ledger,* November 2, 1915.

27. Etheridge, *Butterfly Caste,* p. 95.

28. Guy James to Governor Earl Brewer, August 15, 1915, Guy James Pardon File, RG 27, no. 390, MDHA.

29. De Kruif, *Hunger Fighters,* pp. 355–361.

30. Etheridge, *Butterfly Caste,* p. 96; W. F. Minor, "They Ate Their Way to Freedom," *Times-Picayune New Orleans Statesman Magazine,* January 9, 1949.

31. W. H. Rucker to Governor Earl Brewer, September 16, 1915; W. R. Cooper to Brewer, September 16, 1915: both in James Pardon File.

32. Craddock Goins, "Blood Harvest in Mississippi," copy on file at MDAH; "Shooter's Chance," *Time,* January 23, 1950, p. 15.

33. "Board of [Prison] Trustees Minutes Book," 1906–1916, pp. 305, 312, RG 49, vol. 31, MDAH.

34. J. F. Thames, "Remarks on Prison Conditions in Mississippi," *Proceedings of the Annual Congress of the American Prison Association* (1925), pp. 81–86.

35. J. W. Williamson to Gov. Theo Bilbo, July 26, 1929, Andrew Coleman Pardon File, RG 27, no. 579, MDAH.

36. O. G. Tann to Governor Sennett Conner, September 2, 1933, Andrew Coleman Pardon File, RG 27, no. 721, MDAH.

37. "Mississippi's Prison Experience," *Mississippi Law Journal* 45 (1974): 697; William McWhorter, *Inmate Society: Legs, Half-Pants and Gunmen: A Study of Inmate Guards* (1981).

38. Frank K. Wallace, "A History of the Conner Administration" (master's thesis, Mississippi College, 1959), pp. 59–60.

39. Frank Smith, *The Yazoo River* (New York, 1954), p. 215.

40. *Vicksburg Evening Post,* April 19, 1935.

41. Vernon Rowe to Governor H. L. Whitfield, September 1, 1926, Charlie Bennett Pardon File, RG 27, no. 691, MDAH.

42. Circuit Court, October Term, 1905, Montgomery County, Indictment 1395, Charlie Bennett Pardon File, MDAH.

43. Governor Whitfield to Vernon Rowe, August 28, 1926; Rowe to Whitfield, September 1, 1926: both in MDAH.

44. Charlie Bennett to Governor Theo Bilbo, August 4, 1931, MDAH.

45. T. M. Thompson to Governor Sennett Conner, January 1, 1933, MDAH.

46. C. A. Hudson to Governor Conner, January 21, 1933, MDAH; *Vicksburg Evening Post,* May 9, 10, 1935.

47. John Dollard, *Caste and Class in a Southern Town* (New Haven, 1937), p. 140; Hortense Powdermaker, *After Freedom* (New York, 1939), pp. 23–24, 144; McMillen, *Dark Journey,* pp. 205–206.

48. *Drew Leader,* January 7, 1926.

49. R. B. Smith to Governor Sennett Conner, March 28, 1935, John Randolph Pardon File, RG 27, no. 720, MDAH.

50. "Hearing for John Randolph at Parchman, Miss.," March 27, 1935, Randolph Pardon File, MDAH.

51. *Jackson Clarion-Ledger,* March 27, 1935.

Chapter 9: Executioner's Song

1. Craddock Goins, "The Traveling Executioner," *American Mercury* (January 1942): 93–97; "Traveling Executioner Held One of State's Weirdest Jobs," *Jackson Clarion-Ledger,* March 31, 1985.

2. *Memphis Commercial-Appeal,* quoted in *American Mercury* (January 1941): 109.

3. William J. Bowers, *Legal Homicide: Death as Punishment in America* (Boston, 1984), p. 14; William B. Taylor, *Brokered Justice* (Columbus, Ohio, 1993), p. 146.

4. *Jackson Clarion-Ledger,* October 13, 1940; Goins, "Traveling Executioner," p. 95.

5. Florence Mars, *Witness in Philadelphia* (Baton Rouge, 1977), p. 17. I am deeply grateful to Jan Hillegas of Jackson, Miss., for providing me with an exhaustive list of every person executed in Mississippi from 1795 to the present. The list contains the date, place, and method of execution; the person's sex, race, and crime; and the sex and race of the victim of the crime for which the person was executed.

6. Goins, "Traveling Executioner," p. 93.

7. *Jackson Clarion-Ledger,* January 5, 1947.

8. See, for example, James Marquart, Sheldon Ekland-Olsen, and Jonathan Sorensen, *The Rope, the Chair, and the Needle: Capital Punishment in Texas, 1923–1990* (Austin, 1994); W. Fitzhugh Brundage, *Lynching in the New South* (Urbana, Ill., 1993).

9. Hillegas, Mississippi Execution List.

10. Ibid. Eight people were executed for "rape and murder" in Mississippi, and nine were executed for "armed robbery" that did not involve murder. All were black males.

11. Walter Pittman, Jr., "The Mel Cheatham Affair: Interracial Murder in Mississippi in 1889," *Journal of Mississippi History* 43 (1981): 127–133.

12. Ibid., p. 131.

13. Arthur Raper, *The Tragedy of Lynching* (Chapel Hill, 1933), pp. 3–23; Stewart Tolnay and E. M. Beck, *A Festival of Violence* (Urbana, Ill., 1992), pp. 86–113; Marquart, Ekland-Olson, and Sorenson, *Rope, Chair, and Needle,* pp. 1–18.

14. Hillegas, Mississippi execution list; James E. Cutler, *Lynch-Law* (New York, 1905), p. 183. For lynchings and legal executions as forms of social control, see George C. Wright, *Racial Violence in Kentucky, 1865–1940* (Baton Rouge, 1990); Charles D. Phillips, "Exploring Relations among Forms of Social Control: The Lynching and Execution of Blacks in North Carolina, 1889–1918," *Law and Society Review* 21 (1987): 361–374.

15. *Jackson Clarion-Ledger,* February 12, 13, 14, March 5, 1934; *New York Amsterdam News,* February 14, 1934.

16. *Jackson Clarion-Ledger,* March 10, 1934; "Hernando Hangman," *Time,* March 10, 1934, p. 14.

17. Ibid., March 16, 1934.

18. Ibid., March 11, 1934; "Mississippi: Father's Right to Kill Approved by Senate," *Newsweek,* March 17, 1934, pp. 10–11.

19. *Jackson Clarion-Ledger,* March 13, 1934.

20. Ibid., March 17, 1934.

21. Ibid.

22. Ibid.; "Hernando Hanging (Concl.)," *Time,* March 24, 1934, p. 13; *Louisville Courier-Journal,* March 17, 1934.

23. Ibid.

24. "Capitalizing Capital Punishment," *Literary Digest,* August 21, 1915, p. 338.

25. " 'Sign' Didn't Save Him from Gallows," *Jackson Clarion-Ledger,* August 5, 1979. On Hillegas, Mississippi Execution List, the executed man is listed as Charles Harveson.

26. August Mencken, *By the Neck: A Book of Hangings* (New York, 1942), pp. 49–57.

27. *Hinds County Gazette,* November 21, 1877.

28. *Vicksburg Evening Post,* September 25, 26, 1902; *Jackson Clarion-Ledger,* October 2, 1902.

29. For Pattie Perdue, see *Forest News-Register,* January 18, 1922; for Mary Holmes, *Deer Creek Pilot,* April 30, 1937; for Mildred James, *Vicksburg Evening Post,* May 19, 1944. See also Bowers, *Legal Homicide,* appendix A.

30. *Greene County Herald,* October 13, 20, 1922.

31. *Natchez Democrat,* December 7, 12, 13, 1934.

32. Allison Davis, Burleigh Gardner, and Mary Gardner, *Deep South: A Social Anthropological Study of Caste and Class* (Chicago, 1941), pp. 528–533.

33. Ibid., pp. 529–530.

34. *Vicksburg Democrat,* December 7, 1934.

35. Gardner, and Gardner, Davis, *Deep South,* pp. 536–538.

36. Ibid., pp. 534, 538.

37. For Stagolee verses, see Alan Lomax, *Land Where the Blues Began* (New York, 1993), pp. 202–203; Lawrence Levine, *Black Culture and Black Consciousness* (New York, 1977), pp. 414–415. Levine provides an excellent analysis of Stagolee as a black "bad man." See also H. C. Brearley, "Ba-ad Nigger," *South Atlantic Quarterly* 37 (1939): 75–81.

38. *Bolivar* (Miss.) *Commercial,* December 14, 1934.

39. David Cohn, *Where I Was Born and Raised* (South Bend, 1967), p. 75.

40. Ibid., pp. 68–77.

41. *Bolivar Commercial,* January 18, March 8, 1935.

Chapter 10. A Farm with Slaves

1. *Biennial Report of the Superintendent and Other Officers of the Mississippi State Penitentiary,* 1935, p. 15; *Biennial Report of the Superintendent and Other Officers of the Mississippi State Penitentiary,* 1957, p. 8.

2. *Jackson Clarion-Ledger,* July 5, 1934.

3. William B. Taylor, *Brokered Justice: Race Politics and Mississippi Prisons* (Columbus, 1993), pp. 113, 134.

4. *Jackson Clarion-Ledger,* October 28, 1965.

5. *Mississippi Baptist Record,* September 24, 1947; Ann Waldron, *Hodding Carter: The Reconstruction of a Racist* (Chapel Hill, 1993), pp. 187–88.

6. *Indianola Enterprise,* August 16, 1951, *Jackson Clarion-Ledger,* July 31, 1948; *Memphis Commercial-Appeal,* November 11, 1928.

7. See Eric Newhall, "Prisons and Prisoners in the Works of William Faulkner, Ph.D. thesis, UCLA, 1975, p. 35–38.

8. Ibid., pp. 61–182; William Faulkner, *The Mansion* (New York, 1955), p. 49.

9. Shelby Foote, *Follow Me Down* (New York, 1950). I am indebted to William B. Taylor for bringing this book to my attention.

10. Interview with Matthew Winter; interview with Horace Carter.

11. Tony Dunbar, *Delta Time* (New York, 1990), p. 150.

12. Taylor, *Brokered Justice,* p. 123.

13. Ibid; *Jackson Clarion-Ledger,* January 19, 1947.

14. Interview with Matthew Winter.

15. Stephen Whitfield, *A Death in the Delta: The Story of Emmett Till* (New York, 1988), pp. 9, 35.

16. John Dittmer, *Local People: The Struggle for Civil Rights in Mississippi* (Urbana, Ill., 1994), pp. 45–53.

17. Whitfield, *Death in the Delta,* pp. 15–50.

18. David Halberstam, "Tallahatchie County Acquits a Peckerwood," *Reporter,* April 19, 1956, pp. 26–30.

19. *New York Times,* June 6, 19–20, 1958; Richard Bardolph (ed.), *The Civil Rights Record: Black Americans and the Law* (New York, 1970), pp. 478–479; Whitfield, *Death in the Delta,* p. 18.
20. Ronald Hollander, "One Mississippi Negro Who Didn't Go to College," *Reporter,* November 8, 1962, p. 34.
21. Ibid., pp. 30–34; Mrs. Medgar Evers, with William Peters, *For Us, the Living* (Garden City, N.Y., 1967), pp. 214–225; Dittmer, *Local People,* pp. 79–83.
22. *Jackson Daily News,* June 24, 1961.
23. James Farmer, *Lay Bare the Heart: An Autobiobraphy of the Civil Rights Movement* (New York, 1985), p. 22.
24. Seth Cagan and Philip Dray, *We Are Not Afraid* (New York, 1988), pp. 128–29; Jim Peck, *Freedom Ride* (New York, 1962), pp. 133–53; Taylor Branch, *Parting the Waters: America in the King Years, 1954–63* (New York, 1988), pp. 482–485.
25. Howard Zinn, *SNCC: The New Abolitionists* (Boston, 1964), pp. 54–58; August Meier and Elliott Rudwick, *CORE: A Study in the Civil Rights Movement, 1942–1968* (New York, 1973), pp. 141–142; Farmer, *Lay Bare the Heart,* pp. 22–23.
26. Farmer, *Lay Bare the Heart,* p. 23.
27. Ibid., pp. 28–29.
28. Ibid., p. 30.
29. Charles Payne, *I've Got the Light of Freedom: The Organizing Tradition and the Mississippi Freedom Struggle* (Berkeley, 1995), 103–316; Dittmer, *Local People,* pp. 70–337; Evers, *For Us the Living,* p. 302.
30. Dittmer, *Local People,* pp. 353–362.
31. Statement of Samuel Carter, Natchez File, Freedom Information Library Project, Jackson, Mississippi.
32. Statement of Annie Bell Tillman, Natchez File.
33. Francis Stevens and John Maxey, "Representing the Unrepresented: A Decennial Report on Public-Interest Litigation in Mississippi," *Mississippi Law Journal* 44 (June 1973): 339–342; interview with Ronald Welch.
34. Stevens and Maxey, "Representing the Unrepresented," pp. 341–343; Ronald Welch, "Developing Prisoner Self-Help Techniques:

The Early Mississippi Experience," *Prison Law Monitor* (October 1979): 105, 118–122.

35. Tony Dunbar, *Delta Time: A Journey Through Mississippi* (New York, 1990), p. 46.

36. "Biological Data—William Colbert Keady," William C. Keady Subject File, Mississippi Department of Archives and History, Jackson, Mississippi. Also see Keady's privately published autobiography, *All Rise: Memoirs of a Mississippi Federal Judge,* Recollections Bound, Inc., (Boston, 1988).

37. *Greenwood Commonwealth,* May 22, 1983.

38. *Jackson Clarion-Ledger,* July 10, 1983.

39. *Jackson Daily News,* June 15, 1986; *Jackson Clarion-Ledger,* April 26, 1983.

40. Interview with Welch; interview with James Young.

41. See "Plaintiff's Proposed Joint Trial Plan for Order of Calling Inmate Witnesses: Incident List," May 11, 1972, *Gates* v. *Collier,* GC 716-K, folder 4, Federal Courthouse, Greenville, Mississippi.

42. Interview with Welch.

43. Nazareth Gates to Roy Haber, July 11, 1971, *Gates* v. *Collier,* folder 2.

44. "Incident List" and "Motion for Temporary Restraining Order," July 16, 1971, in *Gates* v. *Collier,* folder 2.

45. General Legislative Investigative Committee, "Mississippi State Penitentiary," 62; 1971; David Lipman, "Mississippi's Prison Experience," *Mississippi Law Journal* 5 (June 1974): 698–699; interview with Young.

46. See *Nazareth Gates et al.* v. *John Collier et al.,* no. GC 71-6-K, 349 F. Supp. 881, 1972, pp. 881–905.

47. Interview with Young.

Epilogue

1. David Lipman, "Mississippi's Prison Experience," *Mississippi Law Journal* 5 (June 1974): 743; Ronald Welch, "Developing Prisoner Self-Help Techniques: The Early Mississippi Experience," *Prison Law Monitor* 2 (October 1979): 118–122; Stephen Gettinger, "Mis-

sissippi Has Come a Long Way, But It Had a Long Way to Come,"
Corrections Magazine (June 1979): 7.

2. Gettinger, "Mississippi Has Come a Long Way," p. 5.
3. William B. Taylor, *Brokered Justice: Race, Politics, and Mississippi Prisons, 1798–1992* (Columbus, Ohio, 1993), p. 220
4. Ibid.; Mississippi Department of Corrections, *Annual Report* (1990), pp. 33–39; L. C. Dorsesy, *Cold Steel* (Jackson, Miss., 1980), p. v. Parchman officials claim, with some justification, that these injury figures are misleading because the prison is now required to report all injuries, no matter how minor. "The overwhelming number of these cases are small run-ins," said one. "Convicts don't roam around here throwing each other off buildings." Interview with Dwight Presley. For a superb analysis of prison violence, its causes, and possible remedies, see John J. Dilulio, Jr., *Governing Prisons* (New York, 1987).
5. Gettinger, "Mississippi Has Come a Long Way, pp. 14–15.
6. Ibid., p. 4.
7. Ibid., p. 17.
8. Richard A. Wright, *In Defense of Prisons* (Westport, Conn., 1994), pp. 25–36.
9. Interview with Dwight Presley.
10. For interviews with Parchman prisoners, see Benjamin Y. Lee, "A Case Study of Prisonization at the Mississippi State Penitentiary," masters thesis, University of Mississippi, 1975.
11. Interview with Presley: interview with Eugene Mealy.
12. Interview with Presley.
13. Interview with inmates Horace Carter, Delbert Driskill, James Louis, Robert Phillips, and Matthew Winter.

✠

Index

Index

Graves, Alex, 46
Gray, Jimmy Lee, 253
Grayson, Gen. T. J., 210–11
Great Northern Railroad, 59
Greene County Herlad, 217
Greenville: Saturday night violence in, 129; yellow fever epidemic in, 112
Greenville and Augusta Railroad, 59–60
Greenville Railroad, 44
Greenwood Enterprise, 86
Gregory, Dick, 232
Grenada, imprisoning of blacks in, 34
Grey, Will, 217
Griffin, Walter, 243
Grisham, John, 1
Growing Up in the Black Belt (Johnson), 122
Gulf and Ship Island Railroad, 43, 50

Haber, Roy, 241–45, 248
Halters, 5
Hamber, Robert, 41
Hamer, Fannie Lou, 237
Hamilton, Col. Jones S., 43–44, 49, 50
Hamilton, Mary, 111, 114
Hangings, 5, 33, 105, 206, 209, 212–13, 214, 215–17, 222, 223
Harrington, James, 47
Hartfield, John (of Ellisville), 106
Hartfield, John (white trusty), 141n
Harveston, Clyde, 214
Hayes, Jessie, 242
Hearn, David, 42
Hendersen, T. S., 62
Herrin, Clarence, 130
Hicks, Alma, 171
Higginbotham, Walter, 75–76
Hitt, Ollis, 242
Hoffman, Frederick, 96
Holbert, Luther, 101–2
Holly Springs Banner, 6
Holmes, Mary, 216
Holmes, Willie, 245
Homosexual behavior, 153–54, 158, 159n
Horn, John, 242
Horton, Squire, 186–87
House, Eddie "Son," 1, 128
House arrest, 176
Howard, Isaac, 211, 212–13
Hoy, Julius, 42
Hudson, C. A., 200
Hudson, Josie, 198, 200
Humes, George, 243
Humphreys, Gen. Benjamin G., 20

Ills of the South, The (Otken), 93
Independent, 98
Indianola, racial conflict in, 88–89, 102
Indianola Rotary Club, 163n
Inmate 5157 (Parchman Farm), 144
Interdancing, 122
Intermarriage, 21, 122
Ivy, J. P., 100

Jackson: Civil War destruction of, 12; lawlessness in, 23–24; state penitentiary at, 6–7, 35, 36, 41, 46, 48; treatment of sharecroppers at, 120–21
Jackson, Ida Joyce, 96–97
Jackson, Jane, 125
Jackson Clarion-Ledger, 101, 104, 106, 151, 158, 206, 211
Jackson *Daily News,* 229, 233
Jacobs, Silas, 149
James, Guy, 192, 193
James, Mildred, 217
Jeter, Ben, 182
Jim Crow laws, 13, 20–22, 23
John (lynching victim), 103–4
Johnson, Ada, 187
Johnson, Andrew, 20, 22, 24
Johnson, Charles S., 122, 123
Johnson, Frank, 50, 241
Johnson, Richard, 130
Johnson, Robert, 128
Johnson, William, 3
Jones, Sheriff (executioner), 209
Jones, Abe, 136, 195
Jones, Elmer, 130
Jones, Fred, 234
Jones, J. F., 53
Jones, Johnnie, 211, 212–13
Jones, Selwyn, 121
Jordan, Will, 136
Juvenile Reformatory Association, 266n. 37

Keady, William C., 223, 239–41, 245–48, 249, 250, 251
Kennard, Clyde, 231–33
Kennedy, J. Preston, 176
Key, V. O., Jr., 1, 276n. 12
King, Clennon, 231
King, Martin Luther, Jr., 232
Kizart, Lee, 129
Knight, Ann, 217
Knight, John, 217
Knowles, Henry, 186
Ku Klux Klan, 26–29, 237

Index